PERFORMING TSARIST RUSSIA IN NEW YORK

RUSSIAN MUSIC STUDIES

Simon A. Morrison and Peter Schmelz, *editors*

PERFORMING TSARIST RUSSIA IN NEW YORK

Music, Émigrés, and the American Imagination

Natalie K. Zelensky

INDIANA UNIVERSITY PRESS

This book is a publication of

Indiana University Press
Office of Scholarly Publishing
Herman B Wells Library 350
1320 East 10th Street
Bloomington, Indiana 47405 USA

iupress.indiana.edu

Manufactured in the United States of America

Cataloging information is available from the Library of Congress.

ISBN 978-0-253-04118-0 (cloth)
ISBN 978-0-253-04119-7 (paperback)
ISBN 978-0-253-04120-3 (ebook)

1 2 3 4 5   24 23 22 21 20 19

CONTENTS

ACKNOWLEDGMENTS

THIS BOOK COULD NOT HAVE BEEN WRITTEN WITHOUT the help and generosity of many people. From the individuals whom I encountered within the academic sphere to those who opened to me their homes and likewise their memories, I remain humbled and deeply grateful.

Since starting my graduate studies at Northwestern University, I continue to be greatly appreciative of the mentorship and guidance of Inna Naroditskaya, whose generosity, rich perspective on life, and astute advice in both academic and personal matters have helped me grow in ways in which I could not have imagined when I first began graduate school. It is hard to conceive of a better mentor and colleague, and, to Inna, I extend a heartfelt thank you. The inspired teaching and subsequent intellectual exchange with Linda Austern sparked my interest in music academics to begin with and has opened to me doors for which I am forever indebted.

To the erudite guidance and sharp advice of Jesse Rosenberg and Andrew Wachtel, whose lessons in teaching and scholarship I maintain to the present. For the many long conversations and exchanges and for the inspired night of singing Russian folk music around the dinner table in the suburbs of Seattle, I extend my deepest regard to Elena Dubinets. To the many other colleagues whose work has inspired me and whose wisdom, insight, and spirit have enriched the academic road, I extend a special thank you to Paul Berliner, Patrick Burke, Leslie Chekin, Julie Christensen, Martin Daughtry, Sam Dorf, Jon Dueck, Jeffers Engelhardt, Katya Ermolaev, Roseen Giles, David Goldfrank, Gini Gorlinski, Katie Graber, Olga Haldey, Eduardo Herrera, Damascus Kafumbe, Masha Kisel, Maurice Jackson, Alejandro Madrid, Margarita Mazo, Megan Guenther McFadden, Rebecca Bennett Meador, Tanya Merchant, Tamara Roberts, Griff Rollefson, Fritz Schenker, Richard Taruskin, Christina Taylor Gibson, Jeff van den Scott, Pat Warfield, Sarah Williams, Sunmin Yoon, Elizabeth Zelensky, and Svetlana Zvereva.

I am likewise grateful to the many supportive and vibrant colleagues I have met at Colby College, whose enriching conversations have shaped my thinking in critical ways. I extend a special thank you to the members of my writing group, Britt Halvorson and Brett White, and to the members of the music department, Steven Nuss, Steve Saunders, Jon Hallstrom,

Lily Funahashi, Eric Thomas, Todd Borgerding, Eva Linfield, and the ever-helpful Margaret Ericson.

When I first proposed this project to Indiana University Press, then-editor Raina Polivka met my ideas with much support and enthusiasm and helped the book through its initial stages. Her post was seamlessly picked up by Janice Frisch, whose targeted comments and support have helped shape this book into what it is. The swift responses of assistant editor Kate Schramm have further helped this entire process go smoothly. I am indebted to the two outside reviewers, whose astute comments helped refine this manuscript in vital ways. Their generosity of time and energy was made evident in their comprehensive and well-thought-out comments, and to them I remain deeply grateful.

Research for this work was supported in part by Colby College and by the National Endowment for the Humanities. I am grateful to Colby for supporting a yearlong sabbatical (2015–2016)—during which time I plunged into the writing of this manuscript—as well as for funding numerous research trips and trips to conferences, at which I presented various parts of this work. The NEH fellowship I received in 2013 for a monthlong residency at Columbia University's Harriman Institute played a critical role in shaping my research and thinking about this book. I thank Ed Kasinec and Robert Davis Jr. for organizing this fruitful session ("America's Russian-Speaking Immigrants and Refugees: 20th Century Migration and Memory"), and for the astute and diverse insights of my fellow participants, the interaction with whom, in both official and unofficial capacities, has enriched my thinking about the Russian diaspora in innumerable ways.

During my fellowship at Columbia, I had the opportunity to comb through a number of collections at the Bakhmeteff Archive, one of the preeminent repositories of Russian émigré material, and I am thankful to Tanya Chebotarev for helping me to navigate this process. My regular visits to the Music Division and Recorded Sound Research Center at the Library of Congress were enriched by the incredibly helpful and knowledgeable librarians, and I extend a special thank you to Cait Miller and Karen Fishman, whose help often went above and beyond and whose friendly disposition made my work light. I thank the staff at the Music Division of the New York Public Library, and I extend a heartfelt thank you to Alexis Liberovsky, archivist and director of the Archives of the Orthodox Church of America, who helped make my research stays both fruitful and comfortable. Thank you also to Eleana Silk at the St. Vladimir's Orthodox Theological Seminary

Library and to Claude Zachary at the University of Southern California Special Collections for his help in tracking down rare images from New York's Russian nightclub scene.

I am indebted to the many consultants I met throughout this project, whose perspectives lent not only depth and nuance to my understanding of the Russian emigration but also a human dimension to the research process. I extend a special thank you to the Sarandinaki family, especially Masha and Tanya, who opened to me their homes and met me with immense warmth. Tanya's navigation through the current world of Russian New York, as well as the extended Sarandinaki-Tolstoy dinner organized by Masha, went beyond anything I was expecting and helped my thinking about the Russian emigration in the early stages of this project. To the late David Pavlovich Chavchavadze and Zhenya Chavchavadze I extend sincere gratitude for the many times they had me to their home. I will never forget David Pavlovich's deep, resonant voice as he spoke about his interactions with dissident Soviet poets, musical evenings (*vecherinki*), and his beloved nanny (*nianiushka*), while Zhenya's recollections of growing up in Russian Harlem with her grandfather, Captain Vladimir de Smitt, at the helm of this émigré enclave, brought to life accounts I had read about in archives. Thanks also to the late Alesha Zacharin, from whom I learned so much about life in the displaced persons camps and then in postwar New York, and who assured me that in those years one required only three words to get around the city: "Broadway, subway, OK." I am likewise grateful to Natalia Lord and to her late mother, Tatiana Nikolaevna Kamendrowsky, whose work as a member of New York's Russian theaters, announcer for Radio Liberty, unofficial guide to touring musicians from the Soviet Union, and wife of a member of the Don Cossack Choir offered valuable perspective to my project. To Natalia Montviloff, for her generous sharing of stories of growing up in postwar New York as well as of the physical concert programs and recordings of Soviet music tours of the 1950s, both of which offered an important glimpse into the post-World War II musical world of the Russian emigration. I am grateful also to Kir Karouna, whose reminiscences growing up in Russian Harlem lent an important firsthand perspective and whose regular mailing of clippings from the Martianoff Calendar—itself a cultural institution within the Russian émigré world—were always a welcomed surprise.

I extend a sincere thank you to Xenia Woyevodsky, active advocate of Russian émigré culture, whose vivid accounts of social gatherings in the 1960s and 1970s among young Russians in the United States, London, and

Paris offered important comparative insight to my work, and to the late Marina Ledkovsky, who generously opened to me her husband's papers and shared with me stories of parish life in postwar New York.

The world of research sometimes graces us with moments of serendipity, and I continue to marvel at these turns of fate. When presenting my work at the 2012 American Musicological Society annual conference, I received an enthusiastic response from Margarita Mazo, who reported that she was acquainted with the son of one of Russian Harlem's musicians whom I featured in my presentation. I soon developed a close working relationship with George Kalbouss, the musician's son and now renowned professor emeritus of Slavic Studies, whose generous sharing of stories and photographs proved to be invaluable to my project. Interviewing George, I later learned that he had been close friends with Zhenya de Smitt (Chavchavadze) in his youth, the exuberant bond between whom is captured in a photograph that I include in this book. For these and the many other people whom I interviewed for this project I extend my sincere thanks and *zemnoi poklon*.

A life in academe often means a life that is less conventional and more consuming than that demanded by other professions. I express my profound gratitude to the many friends and family members who have helped me navigate this course with their love, support, and humor. With fond recollections and appreciation, I think of my enduring friendships with Anna Nazaretz Radjou, Sharon Eldridge, Inna Cook, Sasha Lezhnev, Ksenia Selemon, and Anton Thacker and their wonderful partners. To Marina Zacharin; my cousins, Gene, Liz, and Sasha; and to Aunt Barbara, who help broaden life's perspective and whose sense of humor never fails to uplift. To Kathy and Dave Brewer (and the extended Brewer/Munson/Martinez family), whose love and support have given the term "in-laws" a different connotation—thank you for making me feel like part of the family from the beginning. To my grandparents, Natalia and Eugene Kristofovich, Tatiana and Paul Zelensky, and my great aunt, Svetlana Constine, whose accounts of the past, love for Russian culture, and determination that their grandchildren should too somehow appreciate this abstract realm helped inspire my interest in the Russian emigration to begin with. I remain in deep admiration of their fortitude, love of life, and ability to see life's bigger picture. To Paul Zelensky, my brother and friend—I have yet to meet someone with such heart and wit—and to Kate for her love, vivacity, and sense of humor—and to sweet Zoe. To my parents, Elizabeth and Nikita Zelensky, who inculcated from the beginning a sense of adventure, love of learning, and admiration of the sublime. Your insights have helped my work immeasurably, and your ever-present love and support have made me who I am today—words cannot adequately express my gratitude.

To Nicky, our sunshine, who brings great joy and beauty to the everyday. And finally, to Jared, whose careful eye and loving heart helped bring this book to fruition. As we learned long ago, life exists in the prosaic. From babysitter to ever-scrupulous editor, I cannot think of anything more so than your help over the course of this project. It is not in the grand narrative but in such everyday acts that we witness true joy, which passes "like gold in sand."

With deep gratitude and love,
I dedicate this book to my family,
past and present.

NOTE ON TRANSLITERATION

THE TRANSLITERATION SYSTEM USED THROUGHOUT THIS BOOK RELIES primarily on that of the Library of Congress. Exceptions are made for individuals who have adopted specific spellings utilizing the Latin alphabet or whose names have acquired common spellings (for example, *Rachmaninoff*, *Chaliapin*, or *Tolstoy*). All translations are my own unless otherwise noted.

PERFORMING TSARIST RUSSIA
IN NEW YORK

INTRODUCTION

IN THE SPRING OF 2009, I HAD THE opportunity to meet with the great-grandson of Count Leo Tolstoy, Sergei Tolstoy, in his Florida home. Standing in front of a photograph of his great-grandfather wearing a long Russian peasant shirt and holding a pale blonde toddler (Sergei's mother, Countess Vera Tolstoy) on his lap, Sergei met me with a present. In his hands, the smiling octogenarian held a record concealed in an unmarked, cream-colored jacket. Its nondescript outward appearance belied the value of its content. Carved into the record's grooves were the voices of Sergei's mother; his uncle, Ilya Tolstoy; and his aunt, Alexandra Tolstoy, Leo Tolstoy's youngest and favorite daughter, singing a medley of prerevolutionary Russian gypsy songs, romances, and upbeat folk songs and *chastushki* (rhyming ditties).[1] The jaunty sounds of Vera's *garmoshka* (concertina) can be heard on several pieces, and the deep, cavernous sounds of an old piano, played by the steady fingers of Alexandra, accompanies the majority of the songs. Many of these pieces were ones that Vera, Ilya, and Alexandra had heard from the lips of peasants and Roma they encountered on their beloved estate, Yasnaya Polyana (bright meadow), in the early years of the twentieth century—long before the First World War (1914–1918), Bolshevik Revolution (1917), and subsequent Civil War (1918–1922) would destroy this "noble's nest."

This recording, however, was made on another *polyana*, one several worlds from the Tolstoy family estate. Fleeing Soviet Russia in the 1920s and now living in the United States, the members of the trio performed on the premises of Reed Farm of the Tolstoy Foundation, the Russian refugee center in Valley Cottage, New York, founded by Alexandra Tolstoy in 1939. Established with the help of well-known Russian émigrés Sergei Rachmaninoff (1873–1943), Igor Sikorsky (1889–1972), and Boris Bakhmeteff (1880–1951), the center sponsored Russian refugees, giving them a temporary place to live and assisting them in establishing a new life in the United States. By the time the recording was made in 1952, Reed Farm was a thriving Russian community, now populated largely by displaced persons recently arrived from war-torn Europe. Listening closely to the recording, one can intermittently hear the voices of these refugees supplying the "gypsy choir" responding to Vera's impassioned contralto solos.

Often sitting under the piano at these musical gatherings was a young Maria (Masha) Tolstoy, great-granddaughter of the novelist. Listening to this music, Masha would often cry to the strains of the songs performed by her aunts and uncles, pieces that, as she would much later relay to me, "rooted themselves deeply into my soul."[2] Contrary to the music Masha heard at her aunt's refugee center, she found many of the operatic, salon Russian romances performed at her church's fundraising events in Nyack, New York, to be quite "boring," preferring instead the so-called Russian gypsy songs of the family gatherings or the gutsy sounds of folk singer Serafima Movchan-Blinova (1908–2002). Even further from the repertoire of Russian music embraced by her parents and grandparents were the Soviet songs that Masha and her fellow second-generation émigrés first heard in New York's Russian scout camps from the recently arrived displaced persons and their children. Patriotic Soviet wartime songs such as "Blue Kerchief," the folklike "Katiusha," followed a bit later by the tranquil "Moscow Nights" would soon join White Army marches and prerevolutionary romances in the songs performed by campers.[3]

By the time Masha's own children were growing up in the early 2000s, the possibilities of hearing Russian music in the diaspora had multiplied, owing to the internet, globalization, and the collapse of the Soviet Union in 1991. Alongside Soviet wartime songs, Russian gypsy romances, and folk music, Masha's youngest son grew up eagerly surfing the internet for the latest popular music coming out of Russia, songs that he would share with his friends and cousins (some of whose families had temporarily returned to Russia as bilingual bankers and financial consultants) through the then-popular Instant Messenger program. Indeed, the collapse of the Soviet Union and the opening up of Russia's borders has resulted in a circulation of goods and people previously unimaginable, complicating the idea of Russian culture as it had been defined by the anti-Bolshevik, First Wave diaspora to which Sergei's great-grandparents, aunts, and uncles belonged. One constant marker remains to this day, however: the Tolstoy family members maintain their self-identification as members of the First Wave emigration, the descendants of the approximately one and a half million people who fled Russia after the Bolshevik Revolution and ensuing civil war.

I begin with these snapshots of the Tolstoy family in New York as a way of introducing the First Wave Russian diaspora (alternatively known as

"Russia Abroad" or the "White Russian emigration") and as an invitation to the reader to reflect on the multiple narratives that have made up its musical life. The journey of this diaspora and of this music has been neither simple nor straightforward. Multiple routes—musical, migrational, and cultural—mark its evolution from the 1920s to the present.

This book addresses many of the key issues surrounding music's role in defining a diasporic group. What was the music culture that developed among the postrevolutionary Russian exiles? How did the idea of "Russia Abroad" take shape over time, and in what ways has music helped delineate and change its boundaries? How did the musical repertoire change over time, and how did these changes mirror broader migratory patterns? What was the role of music in defining and mediating interactions between different generations and waves of emigrants? How has music created spaces (sonic, discursive, performative) that continue to connect its listeners, dancers, and performers to the concept of prerevolutionary Russia? How has the site of migration (specifically, the American context and New York City in particular) influenced this music culture?

I explore these questions by looking at five major developments in the history of the First Wave community in New York City: the establishment of Russian Harlem in the 1920s (chap. 1); the vogue for things Russian that took New York by storm in the 1920s and 1930s (chap. 2); the arrival after World War II of Russian displaced persons and the popular songs from the Soviet Union that accompanied them (chap. 3); the involvement of émigré musicians in America's Cold War radio broadcasting in the 1950s and 1960s (chap. 4); and, finally, enactments of "Old Russia" as they take place in the post-Soviet era, specifically looking at today's Russian balls in Manhattan (chap. 5). I examine each period through a particular repertoire: Russian gypsy and folk music (as it was performed in Russian Harlem and soon made its way onto the American stage, New York's restaurants, and sheet music industry); Soviet popular songs of the wartime era; the specific compositional output of Vernon Duke for Radio Liberty; and the music that predominates at Russian balls today.

What becomes clear almost immediately is that this music has been neither simply "Russian" nor an exclusive vestige of the prerevolutionary past, but rather, emerges from a deep entanglement between prerevolutionary Russian, American, Soviet, and now post-Soviet cultures. The intersecting influences of prerevolutionary Russia, present-day Russia (at whatever stage), and nation of residency point to what Greta Slobin has described as the "triangulated" points of orientation at play in the cultural development of the Russian émigré diaspora.[4] Citing James Clifford, Slobin writes: "As we follow the triangulated perspective . . . it will be evident that the complex process of [the diaspora's] formation was not that of 'absolute othering' but rather of entangled tensions.'"[5] The music culture that developed and evolved in the Russian émigré community in New York both demonstrates the "entangled tensions" at work and the potential of music to serve as a space for mediating these differing points of orientation and, subsequently, for developing new modes of being Russian abroad.

This book looks at such tensions and interventions as they have been enacted, experienced, and articulated within the sphere of Russian popular music production surrounding the First Wave Russian community in New York from the 1920s until the present day. Although by now, this group operates more by what Khachig Tölölyan has described as "diasporic trans-nationalism" than by "exilic nationalism," with the homeland no longer serving as an "ideal space of belonging" or necessitating a comprehensive and active commitment, the trope of prerevolutionary Russia remains a central reference point around which cultural discourses evolve.[6]

Without countering the multiple ways individuals can signal belonging to the diaspora, we see the trope of precataclysmic homeland remaining central in unifying the First Wave diaspora. In her work on the Armenian diaspora, Sylvia Alajaji explores this paradox between multiplicity and singularity, explaining that the diversity of lived diasporic experience is often "muted into a forceful singularity—an essentialism that presents the collective as united by a singular narrativizing identity."[7] These singular identities often take on a teleological contour, whether, as in the case of the Armenians, a lineage from the early Armenian kingdom, through outside rule, genocide, and exile, or, as with the First Wave Russian émigrés, an idea of continuity stemming from a mythologized Imperial Russia disrupted by revolution and civil war and followed by dispersal from this mythic time-space. Both groups depend on unifying tropes (the genocide in the former and prerevolutionary Russia in the latter) as the loom on which these narrative threads are woven together into a singular, unifying tale.

The purpose of this book is to identify these narrative threads as they have informed and have been informed by musical acts and to examine the ways that music has been deployed to assert, reify, and shift the boundary of Russia Abroad. While the production of the music culture associated with Russia Abroad has involved multiple genres, generations, and groups of emigrants, it has revolved around two common points of reference: the idea of "prerevolutionary Russia" and of being "Russians outside of Russia." The how and why behind this process and the effect thereof is the subject of this book.

Here, a point of explanation is in order. The culture under study is not the comprehensive, nor is it the definitive iteration of the Russian diaspora. For the Russian diaspora in the broadest sense, and as it has typically been categorized by scholars, includes five, and possibly now six, waves of emigrants—including the pre–World War I migration (made up primarily of persecuted Jews and some Russian peasantry); the First Wave (whose members left after the Bolshevik Revolution and civil war); the Second Wave (which emerged during World War II); the largely Jewish Third Wave (whose emigration in the 1970s and early 1980s was enabled in part by the Jackson-Vanik Amendment and by increased attention to human rights); the post–Soviet Fourth Wave; and a recent wave eager to leave the current repressive climate.[8] These respective waves and their individual members have held different (even vehemently opposed) conceptions of Russia and varying degrees to which they identify with their former homeland and fellow diasporans. (As one woman from the Fourth Wave firmly told me, the descendants of Russians who grew up in the United States simply are "not Russian," while another descendant of First Wave émigrés stated that Fourth Wave Russians "are not exactly us, and we are not exactly them.")[9] Indeed, the First Wave representations of Russia and Russianness that present the focus of this book are part of a wider realm of iterations of the diasporic experience of émigrés from the Russian Empire, the Soviet Union, and post-Soviet Russia, the range of which is reflected in the variety of musical activities that have been engaged within the Russophone diaspora in the United States.[10]

The purpose of this study is not to present a comprehensive view of the Russian diasporic experience and the multitude of subject positions that lay therein, but rather to explore the trope of prerevolutionary Russia as it has been expressed musically by self-defined First Wave émigrés and their descendants and informed through their interactions with other Russian diaspora groupings and the American host culture. Two main themes inform this study: the role of music in creating and sustaining the First Wave Russian émigré community in New York and the musical representation of Russia in American culture, which both mirrored and transformed this role.

Russia "Beyond the Boundary"

As a singer at the Scheherazade nightclub in occupied Paris, Vera Ilinyshna Tolstoy often worked late into the night. At dawn, as the pinks and grays painted the eastern sky, Vera Ilinyshna would hike up her gown under her belt so as not to get it caught in the spokes of her bicycle and quickly pedal her way home across Paris. Singing Russian gypsy songs for well-off clientele was just one in a series of jobs Tolstoy held, all of which would have been considered unimaginable for a countess in prerevolutionary Russia. After fleeing Russia with her mother immediately following the Bolshevik Revolution, Tolstoy worked as a hairdresser in Prague and later began singing at one of Paris's Russian cabarets before immigrating to New York in 1949. Once in New York, Tolstoy sold perfume for Elizabeth Arden and later moved to Washington, DC, where she worked as an announcer for over twenty years at the Voice of America.

As unusual as Vera Tolstoy's course through the world of Russian cabarets in Paris, high-end salons of New York, and Cold War radio broadcasting in Washington, DC, might seem, it was far from unique. Similar stories abound among people who fled Russia in response to the Bolshevik Revolution and subsequent civil war. Who made up this group of exiles from the former Russian Empire? Although the vast majority of First Wave émigrés (and hence the demographic on which this book primarily focuses) were ethnically Russian, Russian Orthodox, and came from the intelligentsia and upper classes, there was some political, ethnic, and social diversity within this group. Political views ranged from Menshevik to monarchist; social classes included both peasant and aristocrat; among its ranks were Jews, Ukrainians, Kalmyks, and other ethnic minorities; professionally, there were landowners, bankers, lawyers, merchants, former Imperial guards, ballerinas, and musicians, among others.[11]

Nevertheless, the First Wave diaspora rested on several ideas that would be fundamental to creating what Marc Raeff has described as a "society" in exile.[12] At least initially, most members of the emigration shared an antagonism toward the Bolshevik regime, a belief that exile from Russia would be temporary, and a commitment to maintaining certain aspects of prerevolutionary Russian culture. These points unified the individuals strewn throughout the world into a transnational community of former conationals. As Raeff writes: "[The émigrés] were determined to act, work, and create as part and parcel of *Russia*, even in a foreign environment. . . . Russia

Abroad was a society by virtue of its firm intention to go on living as 'Russia,' to be the truest and culturally most creative of the two Russias that political circumstances had brought into being" (italics in original).[13] Even the name conferred to this group by First Wave philosopher Piotr Struve (1870–1944), *russkoe zarubezh'e* (Russia abroad) or *zarubezhnaia Rossiia* (Russia beyond the borders), centered on the idea of *rubezh* (border), with the geographic border of the now-closed homeland serving as a literal and metaphoric divide between here and there, now and then, and the Russian concepts of *svoe* (something one's own, familiar) and *chuzhoe* (unfamiliar, strange, other).

The idea of prerevolutionary Russia in particular would remain crucial in defining the First Wave diaspora over time. Indeed, central to what Robin Cohen has categorized as "victim diasporas," the precataclysmic homeland often remains a salient symbol around which discourses of nostalgia, collective memory, and cultural ownership develop.[14] Music presents an especially potent sphere in which these discourses can play out. Adelaida Reyes has shown the stringent boundary drawn between precommunist and postcommunist songs in her work on Vietnamese refugees. Demonstrating how precommunist songs offer their performers a forum for upholding their "mission" of preserving the "'true' Vietnam," Reyes's case study echoes the rhetoric that had likewise dominated discourses within the Russian diaspora.[15] More recently, Alajaji has shown how Armenian folk songs likewise have stood as sonic and symbolic markers of the Armenian diaspora through their signification of a "'true' Armenian sound."[16] Within the Russian diaspora, music has too been deployed as a sonic and discursive means to underscore the boundary surrounding Russia Abroad.

Yet, just as it can divide, a boundary can also be the site in which new modes of identity are forged. Described by Yuri Lotman as the "hottest spots for semioticizing processes," boundaries emerge as potent sites with generative capacities that are enabled through their liminal position. Describing this potential, Lotman writes, "the notion of boundary is an ambivalent one: it both separates and unites. It is always the boundary of something and so belongs to both frontier cultures." He goes on to state, "the boundary is a mechanism for translating texts of an alien semiotics into 'our' language, it is the place where what is 'external' is transformed into what is 'internal.'"[17] As I demonstrate throughout this book, the interchange between "external" and "internal" cultural forces has provided the momentum to maintain the idea of Russia Abroad for now nearly a century, despite fundamental changes within and outside of the First Wave Russian diaspora.

One of the ways in which this book departs from earlier studies of the Russian emigration is in its extension of the chronological existence of the First Wave Russian diaspora beyond World War II and up to the present day. In his seminal work on the Russian emigration, for example, Marc Raeff describes the termination of Russia Abroad in the following manner: "The final blow to Russia Abroad was dealt by the outbreak of World War II in 1939, and more specifically by the German invasion and defeat of France in May-June 1940. . . . Individual Russian émigrés, of course, survived the war; many gallantly fought for the country that had given them asylum. But the Russia emigration could not survive as a "society in exile" with a vital life of its own."[18]

Although in subsequent writing, Raeff notes the shift of the "émigré cultural center" from Europe to the United States during this period, he nevertheless marks World War II as the stopping point of "Russia Abroad's sense of identity and cohesiveness."[19] Other historians of the Russian emigration have likewise marked World War II as the end point to the existence of the First Wave diaspora.[20]

I argue that, rather than ending with World War II, the First Wave emigration shifted in its function, geography, and, to a certain degree, its makeup during this time while still maintaining an active cultural life centered around an idea of prerevolutionary Russia. While World War II may have marked an end to a realistic goal of returning to the homeland and the waning of certain First Wave enclaves, the movement of First Wave Russians from Europe to North and South America following World War II resulted in a reinvigoration of émigré communities throughout the New World (a point I explore with regard to Harlem's Russian community in chap. 3). Indeed, if we shift our focus away from the Russian émigré communities in pre–World War II Europe to those in postwar America, and in New York in particular, we find thriving cultural institutions, such as Russian schools, parishes, theaters, radio programs, and forums for publication, that would allow for a continued intellectual and cultural life revolving around the ideas of being Russians outside of Russia and of preserving prerevolutionary Russian culture.

This book thus presents a response in the form of a case study to the question raised by William Safran: namely, how long does diasporic consciousness last within a community, and what is required for its survival?[21]

In brief, I argue that a diasporic consciousness lasts as long as there exist collectively recognized tropes that reference the diasporic condition. Sustaining these tropes requires modes of engagement that retain a salience for their practitioners. Scholars have pointed out the myriad properties specific to music that have made it a particularly potent sphere for maintaining a semblance of collectivity among diaspora groups. That it is easily transportable, triggers memories of an actual or imagined past, and is socially unifying, emotionally engaging, and even therapeutic have been long recognized as qualities enabling music to shape the diasporic experience. As Martin Stokes eloquently puts it, music has a fundamental capacity to "transcend the limitations of our own place in the world."[22]

Music simultaneously operates in a number of seemingly oppositional ways that allow it to mediate complex modes of existence and identity common to the diasporic condition. The writing of John Baily and Michael Collyer points to these multivalent processes, including serving to comfort (through repetition) and engage (through innovation); to divide and unite; and to inform (inner-directed) and showcase (outer-directed) collective modes of identity.[23] We see these processes at work in the First Wave Russian diaspora, propelling it forward amid the triangulated forces at play discussed earlier.

To fully appreciate Safran's question of diasporic longevity, however, one might consider the nonessentialist possibilities afforded through the musical experience itself, in which social, emotional, and personal resonance can occur through the *practice* of music. J. Lawrence Witzleben has alluded to the fundmanetally different model of diaspora advanced by this line of thinking. As he writes: "Diasporas are unquestionably understood primarily as groups of people, but is a set of instruments or a repertoire performed in a location distant from its homeland not in some sense a diasporic representation of that homeland, irrespective of the people doing the performing?"[24] Witzleben's notion of a metonymic nonessentialism offers a new perspective for understanding how and why diasporas can remain relevant through musical acts, despite inevitable changes in their initial makeup and positioning.

Extending Witzleben's model of inclusion beyond musical instruments and repertoiries to music makers and listeners, I argue that the act of musicking (following Christoper Small) allows participants to engage with collective signs of identity, regardless of migratory, ethnic, or cultural background. Applying Small's concept of "musicking," in which "to music is to take part, in any capacity, in a musical performance," to a diaspora opens up a multitude of possibilities with regard to membership and participation, positioning music itself—and not its specific performers—at the center of this leveling process.[25] As Small states, "the act of musicking establishes in the place where it is happening a set of relationships, and it is in those relationships that the meaning of the act lies."[26] Without denying the very real experience of flight and dispersal among the postrevolutionary Russian exiles, we also see the possibility through music of engaging with the trope of a precataclysmic homeland ("Old Russia") as it unfolds over time through acts of singing, listening, playing, and dancing among their descendants, members of other emigration waves, and those without any historical connection to Russia at all.

Music in Russia Abroad

When approximately three thousand Russian exiles settled in the vicinity of Mount Morris Park in Harlem in 1923, one of the first things they did was to organize weekly cultural evenings. Held initially in the basement of St. Andrew's Episcopal Church (127th Street), these evenings entailed poetry readings, dancing, and musical medleys of Russian gypsy romances, folk songs, and opera numbers. The fact that these refugees—many of whom had fought on the front lines of a civil war and then found themselves stateless and destitute in Constantinople, and who now worked long days as janitors, painters, and seamstresses in New York—would take it upon themselves to organize something as seemingly frivolous as evenings of entertainment, might seem, at first glance, an odd allocation of time and energy. Yet, these evenings quickly became a regular, centrifugal force in the Russian émigré community, not only bringing together members of this immediate group through regular social interaction, but also, through them developing a discourse on the importance of music for preserving a sense of Russian émigré identity.

In his recent work, *Russian Music at Home and Abroad*, Richard Taruskin asks: "can one speak collectively of 'Russia Abroad' when speaking of music, or only of various Russians abroad?"[27] Taruskin succinctly states the problem of a musical Russia Abroad: namely, the lack of institutional support and financial funding and the uncertain position occupied by Russian art music composers teetering between the national and the cosmopolitan that inhibited the development of a "Russian school" of composers outside of their homeland.

Yet, if we shift our focus away from the professional, formal output of composers like Igor Stravinsky (1882–1971) and Sergei Prokofiev (1891–1953) and toward amateur, social, and local music-making practices, another picture emerges. Whether considering the weekly concerts put on by Russian émigrés in 1920s Harlem, Vera Tolstoy performing alongside a choir of Russian displaced persons at Reed Farm, or the boisterous dancing that takes place at today's Russian-themed balls, we see a different musical composite of the emigration. Well-known musicians also were not impervious to the draw of the more recreational arts in evoking memories of the lost homeland. In attempting to create a "microcosm" of Russia in his various New World residencies, Rachmaninoff, for example, hosted parties at his New Jersey summer home that would go late into the night and at which the sounds of Russian gypsy romances could be heard rising from beneath the pianist's fingers as he accompanied his friend, Feodor Chaliapin.[28] These more intimate moments of listening, performing, and receiving bring another perspective in understanding how music could contribute to creating a vibrant and sustained idea of Russia Abroad.

Few scholars have approached the subject of Russian popular music (most have been historians, rather than musicologists or ethnomusicologists), and practically none to date have tackled the subject of popular music culture within the Russian emigration.[29] Indeed, most scholars of Russian music have overlooked the diaspora as a community, while studies of the emigration largely forgo an extensive discussion of music. And, although initially, it may have been true that, as Marc Raeff claims, "literature became even more crucial to the émigrés' collective identity, for language is the most obvious sign of belonging to a specific group," it is clear that later generations require less-mediated yet emotionally salient modes for informing a collective identity, explaining why music, especially that which is participatory, has played such a crucial role in maintaining the First Wave diaspora over multiple generations.[30]

Representing Russia in American Culture

The second thread that runs through this book is the musical representation of "Old Russia" as it is filtered through the lens of American popular culture and politics. As Harlow Robinson demonstrates in his work on Russian-themed Hollywood films, this attention to Russia has been instigated by an almost perverse interest in the political and cultural "enemy"— the "primary 'other' in the American consciousness."[31] With regard to the post-Bolshevik émigrés in particular, American interest in this group also rested on the exiles' association with a Russia of the past—a construct of samovars and troikas, balalaikas and palaces. As Catriona Kelly writes, the attraction to things Russian that followed the émigré exodus "came about through Westerners' preoccupation with the exoticism of a life that seemed still more attractively remote now that it had apparently been destroyed by the Revolution" and the manifestation of which could be found in films, ballet, clothes, and "especially in the Russian restaurants of Paris and New York."[32] As both a mirror to and a productive site for crafting stereotypes, American popular culture—whether in the form of films, fashion, or music—has served to construct and reify prevalent ideas about Russian culture and Russian people.

The conception of Old Russia that circulated in various realms of cultural production in the United States, however, was not merely devised from the outside and projected onto postrevolutionary exiles from the Russian Empire. Instead, the émigrés themselves often took an active part in mediating these representations and fashioning themselves to fulfill American expectations of this exiled Russianness. Similar to Robinson's "double story" approach to the Russian vogue in film, this book likewise examines representations of Russia as they have been generated from outside and from within the Russian émigré diaspora.[33]

Echoing scholarship on the potential of musical spaces for enabling performative iterations of ethnicity specifically, this book situates music as a site rife for crafting and presenting a strategic otherness. The recent work of Natasha Pravaz and Thomas Solomon (on the performance of "diasporic" and "indigenous" identities respectively), for example, highlights the potential of musical performance to serve as a heightened space for executing the "stylized repetition of acts" notably described by Judith Butler as being central to the development of conventional (gendered) subjects.[34] As Pravaz explains, "in its performative capacity, music mirrors identity practices such as gender, whose doing produces the illusion of an essential core through a discontinuous and stylized repetition of acts."[35] Solomon, moreover, underscores the potentially strategic dimension of such acts, which can be deployed in "self-conscious practices of strategic essentialism" and through which people can "engage in role-playing, depending on the intended 'audience.'"[36]

Examples of such "role-playing" abound within the White Russian diaspora, the American context of which only heightens the salience of these self-representations: Vernon Duke's work singing Russian gypsy romances in a red silk shirt (purchased for seven dollars on Eighth Avenue) at a "pseudo-Russian" club in Midtown Manhattan; Elena Vorontsova's performance of Russian folk music alongside a balalaika quartet led by one of Victor Records's in-house conductors for ethnic recordings; and Yul Brynner's spirited declaration from the 1959 Hollywood film *The Journey*— "Tractors and Marxism are not the only thing a Russian cares for—there's always time for music. And when there's music, we sit down and listen, and we feel sad, which is the best way of feeling good."[37] Such performances of an exotic Other gave way to codified iterations of Russianness, helping define Old Russia both within and outside of the First Wave diaspora. Strategic presentations of ethnicity rooted in a mythical past complicate straightforward correlations between musical acts and nostalgia and suggest a more dynamic and pragmatic model of diaspora. Indeed, Russianness as it was articulated within the emigration was often situated somewhere between acts fueled by nostalgia and those spurred by financial or social considerations, the line between the two often blurred and traversed within a single performance.

Earlier Émigrés from the Russian Empire

And so, we return to New York, a city with tens of thousands of former subjects of the Russian Empire living in its boroughs by the time the First Wave émigrés arrived in the early 1920s. The majority of the earlier group entailed the nearly two million Russian Jews who came to the United States from the Russian Empire mostly between 1881 and 1914 for better economic and social opportunities and to escape persecution and the pogroms that ravaged the Pale of Settlement.[38] They established distinct communities, which were located primarily in the Lower East Side of Manhattan, with a smaller enclave existing in East Harlem, just south of what would later become the site of the White Russian émigré community.[39] Out of the bustling Lower East Side sprang a burgeoning of Jewish periodicals, a lively music culture, and a vibrant Yiddish theater, which served as "educator, dream-maker, chief agent of charity, social center, and recreation hub."[40] This area was rich not only in its cultural life but also in the diversity of its Jewish subcultures, with distinct Russian, Hungarian, Galician, Romanian, and Levantine Jewish enclaves in Manhattan's eastern nook that formed a collective of three hundred thousand Jews already by 1893.[41]

Another part of the earlier emigration group included the approximately sixty thousand ethnic Russians who came mostly from the peasant class and had left Russia in the late nineteenth and early twentieth centuries in pursuit of economic betterment.[42] Eventually referring to themselves as members of the "Old Colony" with respect to the White Russian émigrés, the earlier immigrants also lived primarily in the Lower East Side, congregating around East Houston Street.[43] These Russians came to distinguish themselves as the "poorer Russian immigration" that settled in downtown, as opposed to the "aristocratic center" of Russians living uptown.[44]

Hence, unlike Paris, Berlin, Prague, or other hubs of First Wave emigration, New York City had a large and well-established presence of former subjects from the Russian Empire by the time the émigrés first arrived. While much has been written about the largely Jewish pre–World War I emigration from Russia to New York, scholars have yet to systematically study the interaction between the prewar émigrés and members of the First Wave—a topic that would, undoubtedly, serve as a rich field of inquiry. What we do know is that interaction between members of these two groups, though not extensive, did exist and that these exchanges often played a significant role in shaping the lives of White Russians in New York.

Through much effort, Russian-born Jewish impresario Morris Gest (1875–1942), for example, brought former Ballets Russes choreographer Michel Fokine (1880–1942) to the United States in 1919 to choreograph Gest's production of *Aphrodite*.[45] Gest's efforts spawned the beginning of Fokine's successful American career. Gest's subsequent project of bringing Nikita Balieff's (1877–1936) vaudeville-like *Chauve-Souris* from Paris (to which Balieff had emigrated after fleeing war-torn Russia) to Broadway was a decidedly more uncertain endeavor, as it featured a nearly all-Russian script, yet proved instrumental for both Balieff's life in the emigration and for American interest in things Russian. Initially contracted to run for five weeks, the show's continuous sixty-five-week production created a magnificent stir among audiences and instigated what would become a Russian vogue in 1920s New York.

The frequenting of First Wave cultural affairs by already established prewar Russian Jewish émigrés and their children—artists like Al Jolson (1886–1950), Jacob Ben-Ami (1890–1977), and George (1898–1937) and Ira Gershwin (1896–1983)—only added cultural weight to such First Wave endeavors as *Chauve-Souris* and points to the potential of artistic spaces as sites of interaction between the two waves. The *Chauve-Souris* shows, Nicholas Remisoff's (1887–1975) exotic Club Petroushka in Midtown Manhattan, and the later Russian productions organized by Sol Hurok (1888–1974) were all sites in which prewar and First Wave émigrés encountered one another. Hurok in particular was known for going to great lengths to attract Russian Jewish East Side dwellers ("the Hurok audience") to his productions, supplying various stores, bakeries, and cafés with tickets to his shows, while First Wave émigrés and their children swarmed to these events for a glimpse of Russian culture.[46]

The interaction between the earlier and First Wave émigrés at times took on a personal dimension as well. Hurok, who left Pogar (then Ukraine) for New York in 1906, fell madly in love with and later married First Wave singer Emma Rybkina (1897–1974), whom he met at a concert in Berlin in 1929 and whom he soon enticed to move to New York.[47] Another close and long-standing friendship developed between First Wave composer Vladimir Dukelsky (Vernon Duke) and George Gershwin (son of Russian Jewish immigrants) soon after Dukelsky immigrated to New York from Constantinople in 1921 (a relationship on which I elaborate in chap. 4).

Hence, the realm of the arts emerges as especially fertile ground for interaction between First Wave and prewar émigrés. Despite these exchanges, however, the two groups overall maintained differing relationships to their country of origin, which in turn affected collective discourses and memory, as well as representations of identity.

Chapter Overview

One of the primary questions addressed in this book is how music defines and sustains a diasporic group over time. The first chapter ("Performing *a la Russe*: Music, Migration, and the White Russians in 1920s Harlem") examines this process from the early stages of the First Wave emigration's existence as it played out on the ground (or, more specifically, on the stage). Looking at the origins of the First Wave Russian enclave in Harlem, this chapter presents one of the few existing studies of this community.[48] As one of the "small Russian communities" singled out by Marc Raeff as being underrepresented in the history of the emigration, New York's Russian émigré community presents a fruitful focus of study, augmenting earlier scholarship on the influence of the particular context of migration on the development of Russian culture abroad. Comprehensive histories of Harlem, including Jonathan Gill's four-hundred-year overview, and more focused histories, such as on Harlem's white occupants in the 1920s, have likewise overlooked this group.[49]

Chapter 1 goes beyond documenting the development of this community to delve into the ways that the idea of exile as a unifying symbol can emerge through the musical practices of a group. In particular, this chapter examines the Russian gypsy and stylized folk repertoire that dominated the cultural evenings of Russian Harlem, its performance practice, and the discourses that developed around this music to explore how music became a critical means for unifying these exiles. Using Victor Turner's concept of metacommentary and Svetlana Boym's work on nostalgia, I demonstrate the ways that émigrés developed collective narratives around the precataclysmic homeland ("Old Russia") and of being Russian abroad through this repertoire.

The music culture that developed among the émigrés in Harlem, however, did not exist in a diasporic vacuum—a sonic cavern of nostalgia evoked in performances made by and for émigrés. Indeed, looking at this material, it is sometimes difficult to tease out exactly for whom the performances were intended. Each piece on the Tolstoy recording cited at the beginning of this introduction, for example, is introduced by the resonant baritone of Ilya Tolstoy in English. Surely, had this recording been intended solely for fellow émigrés, then neither would the English be appropriate, nor would the cursory descriptions preceding each piece (i.e., "old Russian gypsy song") be necessary.

It is this self-aware performance of "Russian émigré" and its reception and incorporation within New York's music culture that make up the thrust of the second chapter in this book. As the title of the chapter, "New York's Russian Vogue: The Fox-Trotsky and Other Musical Delights," suggests, this section looks at the vogue for things Russian triggered by the arrival of the émigrés and made manifest in fashion, films, cabarets, and music. The chapter begins with the *Chauve-Souris* phenomenon that hit Broadway in 1922 and traces its impact on New York's popular music industry. Appearing simultaneously as Tin Pan Alley sheet music in English translation, this music soon evolved into swinging jazz numbers penned for *Chauve-Souris* but simultaneously blasted out by hot jazz bands around New York City. This trend also was apparent in the Russian tropes that appeared in the American popular music idiom—including a fox-trot-dancing Russian she-devil in sheet music and the Russian gypsy romance "Dark Eyes" that found its way into everything from jazz tunes to the animated cartoon *Krazy Kat*. As I point out, however, this Russian fashion was also informed by the direct input of the émigrés themselves, a phenomenon I explore through the concept of auto-Orientalism, demonstrating that this deliberate staging of otherness helped the émigrés' aggrandizement of economic and social capital in their new surroundings.

By the dawning of World War II, the Russian vogue that had seized New York ten years earlier had notably fizzled out, while the trope of White Russian had all together become cliché. Of interest to the American public were no longer old Russian gypsy romances sung by destitute aristocrats but the new music coming out of the Soviet Union, which one could hear at the 1939 World's Fair, at movie theaters throughout the city, and in record stores. The shift in public taste mirrored a sea change in the Russian diaspora, for it was during this time that an entirely new group of émigrés—the so-called Second Wave—was to leave Russia (now the Soviet Union) and encounter its First Wave counterparts. The third chapter, "Emigration at the Boundary: Russian DPs, Second Generation Émigrés, and Soviet Song in the World War II Era," examines this encounter as it occurred between members of Russian Harlem and the displaced persons now in New York and the role of music in mediating this moment of exchange. For the first time, the Soviet Union (the primary Other in diasporic discourse) took on a tangible, audible dimension. More than this, the second generation of First Wave émigrés was now coming of age, navigating between holding an allegiance to the United States (many, for example, joined the Armed Forces and intelligence community) and an abstract prerevolutionary Russia—known only through stories, photographs, and songs. The postwar era presents an especially rich moment in the collision of various subjectivities within the diaspora—second-generation émigrés who had grown up in New York, the new refugees from Soviet Russia, and First Wave exiles (who had their own second generation) who came to New York from Eastern Europe. This chapter looks at boundary maintenance and mediation as it was enabled through music, processes that, I argue, ultimately helped shift the boundary of Russia Abroad to include the new music from Soviet Russia and reinvigorate the waning First Wave community.

As Cold War hostility replaced wartime sympathies for the Soviet Union, professional opportunities abounded for First and Second Wave Russians, whose language skills and anti-Bolshevik views presented an ideal combination for American government recruiters. Chapter 4, "Radio Liberty, Vernon Duke, and the 'Internal' Émigré Voice in Cold War Broadcasting," looks at the more pragmatic side of émigré existence in the United States, examining the involvement of Russian émigré musicians in America's Cold War efforts. Focusing on the work of Vernon Duke for Radio Liberty (a relationship that was maintained from 1964 until Duke's untimely death in 1969), this chapter presents an in-depth look at one such collaboration. Based on a close reading of the correspondence between Duke and Radio Liberty personnel, this chapter presents what Peter Schmelz has called an "intimate history" of the Cold War, which, through scrutinizing personal exchanges, can reveal subtle and unconventional details often obscured in grand narratives.[50] With regard to Duke's work with Radio Liberty, a far more complex picture emerges than that of the simple binary ideology of anticommunism framing the emigration and presents a rich example of the "hidden corners" within Cold War radio broadcasting in particular.[51] More broadly, chapter 4 explores the involvement of an anticommunist diaspora in American Cold War cultural production.

Although the majority of this book focuses on the development of the Russian émigré diaspora over the first fifty or so years of its existence, the last chapter skips ahead to present-day New York to explore what vestiges remain of social activities organized around discourses of prerevolutionary Russia. Chapter 5, "Old Russia at The Pierre: Music, Enchantment, and the Dancing Body in Twenty-First Century New York," looks at their manifestation through the phenomenon of Russian balls taking place in Manhattan today. The fracturing of Russia Abroad evidenced in the period surrounding World War II has by now multiplied, with two more waves of émigrés leaving Russia and the ever-more-symbolic engagement of latter-generation Russians with this concept. However, the trope of an idealized prerevolutionary Russia is a pivotal point around which certain activities continue to revolve. The Russian ball offers a particularly rich site for exploring the various enactments of prerevolutionary Russia in the twenty-first century and the ways people relate to this trope through music.

Contributing to the renewed interest among music scholars in dance and of the body more broadly, chapter 5 examines the ways that today's balls allow people to engage somatically with a mythical Russia. Focusing on the dancing body in particular, chapter 5 applies Ann Cooper-Albright's idea of the "slippage" between the physical and the cultural realms to demonstrate the ways that Russian balls can engender a sense of collectivity among their participants while allowing room for emergent and multiple subjectivities.[52]

Perhaps it is apt to conclude a book about political exiles with a chapter on music and dance, for the transience of the dancing body serves as a fitting metaphor and active metonym for migrating bodies and offers ways to play out both "belonging" and "difference."[53] Dance presents a more egalitarian entry point into diaspora, allowing any body to partake, regardless of one's migrational, ethnic, or cultural background. As such, this chapter builds on the work of Ian Macmillan, Natasha Pravaz, Sydney Hutchinson, and J. Lawrence Witzleben, in exploring how physical engagement with music can serve as an entry point to various collectivities signified by these actions.[54] Ultimately, chapter 5 positions the (listening, dancing) body as a central analytic for understanding diasporas and their development over time.

Methodology

The wide temporal range of my topic, as well as my aim in capturing both subjective viewpoints and public discourses surrounding the musical culture of Russia Abroad, requires an interdisciplinary methodological approach. I rely on a combination of archival and ethnographic material to document the music culture that developed within Russia Abroad and to understand what this music has meant for its listeners. In assessing this culture historically, I examine concert announcements and programs, extant recordings, scores, sheet music, radio broadcasts, autobiographies, correspondence, American and Russian American newspapers, and records of the Harlem parish in which many of these concerts took place.

Throughout the book, I supplement these findings with ethnographic material collected from interviews with descendants of Harlem's First Wave Russian community, as well as with subsequent generations and waves of Russian émigrés. In part, this approach presents a response to a concern expressed by scholars regarding the lack of studies dealing with what Jana Evans Braziel and Anita Mannur have cited as the "lived experiences of diasporic subjects," rather than merely theoretical discourse about diaspora.[55] With its close study of a community that relies on representations of identity from the perspective of its members (whether gathered from historical documents or ethnographic fieldwork), this book presents a case study based on such "lived experience." I conducted interviews for this book in English and in Russian between 2005 and 2016 in the greater areas of New York City and Washington, DC. Between 2007 and 2016, I attended Russian balls in New York as part of my fieldwork.

Finally, I would like to explain my own position in relation to the subject matter of this book. Like many of the individuals interviewed and researched for this project, I too was raised as part of a Russian émigré community (though in Washington, DC, rather than New York). The First Wave emigration is the one I am most familiar with, since three out of four grandparents belonged to this subset of the Russian diaspora. It was the music I heard in their midst that first inspired me to write this book. In many ways, my status as an insider helped my research process, for I was able to gain access to the community with relative ease, while considering issues that have taken years of personal reflection to formulate. Yet the American context shed new light onto the "Russian émigré" narrative as I understood it through family stories (which were rooted in the Eastern European experience). Indeed, the longer I researched the Russian community in New York, the more nuanced and messy the subject became and the more acutely I felt a distance developing between myself and the subject of my study. Regarding his work on Jewish congregations in Boston, Jeffrey Summit poignantly articulates this sense of distance, stating, "throughout this research I was encountering people who were simultaneously 'me' and 'not me.'"[56] It is this dialectic between self and/as Other that I not only encountered in interviews, but which forced me to reconsider my own subject position and thinking about the Russian emigration, a process that has made me both sadder and wiser. I have incorporated my voice when appropriate, while striving to give my subjects a voice of their own to explore the myriad ways of relating to Russia Abroad.

And so, to return to Yul Brynner, "when there's music, we sit down and listen, and we feel sad, which is the best way of feeling good." At once playing off a cultural stereotype centered on Russian music, as articulated by a White Russian émigré—Brynner himself—playing "Russian" for American audiences, and in this case, complicated further by Brynner's role as a Soviet army major for a Hollywood film put on by fellow émigré Anatole Litvak near the height of the Cold War, this statement and the context of its utterance encapsulates the complexities of Russia Abroad as it developed on American soil and music's place within its signification, the many layers of which are explored throughout the pages of this book.

Notes

1. Throughout this book, I use the term "gypsy" as it has been applied by other scholars to refer to specific genres of music and their associated performative tropes. When discussing members of the Romani ethnic group, I use the term "Roma." For a useful discussion within music scholarship of the terms "gypsy" and "Roma" and insider/outsider assignation, see Carol Silverman, *Romani Routes: Cultural Politics and Balkan Music in Diaspora* (New

York: Oxford University Press, 2012), 3, 295n1. See also: Anna G. Piotrowska, *Gypsy Music in European Culture: From the Late Eighteenth to the Early Twentieth Centuries* (Boston: Northeastern University Press, 2013), 1. On the development of the "Gypsy" trope in Imperial Russia, see Alaina Lemon, *Between Two Fires: Gypsy Performance and Romani Memory from Pushkin to Postsocialism* (Durham: Duke University Press, 2000), 31–55.

2. Maria Sarandinaki, interview with author, Oakland, NY, August 15, 2006.

3. For an examination of the repertoire performed at Russian camps in New York, see Natalie K. Zelensky, "Sounding Diaspora through Music and Play in a Russian-American Summer Camp," *Ethnomusicology Forum* 23, no. 3 (December 2014): 306–330.

4. Greta N. Slobin, *Russians Abroad: Literary and Cultural Politics of Diaspora (1919–1939)* (Brighton, MA: Academic Studies Plus, 2013), 14. Although Slobin's work relates primarily to the literary sphere, her useful model can be applied to other realms of émigré culture and to the broader process of collective identity construction within the diaspora.

5. Slobin, *Russians Abroad*, 22 [citing James Clifford, *Routes: Travel and Translation in the Late Twentieth Century* (Cambridge, MA: Harvard University Press, 1997), 250].

6. Khachig Tölölyan, "Beyond the Homeland: From Exilic Nationalism to Diasporic Transnationalism," in *The Call of the Homeland: Diaspora Nationalisms, Past and Present*, ed. A. S. Leoussi, A. Gal, and A. D. Smith (Leiden, Netherlands: Brill Publishing, 2010), 35, 38.

7. Sylvia Angelique Alajaji, *Music and the Armenian Diaspora: Searching for Home in Exile* (Bloomington: Indiana University Press, 2015), 12.

8. See, for example, Henry L. Feingold, *Silent No More: Saving the Jews of Russia, the American Jewish Effort, 1967–1989* (Syracuse: Syracuse University Press, 2007); John Glad, *Russia Abroad: Writers, History, Politics* (Washington, DC: Birchbark Press, 1999); *The New Jewish Diaspora: Russian-Speaking Immigrants in the United States, Israel, and Germany*, ed. Zvi Gitelman (New Brunswick, NJ: Rutgers University Press, 2016); Dennis Elliott Shasha and Marina Shron, *Red Blues: Voices from the Last Wave of Russian Immigrants* (New York: Holmes and Meier Publishers, Inc., 2002).

9. Interview with author, Brighton Beach, New York, August 13, 2006; interview with author, Nyack, New York, August 14, 2006.

10. Beyond the Russian popular music on which this book focuses, other genres that have made up the rich tapestry of music-making practices in the United States by people from Russia and the Soviet Union have ranged from Yiddish songs to sacred and art music. For an excellent study of Jewish popular music in New York, see Mark Slobin, *Tenement Songs: The Popular Music of the Jewish Immigrants* (Urbana: University of Illinois Press, 1996). On Russian Orthodox music, see, Natalie K. Zelensky, "Russian Church Music, Conundrums of Style, and the Politics of Preservation in the Émigré Diaspora of New York," in *The Oxford Handbook of Music and World Christianities*, ed. Suzel Ana Reily and Jonathan M. Dueck (New York: Oxford University Press, 2016), 361–383. On the art music of more recent Soviet and post-Soviet émigrés, see Elena Dubinets, *"Motsart otechestva ne vybiraet": O muzyke sovremennogo russkogo zarubezh'ia* [Mozart Does Not Choose a Homeland: On the Music of the Contemporary Russian Emigration] (Moscow: Muzizdat, 2016).

11. For an overview of the First Wave diaspora's demographics, see Marc Raeff, *Russia Abroad: A Cultural History of the Russian Emigration, 1919–1939* (New York: Oxford University Press, 1990), 5. For specific statistics, see Sir John Hope Simpson, *The Refugee Problem: Report of a Survey* (London: Oxford University Press, 1939), 62–116.

12. Raeff, *Russia Abroad*, 5.

13. Ibid.

14. Robin Cohen, *Global Diasporas: An Introduction*, second edition (New York: Routledge, 2008), 2.

15. Adelaida Reyes, *Songs of the Caged, Songs of the Free: Music and the Vietnamese Refugee Experience* (Philadelphia: Temple University Press, 1999), 47, 97.

16. Alajaji, *Music and the Armenian Diaspora*, 14.

17. Yuri M. Lotman, "The Notion of Boundary," in *Universe of the Mind: A Semiotic Theory of Culture*, trans. Ann Shukman (Bloomington: Indiana University Press, 1990), 136–137.

18. Raeff, *Russia Abroad*, 6.

19. Marc Raeff, "Recent Perspectives on the History of the Russian Emigration (1920–40)," *Kritika: Explorations in Russian and Eurasian History* 6, no. 2 (Spring 2005): 319.

20. See, for example, Catherine Andreyev and Ivan Savicky, *Russia Abroad: Prague and the Russian Diaspora, 1918–1938* (New Haven, CT: Yale University Press, 2004), 196–198; Robert H. Johnston, *New Mecca, New Babylon: Paris and the Russian Exiles, 1920–1945* (Kingston, ON: McGill-Queen's University Press, 1988), 182.

21. William Safran, "Diasporas in Modern Societies: Myths of Homeland and Return," *Diaspora* 1, no. 1 (Spring 1991): 95; William Safran, "Deconstructing and Comparing Diaspora," in *Diaspora, Identity and Religion: New Directions in Theory and Research*, ed. Waltraud Kokot, Khachig Tölölyan and Carolin Alfonso (London: Routledge, 2004), 14–15.

22. Martin Stokes, "Introduction: Ethnicity, Identity, and Music," in *Ethnicity, Identity and Music: The Musical Construction of Place*, ed. Martin Stokes (Oxford: Berg Publishers, 1994), 4.

23. John Baily and Michael Collyer, "Introduction: Music and Migration," *Journal of Ethnic and Migrational Studies* 32, no. 2 (March 2006): 167–182.

24. J. Lawrence Witzleben, "Review Essay: Music and Diaspora," *Ethnomusicology* 57, no. 3 (Fall 2013): 530–531.

25. Christopher Small, *Musicking: The Meanings of Performing and Listening* (Middletown, CT: Wesleyan University Press, 1998), 9.

26. Ibid., 13.

27. Richard Taruskin, "Is There a 'Russia Abroad' in Music?," in *Russian Music at Home and Abroad: New Essays*, ed. Richard Taruskin (Oakland: University of California Press, 2016), 149.

28. Sergei Bertensson and Jay Leyda, *Sergei Rachmaninoff: A Lifetime in Music* (Bloomington: Indiana University Press, 2001), 223.

29. An exception is Kosik Ivanovič's article on the 1920s Russian cabaret scene in Belgrade ["Russkij teatr v restorane: Belgrad 20-h gg. XX v," *Godišnjak za društvenu istoriju* 12, no. 1–3 (2005): 111–127]. Although not academic, two other works that explore the realm of popular music within the emigration are: Mikhail Blizniuk, *Prekrasnaia Marusia Sava: russkaia emigratsiia na kontsertnykh ploshchadkakh i v restoranakh Ameriki* [The Wonderful Marusia Sava: The Russian Emigration on the Concert Stages and Restaurants of America] (Moscow: Russkii Put', 2007) and Konstantin Kazansky, "Russian Chanson in Paris," in *Russkii Parizh, 1910–1960*, ed. Joseph Kiblitsky, E. N. Petrova, and Juan Allende-Blin, 61–63 [Saint Petersburg]: Palace Editions, 2003.

30. Raeff, *Russia Abroad*, 10.

31. Harlow Robinson, *Russians in Hollywood, Hollywood's Russians: A Biography of an Image* (Lebanon, NH: Northeastern University Press, 2007), 3.

32. Catriona Kelly, "Russian Culture and Emigration, 1921–1953," in *Russian Cultural Studies: An Introduction*, ed. Catriona Kelly and David Shepherd (New York: Oxford University Press, 1998), 301.

33. Robinson, *Russians in Hollywood*, 4.

34. Judith Butler, "Performative Acts and Gender Constitution: An Essay in Phenomenology and Feminist Theory," *Theatre Journal* 40, no. 4 (Dec. 1988): 519.

35. Natasha Pravaz, "Transnational Samba and the Construction of Diasporic Musicscapes," in *The Globalization of Musics in Transit: Music, Migration, and Tourism*, ed. Simone Krüger and Ruxandra Trandafoiu (New York: Routledge, 2014), 281.

36. Thomas Solomon, "Performing Indigeneity: Poetics and Politics of Music Festivals in Highland Bolivia," in *Soundscapes from the Americas: Ethnomusicological Essays on the Power, Poetics, and Ontology of Performance*, ed. Donna A. Buchanan (Burlington, VT: Ashgate, 2014), 144–145.

37. Vernon Duke, *Passport to Paris* (Boston: Little, Brown, and Company, 1955), 92.

38. For an analysis of the Jewish emigration from Imperial Russia during this period, see Simon Kuznets, "Immigration of Russia Jews to the United States: Background and Structure," *Perspectives in American History* 9 (1975): 35–124; Eli Lederhendler, *Jewish Immigrants and American Capitalism, 1880–1920: From Caste to Class* (Cambridge: Cambridge University Press, 2009), 1–37. For an examination of prerevolutionary Russian Jewish life, see, for example, Zvi Gitelman, *A Century of Ambivalence: The Jews of Russia and the Soviet Union, 1881 to the Present* (Bloomington: Indiana University Press, 2001), 1–58; Benjamin Nathans, *Beyond the Pale: The Jewish Encounter with Late Imperial Russia* (Berkeley: University of California Press, 2002).

39. Jonathan Gill, *Harlem: The Four Hundred Year History from Dutch Village to Capital of Black America* (New York: Grove Press, 2011), 136–138; Jeffrey S. Gurock, *When Harlem Was Jewish, 1870–1930* (New York: Columbia University Press, 1979), 27–57.

40. Moses Rischin, *The Promised City: New York's Jews, 1870–1914* (Cambridge, MA: Harvard University Press, 1977), 133. For a detailed look at Jewish cultural life in New York during this period, see, for example, Annie Polland and Daniel Soyer, "Immigrant Citadels: Tenements, Shops, Stores, and Streets" and "Jews and New York Culture," in *Emerging Metropolis: New York Jews in the Age of Immigration, 1840–1920* (New York City: New York University Press, 2012), 103–135, 207–243. On music, see, most recently, Michael Ochs, "A Yiddish Operetta Tailored to Its Audience: Joseph Rumshinsky's *Di Goldene Kale*," in *Di Goldene Kale*, ed. Michael Ochs, Recent Researches in American Music, Vol. 80 (Middleton, WI: A-R Editions, Inc., 2017), xiii–lii.

41. Polland and Soyer, *Emerging Metropolis*, 113.

42. G. G. Bernadskii, *Russkaia koloniia v Soedinnenykh Shtatakh* [The Russian Colony in the United States] (New York: n.p., 1992), 8; Raeff, *Russia Abroad*, 26.

43. Ivan K. Okuntsoff, *Russkaia emigratsiia v Severnoi i Iuzhnoi Amerike* [The Russian Emigration in North and South America] (Buenos Aires: Seiatl', 1967), 220; *Orthodox America, 1794–1976: Development of the Orthodox Church in America*, ed. Constance J. Tarasar (Syosset, NY: The Orthodox Church in America, 1975), 219.

44. *The Fiftieth Anniversary of the Historic Second Street Cathedral* (n.p.: Simandron Publications, 1993), 2.

45. For more on the exchange between Morris Gest and Michel Fokine, see Valleri J. Hohman, *Russian Culture and Theatrical Performance in America, 1891–1933* (New York: Palgrave Macmillan, 2011), 86–88.

46. Ibid., 40. Many consultants I interviewed for this project noted Hurok's productions as being important Russian events to attend in New York.

47. For an extensive biography of Sol Hurok, see, Harlow Robinson, *The Last Impresario: The Life, Times, and Legacy of Sol Hurok* (New York: Penguin Books, 1994).

48. Although an excellent starting point on research of the Russian émigrés community in New York, James Hassell's *Russian Refugees in France and the United States Between the World Wars* (Philadelphia: American Philosophical Society, 1991) is relatively limited in scope.

49. Gill, *Harlem: The Four Hundred Year History*; Stephen Robertson, Shane White, and Stephen Garton, "Harlem in Black and White: Mapping Race and Place in the 1920s," *Journal of Urban History* 39, no. 5 (2013): 864–880.

50. Peter J. Schmelz, "Intimate Histories of the Musical Cold War: Fred Prieberg and Igor Blazhkov's Unofficial Diplomacy," in *Music and International History in the Twentieth Century*, ed. Jessica C. E. Gienow-Hecht (New York: Berghahn Books, 2015), 189–225.

51. Ibid., 192.

52. Ann Cooper-Albright, "Introduction: Situated Dance," in *Engaging Bodies: The Politics and Poetics of Corporeality* (Middletown, CT: Wesleyan University Press, 2013), 10.

53. Mauro Van Acken, "Dancing Belonging: Contesting *Dabkeh* in the Jordan Valley, Jordan," *Journal of Ethnic and Migration Studies* 32 no. 2 (March 2006): 205.

54. Sydney Hutchinson, "Breaking Borders/*Quebrando Fronteras*: Dancing in the Borderscape," in *Transnational Encounters: Music and Performance at the US-Mexican Border*, ed. Alejandro Madrid (Oxford: Oxford University Press, 2012), 41–66; Ian MacMillen, "Fascination, Musical Tourism, and the Loss of the Balkan Village (Notes on Bulgaria's Koprivshtitsa Festival)," *Ethnomusicology* 59, no.2 (Spring/Summer 2015): 227–261; Pravaz, "Transnational Samba," 272–297.

55. Jana Evans Braziel and Anita Mannur, "Nation, Migration, Globalization: Points of Contention in Diaspora Studies," in *Theorizing Diaspora: A Reader*, ed. Jana Evans Braziel and Anita Mannur (Malden, MA: Blackwell Publishing, 2003), 7.

56. Jeffrey A. Summit, *The Lord's Song in a Strange Land: Music and Identity in Contemporary Jewish Worship* (New York: Oxford University Press, 2000), 6.

1

PERFORMING À LA RUSSE

Music, Migration, and
the White Russians in 1920s Harlem

A FTER A LONG DAY'S WORK AT THE SEWING machine, embroidering knockoffs of the Parisian *à la Russe* tunics and scarves then the rage in New York, Olga Popoff (1894–1990) entered the large parish house attached to Christ the Savior Russian Orthodox Church in Harlem. She, along with numerous other refugees from the Bolshevik Revolution (1917) and Russian Civil War (1918–1922), met—as they did nearly every Wednesday night since arriving in New York City in 1923—for an evening of music, poetry, plays, and dancing. The daughter of a Swedish industrialist and a Russian mother, Popoff had grown up in Siberia and attended the conservatory before marrying a Swedish diplomat and escaping from Russia in 1918. A whirlwind on-ship romance with White Army officer Eupheme Popoff (1873–1972) ended the Swedish marriage, and here they were, in the Russian Club of Harlem, mingling with other former Russian nobles, officers, and intellectuals who attended these gatherings despite long hours painting houses, scrubbing floors, mixing chemicals, and painting dolls on an assembly line.

These so-called "Russian Evenings" gave the Popoffs and the other Russian refugees in New York a chance to escape their quotidian lives—to meet with one another, speak their native tongue, and reminisce about life in the home country. Similar to the gatherings that occurred in other pockets of the postrevolutionary Russian emigration in such locales as Paris, Belgrade, and Harbin, this fellowship allowed émigrés to talk "for hours of politics, of books, of art, and of dreams."[1] Of these dreams, both immediate and enduring, one loomed above all others: to return to Russia following the collapse of the Bolshevik regime. Although a return to Russia free of communist rule would not become possible during the lifespan of Olga or Eupheme Popoff, the Russians in Harlem found ways to maintain a connection to their homeland: they cooked pots of hot borscht and cabbage-stuffed *piro-zhki*, they founded and named their church in honor of Moscow's monumental Christ the Savior Cathedral (apogee of Tsarist popular support built to commemorate Russia's victory over Napoleon in 1812 and demolished by the communist regime in 1931), and they designed a memorial chapel in which they hung icon lamps as tribute to those who had died for their homeland.[2] Perhaps more than anything else, they listened to their fellow émigrés perform music—strains so compelling that they allowed the dejected exiles to "forget the present and remember our old Russia."[3]

What was this "Old Russia" and how was it, as phrased by Richard Taruskin, defined musically?[4] Even more germane to this chapter, how did music connect exiles to their lost Russia and inform what it meant to be an émigré, or "emigrant," the term embraced by members of the diaspora as a reference to the French exiles of nearly a century and half earlier who had similarly fled their homeland after a bloody revolution?[5]

"Happier days have faded away and the lilac has wilted . . . happiness has vanished, and the heart lives by the past." These words, sung by émigré Emma Hurok (1897–1974) (wife of the earlier Russian Jewish emigrant and later pivotal impresario Sol Hurok), offer a glimpse of the type of repertoire and affect framing the music culture of the Russian émigré community in 1920s New York, which was then situated in Harlem around Mount Morris Park (now Marcus Garvey Park). Musically, the weekly Russian evenings were dominated by Russian folk and so-called gypsy songs, giving form to the elusive Russian soul and *volia* (freedom from any and all restrictions) respectively.

As Alaina Lemon points out, however, volia is a particular kind of freedom worlds away from the more pragmatic *svoboda* (a "more struc-tured liberty from social law").[6] Indeed, volia refers to freedom of one's very core—one's free will—an ontological state of liberation. The Russian gypsy song was long considered a potent site harboring volia—an asso-ciation forged not only through the music's perceived correlation to the Romani people and the supposedly unfettered lives they led, but, as I will show, through the musical and textual content of this repertoire. The Rus-sian gypsy song offered its listeners temporary liberation from the shack-les of exile—a process that worked because of the music's engagement of an even more mysterious affect: *toska*. A mood so dependent on cultural context that it has no direct translation into English, toska can roughly be translated as a languid desire for something that is now absent (usually a lover and happier days, more generally). Toska permeated Russian émigré existence—emerging not only in the Russian gypsy repertoire but in the daily lexicon of the exiles. (Natalia Rachmaninoff, for example, wrote to a friend just before her husband's death, "They say that S[ergei] Vas[ilievich] had a physician who told him that his heart was tired. How true this is, and how so like him. . . . He has become tired from yearning [toska] for Russia. So of course, we understand all of this very well.")[7] Understanding the ways in which toska has been implicated musically presents a critical starting point for better understanding the role of music in shaping the collective outlook of the Russian émigrés.

At first glance, the adoption of Russian gypsy and folk music by members of the predominantly upper-class, largely ethnic-Russian diaspora may appear as an unusual means of self-definition. Yet this music had rolled off the tongue of educated ladies and gentlemen in prerevolutionary Russia and had been ubiquitous on the stages of restaurants and cabarets throughout the Silver Age. Within the halls of the church in Harlem, this music, however, now took on a new dimension, for it was the Russian gypsy and folk music, with their potent evocations of volia, toska, and an idyllic Russia, that helped inform what it meant to be a Russian émigré. This music presented a space for a performative reinterpretation of Russia, with the prerevolutionary marginality of both peasant and gypsy tropes vis-à-vis the Westernized elite now transformed into an appropriate medium through which this elite in exile could express its newly acquired marginalization and perform Otherness in relation to its surrounding cultural milieu.

Perhaps more importantly, the New York émigrés approached Russian folk and gypsy music as discursive sites for developing and circulating collective narratives of the precataclysmic homeland ("Old Russia") and of being Russian abroad. In line with Victor Turner's concept of "social drama," the shared experience, in this case, of revolution, civil war, and migration presented the necessary "conflict" that was processed through the theatrical medium of musical performance.[8] These musical acts, in turn, can serve as forums for creating and articulating social metacommentary, or "a story a group tells itself about itself."[9] Such metacommentary not only reflects social life but also allows participants to reflexively reinterpret and subsequently transform everyday life.

Through this dialectic process, a trope of Old Russia thus came into existence by way of musical performance, which helped the émigrés define and maintain their mission of cultural preservation. Indeed, a kind of "active or 'magic' mirror" the concerts in Harlem served as sites in which Old Russia could materialize through the reflection, projection, and reinterpretation undertaken by their participants.[10] Within a migratory context, this metacommentary often takes on a specific dimension that reifies a perfected (and lost) homeland through musical performance. I call this phenomenon *diasporic metacommentary*, a concept that fuses anthropological and diasporic theory to help elucidate the processes by which a group of émigrés comes to define itself as a singular, recognizable entity through common discursive tropes enabled through artistic acts.

Examining the music that dominated Russian Harlem, its performance practice, and the ways its performances were publicized and received by the Russian-American press, this chapter explores how Russian émigrés in New York used Russian folk and gypsy music as a space for creating a diasporic metacommentary, the rhetoric of which would become a foundational element in defining the First Wave Russian diaspora. More broadly, an examination of the music culture of Russian Harlem presents a case study of how an exiled community chooses to represent the past through music and to address the pressing question of how to maintain a connection—however imagined or tenuous—to the homeland. Framed as "heightened forms of representation for public perception,"[11] musical performance presents a critical forum for the study of how diasporans choose to define themselves around collective symbols of migration, dislocation, and an overriding sense of "not being there."[12]

Harlem's Little Russia

As the anti-Bolshevik White Army suffered defeat after defeat toward the end of the Russian Civil War, growing numbers of people fled their homeland, ultimately reaching a group of approximately one and a half million exiles.[13] One of the main evacuation routes from Russia was through Crimea to Constantinople. This departure entailed people desperately making their way onto overcrowded ships in the hopes of escaping the approaching Bolshevik soldiers. Left behind were crystal glasses, pianos, ever-faithful schnauzers, hunting parties, decadent nights of champagne and caviar, and fathers, mothers, sisters, and brothers.

This mad-rush separation from the *rodina* ("homeland," literally, the place of one's kin), was followed by a more extended pain. This was life in

Constantinople (or, for those with an even more difficult road, along the barren plains of Gallipoli, where tents were erected as makeshift homes for thousands of refugees). Although the American Red Cross and YMCA initially supplied the refugees with food (canned beef and condensed milk were given on board vessels fleeing Crimea, for example), provisions soon ran out, and the refugees were forced to find ways to sustain themselves. Many exiles, including composer Vernon Duke (Vladimir Dukelsky), his mother, and brother, initially survived by selling family valuables (diamonds, in the case of the Dukelsky family). Once these treasures disappeared, the exiles were forced to find other means of supporting themselves, as they peddled water, chocolates, and handcrafted paper flowers; swept dusty streets; and mended the clothes of American aid workers. The lucky few worked as butlers and governesses for Turkish, Armenian, and Georgian households—hired as much for their language skills as for their former positions as members of the Russian nobility. Precious few found work, however, and many maintained a desperate existence on both physical and moral grounds. The usually perky Dukelsky (whose piano skills supplied him with work at "one of the better" restaurants in the European section of Constantinople) remembers the difficulty many Russians faced in the ancient city: "I cringed when I saw former heroes, proud earners of all four Saint George crosses, still bearing the now-obsolete insignia of no-longer existing regiments, in their faded and artlessly patched uniforms, ambling aimlessly and shamefacedly along; or worse, Russian women, many of them still pretty, still hopeful, with the bold flag of Parisian lipstick on parched lips . . . their dresses out of fashion—even in Turkey—their shoes pitifully disguised wrecks, who haunted the Grande Rue de Pera at all hours, window-shopping masochistically."[14] Experiencing the "misery of Constantinople," most refugees scrambled to get out of Turkey, going to whatever countries would accept them.[15]

It was under these conditions that a group of approximately three thousand Russian émigrés left Constantinople for the more promising shores of New York. The large majority arrived on a single ship, the SS *Constantinople*, under the energetic and steady leadership of Vladimir de Smitt (1884–1964), former captain of the Russian Imperial Navy, future founder of Harlem's Russian Orthodox parish, and oceanographer, whose respected work in the field gave him coveted positions at Constantinople's Roberts College, Western Union, and, starting in 1926, at Columbia University. Mirroring the makeup of the broader emigration, the Russian community in

Harlem would include White Army officers and their families, artists, students, and former members of the Russian nobility.[16]

Regardless of their former status, most members of the Russian Harlem community sought a means of earning a living upon arriving in the city, with 90 percent initially finding work as unskilled laborers.[17] Many worked at Brooklyn's Lyon Match Factory (which Dukelsky hailed as being "considered the thing by refugees"), others labored in sewing shops, and some eventually in Igor Sikorsky's helicopter manufacturing plant in Stratford, Connecticut.[18] This change in fortune presented an enticing juxtaposition for the American press, which published such sensationalist pieces as "Noble Russians in Our Garages" and "Title and Talent Exiled, Toil Here in Lowly Tasks." The stereotype of the penniless aristocrat soon emerged as a common image in American sheet music, plays, and films (see chap. 2).[19]

Upon their arrival in New York, the émigrés were met by representatives of the Russian Refugee Relief Society of America, who assisted the refugees in matters of immigration, helped them find work, and oriented them to their new surroundings in exchange for 10 percent of their first month's salary.[20] Initially, the most pressing need was finding a place to sleep, and the émigrés were given two free weeks of lodging in a five-story stone house on Fifth Avenue and 128th Street, where, among others, accordionist and future big-band leader Basil Fomeen (1902–1983) stayed upon coming to New York. The house, which was owned by the Relief Society, included a dormitory and inexpensive dining room. The support system offered by the Relief Society was the initial draw for the émigrés to Harlem and helped establish a Little Russia in the neighborhood. In the words of the émigrés, "in this way a significant, homogenous, and tight colony of Russians was formed around Mount Morris Park."[21]

Although the Russian exiles settled in different pockets of Manhattan, the most concentrated number lived around 125th Street and Fifth Avenue in Harlem, a neighborhood abounding with beautiful brownstones, gothic-style churches, and charming parks. To the Russian exiles, who had lived through civil war, flight from Russia, and horrendous living conditions in Constantinople, Harlem must have appeared a magnificent haven. Indeed, Harlem was at once comfortably predictable—with the beautifully steady hum of work—and utterly modern—with the blaring sounds of jazz emerging mere blocks away from the Cotton Club.

After settling in Harlem, the émigrés rapidly established Russian businesses in the Mount Morris neighborhood. Longing for a book in the native tongue, one could frequent the three Russian bookstores. Or if one desired a palatable treat for the mouth or olfactory reminder of the homeland, one could meander into any of the five Russian restaurants, all opened in the mid-1920s and made more quaint by the diminutives in their names: *Russkii kabachek* (the little Russian tavern), *Khutorok* (the little farmhouse), *Zolotoi petushok* (the little golden cockerel), *Petushok* (the cockerel), and the vaguely Socialist anomaly, *Progress*.[22]

At the center of the Russian community in Harlem stood Christ the Savior Cathedral, a gothic-style church with tall spire that was purchased from the Knights of Columbus in 1927 and which stood on 121st Street between Park and Madison Avenue (see fig. 1.1).[23] Like the renowned Cathedral of Alexander Nevsky on Rue Daru, the "uncontested heart of Russian Paris," Christ the Savior emerged as the hub of émigré life in New York.[24] Indeed, as the "overwhelming majority"[25] of Russian émigrés belonged to the Orthodox Church, it is not surprising that involvement in the church "became essential to the lives of most White émigrés."[26] More than a spiritual center, Christ the Savior Church became a cultural locus—a space for regular social interaction for believers and unbelievers alike.[27]

Although Manhattan already boasted a prominent Russian Orthodox church—the ornate, Muscovite-style St. Nicholas Cathedral on Ninety-Seventh Street, built by Tsar Nicholas II in 1904—the émigrés decided to establish their own church, quite possibly because of the class divide that existed between them and the earlier Russian immigrants who attended St. Nicholas. Despite its lack of longevity and Russian-style exterior, however, Christ the Savior became the church in which it became fashionable for First Wave Russians to be seen, married, and buried (see fig. 1.2). Numerous princes and princesses, counts, and barons held their weddings at the Harlem church, which also served as the site for the final rites for many renowned émigrés, including several artists and musicians. Following the deaths of composers Sergei Rachmaninoff (1873–1943) and Alexander Arkhangelsky (1856–1924), for example, the church held memorial services—two occasions that were widely publicized in the Russian-American press. The funeral of Russian impresario Nikita Balieff was held at the church. Likewise, the funeral of Michel Fokine (1880–1942), the once-daring choreographer of the *Ballets Russes* who came to New York in 1919 through the instigation of impresario Morris Gest, was also held at the church. Considering that, according to his son, Fokine was not a "church man," the choice of Christ the Savior as the site of the ballet master's funeral

Figure 1.1. Christ the Savior Russian Orthodox Cathedral in Harlem, c. 1930. Christ the Savior Papers, The Archives of the Orthodox Church in America.

Figure 1.2. Interior of Christ the Savior Russian Orthodox Cathedral. Christ the Savior Papers, The Archives of the Orthodox Church in America.

further underscores the central social position of the parish in regard to the cultural topography of White Russian New York.[28]

While the church building proper was the site of religious services, it was the adjacent parish house that came to stand as the cultural center of Russian Harlem. There, all manner of artistic, gastronomic, and social happenings took place. With a reception hall that could fit six hundred people, the "Russian Club" housed the headquarters of numerous émigré organizations, dances, and weekly social evenings (fig. 1.3). The building also included a busy restaurant that served "good Russian food and cheap vodka."[29] This fare entailed piping-hot pirozhki (traditional Russian meat pies) and generously stuffed *kulibiaka* (a roulade made of cabbage or ground beef).[30]

From the beginning, both Christ the Savior and its adjacent Russian Club were supported by the generous financial assistance of a number of prominent New Yorkers, including the prerevolutionary Russian ambassador to the United States, Boris Bakhmeteff (1880–1951); the Russophile-philanthropist Charles R. Crane (1858–1939); and the affluent arts patron Addie Wolff Kahn (1875–1949), wife of renowned banker and philanthropist Otto Kahn (1867–1934).[31] Russian émigré musicians likewise made

Figure 1.3. Parish Hall of Christ the Savior Russian Orthodox Cathedral ("Russian Club"). Christ the Savior Papers, The Archives of the Orthodox Church in America.

donations—both monetary and artistic—that helped found and sustain the parish. One of the first donors to Christ the Savior was Sergei Rachmaninoff, who contributed $400 (the equivalent of approximately $5,000 in today's value) to the church in 1925.[32] At that time, Rachmaninoff and his family lived south of Russian Harlem, on Riverside Drive between Seventy-Fifth and Seventy-Sixth Streets. Although it is unclear whether or not Rachmaninoff was a parishioner of Christ the Savior, some scholars speculate that he and his family began to frequent the church after the confiscation of St. Nicholas Russian Orthodox Cathedral by the Soviet "Living Church" in 1926.[33]

Composer Alexander Gretchaninoff (1864–1956), who had fled Russia in 1925 and initially settled in Paris, likewise supported the church in the form of a series of benefit concerts that he conducted in New York City as part of his 1929 American tour, which took him to the very pinnacle of New York musical life: Carnegie Hall. Yet, even in this most revered space, the concert was explicitly publicized as being organized for "The Russian Church in New York," a point made in both concert announcements and programs.

The cultural weight of Gretchaninoff's Carnegie Hall concert and, by extension, the institution that it was supporting, was furthered by the musicians and patrons who took part in the event. The artists included Nina Koshetz (1881–1965), who had finished the Moscow Conservatory in 1913 and began establishing herself as an opera singer in prerevolutionary Russia. Emigrating from Russia to New York via Constantinople in 1920, Koshetz made numerous concert appearances, including at Carnegie and Town Hall and at private parties held by the Astor and Vanderbilt families.[34] By the time of Gretchaninoff's concert, Koshetz had performed throughout the United States, including singing the lead role in the Chicago premiere of Prokofiev's *The Love for Three Oranges*. Further underscoring the concert's social gravitas, Gretchaninoff's concert was supported by members of the Russian nobility, including Grand Duchess Maria Pavlovna (1890–1958), first cousin of Tsar Nicholas II (1868–1918), and Princess Nina Georgievna (1901–1974), great-granddaughter of Tsar Nicholas I (1796–1855), both of whom took an active role in the philanthropic events organized in New York for their fellow émigrés.

Émigré musicians did not merely support the Russian Church in Harlem from a distance but also performed on the premises of the parish. Two weeks before his Carnegie debut, for example, Gretchaninoff conducted the same program at the Russian Club. Several years following Gretchaninoff's concert, Koshetz gave a vocal recital at the Russian Club in February 1932 (see fig. 1.4). The writing on the program emphasizes the close relationship between Koshetz and her contemporaries whose works are featured on the concert, including Rachmaninoff, Gretchaninoff, Nikolai Medtner (1879–1951), and Alexander Scriabin (1872–1915) (see fig. 1.4).[35] The program situates Koshetz in a position of recognition, as it specifies that the songs by these composers were all dedicated to the singer herself. The explanation under the song by Scriabin, moreover, underscores both its rarity and supposed authenticity ("Only song ever written by Scriabine, given to Nina Koshetz in manuscript").

The close relationship between Russian musicians in the emigration (all of the composers featured on Koshetz's concert save Scriabin, who died in 1915, left Russia after the Revolution) as well as the many concerts organized for the benefit of the Russian church in Harlem point to a broader culture of philanthropy that helped define musical life in the emigration. In part, the mutual assistance practiced by the émigrés reflects a continuation of the benefit concert tradition that had been prevalent during

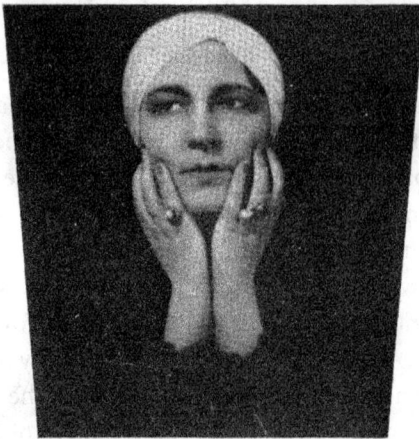

RUSSIAN CLUB, 51 East 121st Street, New York City

Recital of Russian Melodies
given by

NINA KOSHETZ
for the benefit of

RUSSIAN CHURCH OF CHRIST THE SAVIOR

Saturday, February 6th, 1932, 9:30 P. M.

PROGRAM

I.

"Oh, Could I Express in Sound" .... *Malashkine*
Old Valse .... *Bulakhoff*
The Doubt .... *Glinka*
Jamais .... *Dargomijsky*

II.

Back to Thy Home .... *Borodine*
It is not the Wind .... *Rimsky-Korsakoff*
Desire .... *Cesar Cui*
Children's Songs .... *Moussorgsky*

    (a) In the Corner
    (b) With the Doll
    (c) Evening Prayer

III.

On the Yellow Fields .... *Tschaikowsky*
Valse .... *Arensky-Koshetz*
Devotion .... *Scriabine*
(Only song ever written by Scriabine, given to Nina Koshetz in manuscript, now published by Bessel in Paris.)
Daisies .... *Rachmaninoff*
(One of six songs dedicated to Nina Koshetz.)
Spanish Serenade .... *Medtner*
(Dedicated to Nina Koshetz.)

IV.

When the Fields are Swaying .... *Gretchaninoff*
(One of three songs dedicated to Nina Koshetz)
Miniature .... *Nina Koshetz*
(One of the cycle "The Wreath of Miniatures")
Bells of Home .... *Nina Koshetz*
Children Song .... *Strawinsky*

BORIS KOGAN *at the Steinway Piano*

(Songs of Nina Koshetz published by Schirmer, Inc.)
(R. C. A. Victor Records)

AFTER CONCERT — DANCING

Figure 1.4. Russian Club Concert Program, featuring Nina Koshetz, February 6, 1932. Christ the Savior Papers, The Archives of the Orthodox Church in America.

World War I in Russia, serving as a precedent for the countless aid organizations that sprang up amid the émigrés, despite their own often-destitute predicament.[36]

Beyond a mere continuation of practice, however, the philanthropy that predominated in the Russian emigration was a response to the condition of exile—a mutual impulse among émigrés to help one another that was evident in both public and private spheres. Despite her international renown, Koshetz, for example, befriended the little-known Vladimir Dukelsky (who would soon take on the more accessible pseudonym, Vernon Duke) after both settled in New York in the early 1920s. Koshetz actively advocated on Dukelsky's behalf, asking the young composer to play as her accompanist, showcasing his songs, and, on a purely amicable level, inviting Dukelsky to her apartment for food, music, and gossip. The evenings at 33 Riverside Drive made an especially strong impression on the young composer, presenting him with what he recalled as: "a delicious refuge for lost young souls like myself, who often repaired to Nina's after an overdose of poor jazz or synthetic gypsy wailing. We drank oceans of tea and devoured innumerable *pirojki* and other Russian goodies; we talked of Rachmaninov and Scriabin and that impertinent young coxcomb Prokofiev."[37]

With Koshetz a rising opera star while Dukelsky a mere teenager in prerevolutionary Russia, it is doubtful that the two would have crossed paths, let alone have become friends. Yet the common context of being émigrés in New York engendered a camaraderie that would unite the two as well as countless other musicians in the diaspora, including Rachmaninoff and Fokine, who became close friends only after fleeing Russia and settling in New York. Indeed, aside from their common views on art and their mutual respect for one another, the friendship between the two artists was based on a shared feeling of uprootedness.[38]

The bond originating in the common experience of exile and cemented around the samovar was also demonstrated in more public forums. In October 1925, for example, a group of émigré musicians spearheaded by Jascha Heifetz (1901–1987), Leopold Auer (1845–1930), and Alexander Aslanov (1874–1960) published a letter in the nationally circulating Russian-language daily *Novoe Russkoe Slovo* (the new Russian word) calling for "all Russian musicians in America" to join in signing their names in commemoration of composer Alexander Glazunov's sixtieth birthday.[39] As Glazunov had remained in Russia following the Revolution (where he headed the St. Petersburg Conservatory until 1928), the letter was, in part, a means of keeping émigré musicians from being excluded from this occasion, as it emphatically states: "We shall not remain on the periphery of this celebration . . . we, Russian musicians, [who were] strewn in all directions and, in most cases, forced into exile."[40] In addition to seeking inclusion in the Soviet commemoration, the letter reveals a dismissal of the new Soviet regime by its use of the "Old Style" Julian calendar dates (used in prerevolutionary Russia and then consequently replaced by the Soviets with the more accurate and widely used Gregorian calendar) and by describing Glazunov's birthday celebration as one of the "few joys" in today's Russia.

The Glazunov commemoration engages a broader question of cultural ownership and diaspora-homeland politics. The tone of the article, in fact, calls into question the extent to which Glazunov's birthday was not merely a pretext for asserting the voice of musicians in exile. Its writers ask not only former colleagues and students of Glazunov to sign the letter, but all those who "consider themselves tied to Russian musical art, its achievements, and its future." What is especially noteworthy in this letter is the means by which its writers describe the role of music in fostering a connection between musicians in exile and the musical life they left behind: "[Despite] the external separation from the musical life in Russia, which was once so close to us, we are, nevertheless, not separated from it in spirit. By ever-deep roots, with thousands of unseen strands, are we connected with this life and, with the uttermost inner participation, with all of its joys and adversities."[41]

While appearing simply as a birthday greeting, the letter attests to the strong bond that developed among musicians in the emigration and the desire among them for a connection to life in Russia. The notion of "unseen strands" linking musicians in exile to their homeland served as a central part of the discourse defining the Russian diaspora and became a central idea fostered through musical performance.

Performing Russian "Folk" in Harlem

How were the "unseen strands" connecting émigré artists to musical life in Russia made manifest in the daily existence of the émigrés? For the Russians in Harlem, this idea was largely fostered through weekly artistic evenings. One of the earlier such occasions took place on August 30, 1924, and entailed a potpourri of acts featuring soprano Elena Vorontsova (?–1951), folk music sweetheart of Russian New York and, like many women in the audience, wife of a White Army officer; pianist Sandro Corona, a graduate of the St. Petersburg Conservatory; and émigré poet Aleksandr Voloshin, whose oeuvre included poems that playfully relayed life in Russian Harlem:

Katilis' dni, tekli nedeli,	Days passed by and so did weeks.
V Garleme bezhentsy oseli,	The refugees made their home in Harlem,
I vyros russkii gorodok:	And there a little Russian town did grow:
Ne to Lubny, ne to—Mozdok!	A little like Liubny, a little like—Mozdok!
Zakrylis' serdtsa zlye rany,	The wounds of the hearts did close,
Zato—otkrylis' restorany,	Yet—in turn, did restaurants open,
Stolovki, russkikh klubov riad.	Snack bars, and a row of Russian clubs.[42]

According to a write-up in the *New York Times*, the evening was a success, with Vorontsova singing "with a great deal of expression and a voice which had both strength and variety" and Voloshin keeping the audience "in roars of laughter."[43]

The format of this particular Russian Evening in Harlem became typical of the weekly gatherings that followed. Musically, these events entailed Russian art songs ("*romansy*"), excerpts from Russian operas, and Russian gypsy and folk songs. This motley arrangement of musical acts (interjected by comedic sketches, social dances, and, in several cases, even boxing matches), created an informal, carnivalesque air typical of the Estrada variety shows of prerevolutionary Russia.[44]

Of the four genres making up the musical portion of Harlem's Russian Evenings, Russian gypsy and folk music emerge as especially vibrant sites in which the émigrés engaged with their position as exiles and performed nostalgia for a lost homeland. At face value, the Russian gypsy genre—with its immediate association with Romani culture and people—presents a seemingly peculiar choice for the creation of Russian émigré culture. Russian folk music, on the other hand, emerges as a genre long imprinted in the Russian imaginary associated with an ideal, mythologized Russia, therefore presenting the émigrés with a potent sphere in which to play out narratives of nostalgia for Old Russia.

Far from the traditional practices of the Russian village, however, the folk repertoire performed at the Russian Club belongs to the category of stylized folk songs that made up part of the prerevolutionary Russian popular music culture. Consisting of songs either composed in a folk style or rural songs arranged according to harmonic, tonal, and structural rules of Western art music, this repertoire was frequently performed in such urban spaces as restaurants and cabarets in Russia and later in the émigré haunts of New York, Paris, Prague, Berlin, and Constantinople.[45] The Russian Club in Harlem was no exception, featuring such Russian folk standards as "*Svetit' mesiats'* [Brightly Shines the Moon]," "*Vo piru byla* [I Was at the Party]," and "*Ne shei mne, matushka, krasnyi sarafan* [Oh, Mother, Do Not Sew a Red Sarafan for Me]," a piece composed in a folk style by Alexander Varlamov (1801–1848), one of the numerous faux folk composers of the nineteenth century.[46]

The choir of Christ the Savior, which had been led since 1928 by Serge V. Savitsky (1886–1951), performed many such stylized pieces. The program from December 26, 1931, for example, was made up of pieces taken directly from the songbooks of Olga Agrenev-Slavianskii (1847–1920) and Alexander Alexandrov (1883–1946), two figures central in the professionalization of Russia's folk music culture and whose arrangements present cleaned-up versions of folk songs made more palatable to the urban ear though eliciting chagrin in seekers of authenticity. (Tchaikovsky likened the arrangements of Agrenev-Slavianskii to "cartoon versions" of the village originals.)[47] The pieces in Savitsky's December concert include "*Kak vo pole chistom*" (translated in the program as "In the Open Field"), "*Ekhal pan*" ("The Squire Rode"), "*Khodila mladeshen'ka po borochku*" ("The Bride Walked in the Wood"), and "*Akulinushka dusha*" ("Akulina, Darling").[48]

Regardless of whether or not these songs had originated in the Russian countryside, they had undergone various permutations by the time they were sung at the Russian Club. For instance, "*Khodila mladeshen'ka*" is featured in the folksong collection of Nikolai Lvov and Ivan Prach (1790), whose arrangements tend to eschew traditional heterophonic practices in favor of more standard three- and four-part harmonizations. Lvov and Prach's "*Khodila mladeshen'ka*" goes through a common Western chord progression, landing on a deafening dominant seventh chord (anathema to folklorists) on the penultimate beat. "*Khodila mladeshen'ka*" later found its way into the folk song collection of Nikolai Rimsky-Korsakov (1875–1876) and was even arranged by Rimsky-Korsakov and other art music composers into full-scale orchestral works before Agrenev-Slavianskii included the piece in her own songbook.

Savitsky's connection to stylized Russian folk music, however, surpasses mere aesthetic preference. While still a youth in the Pskov Corps of Cadets, Savitsky was inspired to become a choral conductor after hearing the famous folk choir of Prince Dimitry Agrenev-Slavianskii (1834–1908), whose *sarafan*- and caftan-wearing ensemble performed his wife's tightly arranged repertoire in a dramatic manner.[49] Savitsky's connection to Agrenev-Slavianskii was established to an even greater degree after he

Figure 1.5. Elena Vorontsova (?–1951), publicity photograph, *Almanac of Russian Artists in America*, vol. 1 (New York: Nicholas Martianoff and Mark Stern, 1932), 169.

fled Russia and married one of the daughters of the renowned composer while in Constantinople in the early 1920s.[50] Olga Dimitrievna remained a constant companion to Savitsky, singing in Harlem's Russian choir and bringing Savitsky closer to the work of her father.[51] It is not without some irony that Savitsky, who had been forced to pursue a military career in pre-revolutionary Russia, was in some ways liberated through exile to pursue his love of music, as there existed in the emigration a greater need for choir conductors than for former Russian imperial officers.

la ve - cher   mla - da,   na   pi - ru   by - la

Example 1.1. Opening phrase of "*Na piru byla*," transcribed from Elena Vorontsova, "*Na piru byla*," conducted by Leo Shield, Victor 78079, 78 Recording.

Although we do not know what Savitsky's choir sounded like, we do have an idea of how some singers in the Russian community of Harlem performed this repertoire. As early as 1924, for example, Elena Vorontsova recorded "*Vo piru byla* [I Was at the Party]" for Victor Records (see fig. 1.5).[52] The recording opens with the soft sounds of a balalaika ensemble, which instantly frame the piece as "traditional" and "Russian."[53] The quaint introduction is soon interrupted by the strong, belting voice of Vorontsova. Singing the opening phrase, "*Ya vecher mlada* [Last night, I, the young married woman]" in a loud, plucky manner, Vorontsova's initial state-ment is both visceral and colorful and provides a stark contrast to the soft strains of the balalaika ensemble. Vorontsova sings the consequent phrase ("*na piru byla* [was at the party]"), with her chest voice, yet shifts abruptly to her head voice and vibrato to sing the second word ("*piru* [party]") only to return to a rugged chest voice on the last word ("*byla* [was at]") (see example 1.1). Vorontsova continues in this manner throughout the piece, belting out and elongating the first word of each phrase (at which point the ensemble cuts out, making these moments further dramatic) and suddenly switching her vocal production and elongating the second word of each consequent phrase. Vorontsova ends the piece with an upward slide of an octave that she punctuates with a playful, folksy yelp.

The contrast between Vorontsova's different vocal productions results in an interpretation that is stylistically abrupt, and one wonders whether Vorontsova's shift to head voice is one of physical necessity due to a sig-nificant and rapid shift in melodic range.[54] Regardless of the reason for Vorontsova's shifts, her contrast in range and in timbre, dramatic rubato, and concluding spirited yelp produce a highly stylized effect. Further under-scoring the stylized nature of this recording is the fact that the balalaika ensemble is directed not by a fellow Russian émigré but by in-house Victor musician and later film composer Leroy Shield (1893–1962), who conducted many of Victor's ethnic ensembles and is featured on numerous records made by Russian artists.[55] Indeed, rather than a hermetic performance by an émigré artist, the Vorotnsova-Shield collaboration suggests a certain malleability in the production of culture in the First Wave diaspora—in which émigrés drew on their new surroundings, rather than remained isolated in an ethnic enclave.

Folk Music, Nostalgia, and the Russian-American Press

The stylized manner in which singers in Harlem interpreted Russian folk music in no way impeded a perceived correlation between this music and an essential Russia. The Russian-American press emerged as a major force in reinforcing this connection and in codifying the narrative of Old Russia as it was represented by émigré folk music performances. One of Vorontsova's first concert reviews to appear in the New York–based émigré paper, *Russkaia Mysl'* [Russian Thought], for example, describes the power of the singer's repertoire and style to evoke memories of time passed in an idyllic Russia: "Her song, thought out to the utmost subtlety, [and] her voice, which creeps into the soul, draw out and weave many, many memories of Russia—her fields, her forests, and the life of bygone days."[56]

Another review notes the idea of a universally "Russian" heart, while collapsing the past with the geographic locale of the homeland: "[Vorontsova's] songs ... transport the listener to Russia, entwining the Russian heart with dear memories."[57] Such rhetoric—which underscores a connection between folk music, an innate Russianness, and an idyllic landscape—enabled the reification of Old Russia, setting up the listener's expectations to be transported to this idyllic place through the sounds of Russian folk music.

Reviews and announcements of émigré performances in New York continually position folk music as a means of accessing an idealized Russia. Heralding Gretchaninoff's 1929 Carnegie Hall debut (which included two songs composed in a folk style), for example, *Novoe Russkoe Slovo* employed the colorful assertions, "Thus, by way of the concert, the Russian colony is presented with a very rare enjoyment ... authentic Russia in sound and word!" and "What Russian music—to the very marrow of the bones is it Russian."[58] As part of this "authentic Russia," folk music was likewise presented as a means of channeling the equally nebulous Russian spirit. Reviewing the January 1927 New York concert of renowned folk singer Nadezhda Plevitskaya (1884–1940), *Novoe Russkoe Slovo*, for example, remarked on the singer's "utterly unique ability" to relay "the authentic character that the Russian people have poured into their song."[59] Adding further color to this assertion, the writer goes on to ask, "Who can better portray what a peasant is thinking and feeling [than Plevitskaya]?"

Emerging as part of the Herderian nationalism that swept through Russia in the nineteenth century, the prototypical peasant (as later embodied by singers like Plevitskaya) became a central trope of the Russianness cobbled together and imposed by the upper strata of society. At this time, the Russian elite began to "formulate mythological versions of the peasant as a way of defining themselves and their nation," and stylized folk music was a recognized means of channeling a "pure Russian character."[60]

Although the belief in folk music as projecting the "truest expression" of the Russian nation had been established long before the émigrés left Russia, the context of diaspora added a new dimension to this connection.[61] The idealized Russia now rested on a collapse between time and space—Mikhail Bakhtin's "chronotope," which he defines as the "intrinsic connectedness of temporal and spatial relationships" expressed in literature, or in this case, through musical performance.[62] Bakhtin's literary model, based on Albert Einstein's Theory of Relativity, is rooted in an inseparability of space and time: "Time, as it were, thickens, takes on flesh, becomes artistically visible; likewise, space becomes charged and responsive to the movements of time, plot and history."[63] Like the "adventure time" Bakhtin details with regard to ancient Greek literature, the émigré parallel of prerevolutionary time reflects not the actual passage of time but a narrative whose gaps in real time leave "no trace" and present a time sequence in which "nothing changes."[64]

Even closer to the émigré model is Bakhtin's idea of the idyllic chronotope, which he defines as the "special relationship that time has to space in the idyll."[65] The idea of Old Russia as it developed in émigré discourse reflects an idyllic vision with the "unity of place" that "weakens and renders less distinct all the temporal boundaries between individual lives."[66] The predominant descriptions of the Russian landscape in the émigré concert announcements and reviews, moreover, reflect the "common language used to describe phenomena of nature and the events of human life" that further defines this chronotope.[67] Thus, the concept of Old Russia, as it emerged in émigré discourse, was not merely the land mass now thousands of miles away but also a symbol chronologically situated in the prerevolutionary period, paradoxically bound to its position in a timeless and idyllic space.

As a sonic pathway to the lost homeland, the performance of folk music offered émigrés a means through which to define Old Russia and a forum for conveying nostalgia toward this time-space. As such, Russian folk music emerges as a space for what Mario Rey has described as a "staging of nostalgia," in which exiles position themselves as (ethnic/political/gendered) Other, while garnering unified narratives of the past.[68] These narratives are framed by the very event of exile, whose trauma engenders a "corrosive nostalgia" that is rooted in mythologizing the homeland and collapsing space (homeland) and time (pre-cataclysmic past).[69]

The nostalgia for Old Russia incited through the performance of folk music laid the cornerstone for the diasporic metacommentary that defined what it meant to be a part of the Russian emigration. The idealized time-space that was engaged through folk music echoes one of the two categories of nostalgia as defined by Svetlana Boym.[70] Emphasizing *nostos* (the return home) as opposed to *algia* (longing or pain), this "restorative nostalgia" is rooted in narratives of the "truth" that frame a prelapsarian home.[71] Informed through the repetition of customs, which enshrouds it with a semblance of continuity with the past, restorative nostalgia is elicited through "new traditions" that are far more formalized than the "actual peasant customs and conventions after which they were patterned."[72] These "peasant customs" took on a literal dimension in the folk performances in Harlem, as singers played out the folk through stylized songs, performance practices, and costumes. As a conduit for restorative nostalgia, folk music enabled a momentary collapse of distance between Harlem and Old Russia by "intimate experience and the availability of a desired object."[73] The high yelps produced by Vorontsova, the tinny strands of Shield's balalaika players, and the crinkle of the starched *sarafany* worn by Olga Savitsky (née Agrenev-Slavianskii) and other women in Savitsky's folk choir created the "intimate experience" that rendered Old Russia as unified and real. As a multisensory experience, folk music performance brought this Russia to life and allowed its listeners to take part in, as émigré conductor Alexander Alsanov described, "authentic Russia in sound and word."[74]

Folk music performances in Harlem reflect one of Boym's paradoxes of restorative nostalgia: namely, that the "stronger the rhetoric of continuity with the historical past" (in this case, Old Russia), the "more selectively the past is presented."[75] Unlike the fractured nature of Boym's reflective nostalgia, which embraces multiplicity and incongruity, its counterpart relies on a "perfect snapshot" of the past by way of "national symbols and myths."[76] As such, Russian folk music in Harlem mirrors the music of other exiled communities, like those of anticommunist Cuban-American artists, who have employed claims of authenticity and incited nostalgia to construct a "hollowed-out" version of Cuban history.[77] The folk music in

Figure 1.6. Choir of Christ the Savior, c. 1925. Christ the Savior Papers, The Archives of the Orthodox Church in America.

Russian Harlem can be compared to the songs of such Cuban artists as Gloria Estefan, whose 1993 album, *Mi Tierra* (My Homeland) promotes an idyllic prerevolutionary past whitewashed of conflict. This "hollowed-out" history is constructed, in both cases, through musical signifiers of the past (including the use of traditional instruments), romanticized tropes of the homeland (such as birch trees, nightingales and sugar fields, palm trees), and a marketing strategy that frames émigré music as an uncorrupted reproduction of music from a bygone era. Like the music of Vorontsova or Plevitskaya, Estefan's songs acutely reflect this comparison, as they engage both musically and textually the "romantic, even mystical" homeland, promoting a "falsely homogenize[d]" homeland culture.[78]

This perfect snapshot of the past is illustrated on both a literal and figurative plane by a photograph from the mid-1920s of Christ the Savior Choir (see fig. 1.6). Although it is difficult to discern the costumes worn by the men, the women in the ensemble wear the dress of pre-Petrine nobility (*boyari*), donning jeweled headdresses (*kokoshniki*) and ornate sarafany.[79] Having become the rage among society women after the Russian victory over Napoleon in 1812, boyar costumes later became fashionable attire at costume balls and, in a stylized version, official uniforms for ladies-in-waiting at the Romanov courts. They also became the norm for folk ensembles, with a shift in costuming from traditional peasant garb to the more ornate look instigated by Dimitry Agrenev-Slavianskii in the later quarter of the nineteenth century.[80] By the time the photograph of Christ the Savior's choir had been taken, boyar costumes had become typical for folk ensembles, thus conflating pre-Petrine noble culture with music associated with the Russian peasantry and further illustrating the "symbolic formalization and ritualization" of Boym's restorative nostalgia.[81]

The embroidered sarafany were worn time and again at concerts, parties, and balls by women in the diaspora, including Harlem's Olga Popoff, whose mother did indeed sew for her the dress ("Oh, mother, do not sew for me . . ."). As underscored by historian Orlando Figes, it was this perfect snapshot, informed by meticulously sewn sarafany, the buoyant playing of balalaika ensembles, and roughly executed folk songs, which resonated within the Russian émigré communities strewn throughout the world: "In the 'Little Russias' of Berlin, Paris and New York the émigrés created their own mythic versions of the 'good Russian life' before 1917. They returned to a past that never was—a past, in fact, that had never been as good, or as 'Russian,' as that now recalled by the émigrés . . . The émigrés united around the symbols of Russian culture as the focus of their national identity."[82] Folk music provided an ideal forum for acting out this "good Russian life" and the nostalgia that lent poignancy and immediacy to this concept.

However, this kind of restorative nostalgia, as mapped out by Boym, is not always "paranoiac" and driven by a "delusional" belief of persecution and dislike.[83] Indeed, the idealization of the homeland among émigrés in New York was in no small part due to the circumstances under which the Russian diaspora was formed—the unwanted departure from Russia that followed a violent revolution and civil war—and is not uncommon to groups fleeing violent takeovers by communist regimes, including the Polish, Cuban, and Vietnamese diasporas, formed primarily in the 1940s, 1960s, and late 1970s respectively.[84] Such traumatic dispersal complies with the classic understanding of diasporas as it has been articulated by Robin Cohen and Khachig Tölölyan, in which a collective memory of the homeland is central to diasporic identity. Such "exilic nationalism" as laid out by Tölölyan, in which the "practices, mores and values that were considered the core of national identity in the homeland must be preserved in exile [and] must remain 'pure' or 'true' to their origins," emerges, in this case, as a central impetus in defining the time-space of prerevolutionary Russia.[85] For the New York Russians, this "exilic nationalism" engaged a form of cross-dressing, or, perhaps more aptly, class-dressing, through which they could simultaneously perform peasant and aristocrat, nationalist and cosmopolitan, and which enabled them to traverse between Russian countryside and New York nightclub.[86] Like Tolstoy's Natasha Rostova in *War and Peace*, for whom a village song brings to life the Russian spirit lying dormant within her outwardly Westernized, aristocratic self as it does within "every Russian man and woman,"[87] folk music freed the émigrés from the confines of the stone walls of the church in Harlem to tap into what Tölölyan calls the "core of national identity." Like Countess Rostova, the émigrés performed the folk from a position of power, as their upper-class upbringing ultimately situated them within New York's social strata as cosmopolitan desirables with an exotic flair—a paradox that would underlie a strategy of otherness enabled through music and embraced by many on the stages and restaurants of the diaspora.

Longing for a Gypsy Song

Despite the great distance between the émigrés in Harlem and the idyllic countryside they conjured through folk music, the connection between this music and a convention of Russianness is fairly straightforward. A more problematic category of music that defined Russian émigré culture is the so-called "gypsy" romance. Arguably the most popular genre of entertainment in the first decades of emigration and one that dominated Harlem's Russian Evenings, the gypsy romance presents a somewhat curious component of Russia Abroad.

The music's prevalence in the diaspora, however, can be explained by several factors. In part, the answer lies in the unparalleled popularity of gypsy music in prerevolutionary Russia, which grew out of the culture created by the various Romani communities that had migrated into Russian territory beginning in the mid-fifteenth century.[88] Eventually appearing in restaurants, on the estates of the gentry, and in the Rom camps that dotted the outskirts of Moscow and St. Petersburg, the Romani people became associated in the Russian imaginary with enchantment, sensuality, and freedom (volia)—tropes that would predominate in the Russian arts and letters.[89]

Central to this idea, the trope of the Gypsy (and, more specifically, the music she sang) emerged as a conduit for Russians to lose themselves in abandon and free themselves from the trappings of everyday life. As the Russian gypsy romance entitled "Tsyganka" by nineteenth-century poet Stepan Shevyrev (1806–1864) begins: "Oh you, most beautiful Egyptian! How full of feeling is your voice!"[90] From Pushkin's "*Chernaia shal*'" to the works of Dostoevsky, Leskov, and Tolstoy, to the plots of many lesser-known writers, the "beautiful Egyptian," with her seductive songs, had become a stock figure by the time of the revolution.[91] Initially retracted from the Soviet literary canon as a relic of the decadent bourgeois past, she made her way in the luggage of the emigrants to resurrect her song in a new but equally compelling form among Russian émigrés.

This body of work made its way to the far corners of the Mount Morris neighborhood of Harlem and included such standards as "*Chto nam gore* [The Heck with Heartache]," "*Ochi chernye* [Dark Eyes]," and "*Proshchai, proshchai, podruga dorogaia* [Farewell, My Love]."[92] Although there exist different iterations of Russian gypsy songs, the pieces tend to be in a minor key, start off slowly with much rubato, and employ harmonies of diminished seventh chords. The second half of the songs tends to be faster, with long interchanges of dominant tonic chords within the dizzying accelerando endings. Although accompanied by a range of instruments, including piano, accordion, and violin, the instrument most emblematic of the genre is the Russian seven-string guitar. Invented in Russia in the nineteenth century and most likely coinciding with the rise of amateur song performance during that period, the seven-stringed guitar is defined by its tuning system, which differs from that of the six-stringed guitar and facilitates chordal production.[93] Although not exclusively used for Russian gypsy repertoire, the seven-stringed guitar was the instrument of choice for playing such urban songs. This "symbol of Russian city culture" continued to be embraced by the émigrés, and many (including Alexandra Tolstoy (1884–1979), daughter of Leo Tolstoy, as well as Grand Duchess Marie Pavlovna) made it a point to take into exile their seven-string guitars when fleeing Soviet Russia.[94]

Despite their label as "gypsy" songs, however, the actual provenance of many of these pieces is far from clear, as many were unauthored, while others were composed by Russians, with and without the collaboration of Romani musicians. Still others were performed by Romani choruses in a deliberate "gypsy" style, rendered to suit the expectations of the Russian public.[95]

Instead of a necessary derivation from Rom culture, Russian gypsy music is better defined by its subject matter (abounding with references to "gypsy" life), the inclusion of words in the Romani language, and a specific performance practice that emphasizes an affective aesthetic. Singers sigh and groan, employ rubato frequently, and saturate songs with nonsensical utterances (most commonly, "da-ri-dai"). This style is evident on recordings made before the revolution by such performers as the renowned Romani singer Varia Panina (1872–1911) and the great bass Feodor Chaliapin (1873–1938) and would later predominate among singers in New York's émigré scene.

No better way is the circuitous history of Russian gypsy music illustrated than in the route the songs took between the estate of Russian writer Leo Tolstoy and the rolling hills of Valley Cottage, New York. It was there that the children and grandchildren of the author gathered in 1952 to record the Russian folk and gypsy songs they had once heard at Yasnaya Polyana, and the description of whose sounds begin this book.[96] Made on the premises of Reed Farm—one of the major centers for Russian refugees in the World War II era—the recording features Alexandra Tolstoy, who founded Reed Farm in 1939; Ilya Tolstoy (1903–1970), grandson of the author; and granddaughter Vera Tolstoy, who had performed Russian gypsy romances in the renowned Russian émigré club Scheherazade in Paris before immigrating to the United States in 1950.

The recording features some of the songs performed by the Rom who frequented Tolstoy's estate, as well as several pieces either composed or arranged by members of the Tolstoy family. Designated on the jacket notes in English, the pieces include, "Dreams by a Fireplace," "Let Your Pacer Go," "Not for Me to Hear," and "Where Are You, My Gypsy?" The way these songs are presented on the album underscores the often-ambiguous provenance of the Russian gypsy romance. The piece entitled "Not for Me to Hear," for example, is described as an "early 19th century gypsy song" that was "considered by gypsies as their rhapsody." A number of other songs are simply marked as being "quite old" or "very old" with unknown origins and years of composition. The song entitled "Let Your Pacer Go," for example, is simply announced as a "Russian gypsy song" by Ilya Tolstoy on the recording and is described as an "Old field gypsy song, origin and year unknown" on the liner notes.[97] A number of songs on the recording, moreover, are attributed to members of the Tolstoy clan and were, according to the liner notes, "adapted" by Romani musicians.[98] In this way, the album itself serves as an important clue regarding the ways Russian gypsy music was conceived and framed by members of the emigration as well as the complex roots of this music.

Even in Russian gypsy songs of unclear provenance, the so-called gypsy style is instantly recognizable. On "Let Your Pacer Go," for example, Vera Tolstoy employs much rubato, sliding, and frequent turns. The slight quiver in Tolstoy's voice and her use of vibrato further surround the song with a sensual and emotive air. Tolstoy sings in Romani in an affective style, while the "gypsy chorus"—comprised of Russians living on Reed Farm—accompanies the singer. The performative nature of the recording (i.e., former Russian nobility and descendants of the iconic literary figure allegedly playing "gypsy" music for an American audience) is further underscored by Ilya Tolstoy's announcement of the accompanying choir, which he introduces using the Romani word for gypsies (*chavale*), only to promptly translate into English as "gypsy choir."

The Russian gypsy style was so well established that this music continued to be not only sung but also penned in the emigration according to the earlier conventions. After coming to New York in 1922 and singing in the "gypsy" choir at Club Petroushka, accordionist Basil Fomeen (1902–1983), for example, composed numerous Russian gypsy romances. Although his best-known work continues to be "Manhattan Gypsy," Fomeen wrote a number of lesser-known pieces, including thirty-six "Russian Gypsy Songs" as part of his large oeuvre, *Songs of Inspiration* (see fig. 1.7).[99]

One of the set's pieces, "*Vse smutilos'* [Everything Is Hazy Now]," exudes a style typical of the genre, in which the emotions of anticipation, passion, and a live-for-today-for-tomorrow-we-die attitude are translated into musical terms. Set in A minor, the piece begins with a foreboding diminished seventh chord—a harmony that is found throughout the piece. After a short introduction, the vocalist enters to an accompaniment of rolled piano chords followed by quarter rests, which creates a recitative-like effect and enables the singer to take rubato at whim. Much like the other songs in the group, "*Vse smutilos'*" is laden with diminished seventh chords, syncopation, frequent shifts to the subdominant, passing tones, and structurally, a slow introduction (which sets an anticipatory tone), followed by a fast

ПЕСНИ

НАСТРОЕНИЯ

МУЗЫКА и СЛОВА

Василия Фомина

Альбом 5. Ор. 6.

1. ВСЕ СМУТИЛОСЬ.
2. МНЕ ХОЧЕТСЯ ВЕРИТЬ ТЕБЕ.
3. КОЛЬ ДУША БОЛИТ.
4. ЗОЛОТАЯ ЛУНА.
5. РАСПУСКАЛАСЬ СИРЕНЬ.
6. ЗВЕЗДОЧКА ЯСНАЯ.
7. Я ВЕРЮ ТЕБЕ.
8. ПУСТЬ СКРИПКА СТОНЕТ.

Цена 1.00 доллар.

VOGEL
MUSIC CO. INC
113 WEST 44th STREET
NEW YORK

MADE IN U.S.A.

Figure 1.7. Basil Fomeen, *Songs of Inspiration* (Album 5, Op. 6) cover page (Vogel Music Co., 1940). Basil Fomeen Collection, Music Division, Library of Congress.

Example 1.2. Basil Fomeen, "*Vse smutilos'*," measures 1–15. Basil Fomeen Collection, Music Division, Library of Congress.

section that ends in an accelerando climax (see example 1.2). This build-up and release is only furthered by the text, which begins with a wistful declamation ("We live within our fantasies, which enticingly intoxicate the heart"), only to end with the impassioned words, "Who knows what tomorrow may bring; as for today, today I shall love!"

The style in which Fomeen's pieces were performed likewise reflects a continuation of the prerevolutionary performance practice. Shortly after the publication of Fomeen's songs, fellow émigré and friend Adia Kuznetzoff recorded eight of these pieces (two of which are dedicated to the singer as Fomeen's "dearest friend") on an album entitled *Songs of Inspiration*. Performed in an emphatic, affective style, most of the pieces on the recording follow a similar format. The songs tend to open, for example, to the sounds of a wailing violin, accompanied by guitar and piano, which plays rolled chords and glissandi. The entrance of the vocal part is preceded by the violin's dramatic pause on the high point of the opening phrase. The verses are punctuated with Kuznetzoff's rich bass and frequent dramatic pauses in between phrases. The second phrase typically includes either the violin or guitar responding to Kuznetzoff's words with embellished runs and arpeggios. The choruses also follow a standard format, as they start slowly and build in anticipation in both speed and volume. Kuznetzoff repeats each chorus in a round of emphatic vocables ("da-ri-dai-dai") and employs yells, deliberate cracks in the voice, and extensions on high notes for an overall dramatic and soulful delivery.

The performance style of the Russian gypsy romance as exemplified by Kuznetzoff, Tolstoy, and other singers in the emigration, creates a performance site primed for expressivity, a point underscored by Carol Silverman in her work on Rom music and the coding of emotion.[100] As numerous pieces sung by the émigrés were performed using a combination of Russian and Romani texts as well as vocables, these songs often elude exact textual meaning. This aesthetic is only furthered by the style in which the instruments accompany the singers. For the staple of Russian gypsy music—the seven-stringed guitar—this expressivity entails runs of notes weaving a web of bubbling anxiety around the vocalist's pitches and extending the emphatic lines of the voice. The deep bellows of the accordion—as played by Vera Tolstoy, for example—produces heavy sighs. And the violin, present in such songs as those recorded by Kuznetzoff, offers a heart-wrenching wailing.

It is little wonder, then, that such an expressive and semiotically flexible space was associated both in prerevolutionary Russia and later in the diaspora with the emotion of toska, roughly translated as a wistful yearning for something far away. Gypsy music had long been established in the Russian imaginary as inciting desire for days long passed and a time much happier. In his 1951 autobiography, *Speak, Memory*, itself an exercise in the minutiae of nostalgia, Vladimir Nabokov recalls listening to the Russian gypsy romance in his youth:

> On the veranda where our relatives and friends assembled, it emitted from its brass mouthpiece the so-called tsïganskie romansï beloved of my generation. . . . Their natural environment was characterized by nightingales in tears, lilacs in bloom and alleys of whispering trees that graced the parks of the gentry. Those nightingales trilled and in the pine grove the setting sun banded the

trunks at different levels of fiery red. A tambourine, still throbbing, seemed to lie on the darkening moss. For a spell, the last notes of the husky contralto pursued me through the dusk.[101]

In this passage, song melds with landscape as present and past collapse in Nabokov's quixotic haze. The throbbing tambourine and low notes dissolving into darkness vividly illustrate the writer's nostalgia for a sensual reverie incited by Russian gypsy music.

As a Russian parallel to such categories of longing as *saudade* in Portuguese fado, toska inspired by Russian gypsy romances offered a prime performance space for expressing nostalgia.[102] Within the context of diaspora, however, toska associated with Russian gypsy romances was often projected onto the lost homeland—a pattern that was evident on stages spanning from Constantinople to Harlem.[103] In the classic 1925 account of émigré life in Constantinople, Red Cross worker Eugenia Bumgardner describes a scene from a Russian cabaret: "Sacha Macaroff, tall and dark, known to all these Russians in days of old, played his guitar, while Madame Laska, very Spanish in type, in a deep throaty, passionate voice, sang Gypsy songs. The Russian waitresses sat like beautiful statues, their hands clasped in their laps or outstretched on the tables, and in their eyes could be read the tragedy of their lives. More than all else this Gypsy music brought back Russia to them, their lost Russia."[104]

Russian gypsy songs performed in Harlem's Russian Club were likewise positioned as a means of accessing the Russian homeland. A concert announcement for a performance by Nastia Poliakova, one of the few singers of gypsy music in the emigration actually of Rom descent, for example states:

> The Moscow public, which often would drop thousands of rubles at the Yar [renowned Moscow nightclub famous for its Romani performers], could not live without its gypsies, without Varia Panina and without the very young, rising star, Nastia Poliakova. Varia Panina is no longer with us . . . but Nastia is, and we have a rare opportunity to listen to her, to listen to the gypsy song and with it forget the present and remember our old Russia.[105]

This music once again serves as a conduit for connecting listeners to their homeland, as Poliakova is positioned as one who can channel Russia through the evocative strands of the gypsy romance.

As part of evoking the lost homeland, Russian gypsy music operated by eliciting a purely visceral response, literally bringing émigrés to tears.

Eugenie Chavchavadze, the granddaughter of Captain Vladimir de Smitt, for example, remembers the parties of her grandfather at which guests would "cry for Old Russia" through the sounds of the gypsy romance.[106] As a common response to much Romani music and other affective genres like fado, the act of communal crying reinforces the perceived genuineness that is associated with the music and the response it elicits, thus presenting a kind of aural-emotive feedback mechanism.[107] As Ellen Lila Gray has noted in her work on saudade, the tears brought on by fado and, in this case, Russian gypsy music, engage a physical response in which the "soulfulness of the aural is made visibly public," thereby unifying its listeners around collective indices of "feeling" defined by a national "essence" and articulated as a collective national "soul."[108] The affective response anticipated by listeners pushed Russian gypsy music only further into the realm of a quixotic fix to exile. Within the diaspora, then, Russian gypsy music, played on a seven-stringed guitar, itself the embodiment of difference in six-string America, offered an ideal venue for performing nostalgia for Old Russia.

The Sounds of Toska

Aside from a discourse of nostalgia surrounding the performance of Russian gypsy romances, the sounds and lyrics of the songs further delineate the trope of toska. One song that exemplifies toska in its musical and textual language is "*Dve gitary* [Two Guitars]," a piece that was performed time and again in the emigration including by the Don Cossack choir, Yul and Vera Brynner, and eventually by Hollywood actors depicting Russian émigrés. Like many Russian gypsy songs, "*Dve gitary*" is set in a minor key and a slow tempo (see example 1.3).[109] Although, in this rendition, the piece is in A minor, it starts with the subdominant chord of D minor rather than with the expected tonic. The key center remains ambiguous, as the first half of the phrase (m. 3–4) moves from the dominant seventh chord up a step to end with a deceptive cadence on the submediant chord of F major. Without establishing the song's tonality at the beginning of the piece, the opening plays with the listener's expectations, creating an unresolved atmosphere. Not until the end of the verse does the progression fully resolve with the tonic. The overall effect is one of musical uncertainty and desire for a harmonic resolution. The constant vacillation in the melody between notes that are a second apart, moreover, lends the piece an air of melancholy and evokes a kind of musical groaning.

Example 1.3. Opening phrase of *"Dve gitary"* (Melody and harmonies transcribed by author from Don Cossacks Choir, *Folk Songs and Romances*, Hymns of the Russian Orthodox Church and Folk Songs, Disc 3).

Based on the poetry of Apollon Grigor'ev (1822–1864), the lyrics of *"Dve gitary"* further emphasize toska, as they describe the lamentations of a young man to his "seven-stringed friend" as he hears a song that reminds him of days past:

Dve gitary, zazvenev,	Two guitars ring out,
Zhalobno zanyli . . .	Sorrowfully wailing . . .
S detstva pamiatnyii napev,	A song familiar from my youth,
Staryi drug moi—ty li?	My old friend—is it you?
O govori khot' ty so mnoi,	Oh, at least you, speak to me,
Podruga semistrunnaia	My seven-stringed friend,
Dusha polna takoi toskoi	My soul is filled with such longing [toska]
A noch' takaia lunnaia! . . .	And the night is filled with such moonlight! . . .
Ia ot zari i do zari	From one dawn to the next
Toskuiu, muchus', setuiu . . .	I pine, agonize, complain,
Dopoi zhe mne—dogovori	Complete the song for me—do sing to me,
Ty pesniu nedopetuiu.	The song that is unfinished.[110]

Throughout these verses, the guitar takes on an anthropomorphic dimension. There is no human playing this instrument, but rather, the guitar plays itself and comes to life through the song emitted through its body. Becoming both an instrument of toska and a co-sufferer, the guitar emerges as a bridge between the isolated narrator and the surrounding world. As such, the disembodied gypsy romance brought to life through the hidden guitar becomes a voice for the voiceless. There is a certain intimacy between the narrator and the unseen, mysterious guitar that is rooted in shared suffering (i.e., the guitar, too, suffers through the very strains it plays). The poetry of *"Dve gitary"* thus positions the Russian gypsy romance (as symbolized through the seven-stringed guitar) as a kindred spirit and a vehicle for expressing the ineffable, to finally complete the "unfinished" song of a wary soul overcome with toska.

The powerful and long-standing trope of the gypsy romance as simultaneous instigator and alleviator of toska is likewise present in songs composed within the emigration. A number of Fomeen's pieces, for example, focus on the gypsy song (much like the free-flowing wine often cited in these pieces) as both source of and deliverance from sorrow. The chorus of Fomeen's "*Spoi mne pesniu tsyganskuiu* [Sing to Me a Gypsy Song]," for example, exclaims:

Spoi mne pesniu tsyganskuiu grustnuiu	Sing to me a gypsy song, a sad song
Spoi chtob pesnei nadryv zaglushit'	Sing so that the song drowns out my broken heart
Chtoby liubov' moiu odinokuiu	So that my love, my lonely love
V etoi pesne ia b mog zaglushit'!	In this song I can drown out![111]

The gypsy song serves a metonymic role to literally drown out the narrator's sorrow. This sentiment could have easily been transferred to the condition of exile as these songs were performed in the halls of the Russian Club. The sudden shift between minor and major keys, increased volume and tempo, higher register, and emphatic delivery in Kuznetzoff's rendition of the piece, moreover, provides a certain momentum that reinforces the meaning of the text, providing a clue as to how the performance of these songs could have further operated as temporary alleviator to the condition of exile, as émigrés could live through their condition through the sounds of the gypsy romance.

Fomeen's later work, "*Gde zhe ty, milaia tsyganka* [Where Are You, My Dear Gypsy?]" (Op. 21, no. 3) applies the gypsy trope to exile even more explicitly, and one cannot help but wonder the extent to which such music was written in response to the composer's experience of exile. The second verse, for example, states:

Daleko my na chuzhbine	We are far off in foreign climes,
Vse razbrosany sud'boi	Scattered by fate,
I toskoiu po otchizne	And, missing our homeland,
Mysli nas nesut s soboi.	Our thoughts carry us far away.
Ne slykhat' tsyganskikh pesen'	Not to hear the gypsy songs
Ved' tsygane dalekiSince	the gypsies are so far away
Daleki oni, no zhivut oni	Far they are, but they do live on,
Kak nadezhda [v] moei dushi.	Like hope lives on in my soul.[112]

This example further demonstrates the powerful position held by gypsy music in the Russian diasporic imaginary. For one, it is the "gypsy" song and the "gypsy" people that the narrator projects as associations with the lost homeland. More importantly, however, it is the performance of the song itself that sustains this longed-for Russia and brings catharsis to those "scattered by fate."

The toska elicited through Russian gypsy music might have been unbearable (and the genre's popularity in the emigration less explicable) if this longing were not coupled with an ecstatic release. Russian gypsy songs operate on this duality: the volia with which they are associated comes through a catharsis that is reached by living through the toska embedded in the text and music. Common to the Russian gypsy repertoire, this catharsis is reached in the second half of many songs, the piece likened to a locomotive, traveling increasingly faster to the point of derailment. As the vocalist declaims her words louder, the choir responds with ever-greater abandon, lending the song an air of earnest emotionality.

The lyrics of these songs often mirror the idea of release through suffering and abandon, a point that is encapsulated by the iconic "*Chto nam gore* [The Heck with Heartache]." In this piece—sung by Tolstoy, Kuznetzoff, and countless others—fate is stared directly in the eye: "Death? Life? For me, it's the same!" Attained through the suffering that precedes it, this catharsis encapsulates the volia with which Rom people were associated in prerevolutionary Russia and which was, in turn, mapped onto the Russian gypsy repertoire.[113] Whether through words or sound, as a vehicle for engaging volia, Russian gypsy music could momentarily liberate listeners from the confines of exile: "Far they are, but they do live on; Like hope lives on in my soul."

Conclusion: Music in Exile

The embracing of Russian folk and gypsy songs by cosmopolitan elites reflects a long history of the performance and appropriation of these genres within Russian culture. Yet, on the stages of New York, the function and meaning of this music was now transformed through the event and context of exile. The study of popular music culture in the Russian emigration suggests an alternate conclusion to Sybil Milton's question of whether there is an "exile art" or merely "exile artists."[114] Rather than Milton's emphasis on exile artists, the Russian gypsy and folk repertoire performed in Harlem engenders an exile art that create a semiotic framework for defining Russianness abroad.

Central to the notion of exile art is the question of how the past is collectively imagined (in the spirit of Benedict Anderson's "community," which is distinguished not by its "falsity/genuineness" but by the "style in which [it is] imagined") and, especially important for a study on music, how the past is performed.[115] As the very concept of the past is situational and informed by the present, a study of the ways in which a golden age is imagined and represented at any moment is key for understanding the processes of diaspora construction.[116] Within a diaspora, this utopic site is predicated on a "homeland myth" and a "purity associated with home" and is fueled by discourses of exile and of "not being there."[117] For members of the Russian emigration, this golden age was articulated as "Old Russia," a space informed as much by a lost place as it was by a lost time, in which "revolutionary upheaval sundered past from present."[118]

As a prime forum for diasporic metacommentary, the performance of Russian folk music became a space for enacting and defining a mythologized homeland. Indeed, the upbeat strands of *"Svetit mesiats"* reverberating along the walls of the Russian Club as sung by wives of White Army officers in bright sarafany and tall, sequined kokoshniki brought to life a Russia "that never was."[119] In part, the correlation between an idyllic Russia and Russian folk music emerges as part of a long-held association informed through nationalist discourses that began in nineteenth-century Russia and would continue within the diaspora.

Beyond dry discourses, however, it was the performance of folk music that literally brought this Russia to life.[120] As a musical medium engaging "multiple signs" of performance (visual, linguistic, sonic), Russian folk music served as an enhanced space for animating this Russia.[121] Through musical performance, émigrés in Harlem could play out the "urgent problems" of life in exile, engaging Turner's "subjunctive world" to "make sense" of their daily lives now outside of the homeland.[122]

Unlike folk music, Russian gypsy songs evoked not a formulaic Russianness, but the personal and immediate toska, going straight to the heart of the émigré. Operating on prescribed codes of toska and volia, the musical language, texts, and performance practices associated with Russian gypsy romances primed its listeners for a cathartic experience. Within the context of exile, toska evoked through this repertoire and previously associated with lost love was now projected onto lost country. Eliciting a response that was at once socially unifying and deeply personal, Russian gypsy music created a site in which participants could literally sing together a diaspora that was informed simultaneously by individual yearning and a collective discourse of exile. Both tragic and therapeutic, the performance of Russian gypsy music elicited raw emotion (a response long ingrained in the Russian imaginary) that indexed this response, as well as its object of projection (Old Russia), as something "real" and "authentic."

Finally, the analysis of Russian gypsy and folk music performance in the emigration raises the question of the performativity of these productions. Was this a conscientious performance, and if so, then for whom? What was the meaning of Elena Vorontsova's exotic persona or Ilya Tolstoy's announcements—made mostly in English—of the "old gypsy songs" sung by his aunt and younger cousin on the family's recording? There is no question that the diasporic metacommentary surrounding these performances was, in part, created by and for the émigrés themselves. The performance of an idyllic homeland presented émigrés with a coping strategy for emotionally and socially dealing with exile.

Yet, these performances engaged a level of self-awareness and a deliberate positioning of the self as Other, especially as they began to catch the attention of American onlookers. Vladimir Dukelsky's reference to "synthetic gypsy wailing," for example, or casual description of a Russian New Year's Eve party hosted by New York socialite Mrs. Henry P. Loomis in 1929 consisting of "Cossacks, gypsies, oceans of vodka and other Russian trimmings" suggests a certain codification of various tropes into a recognizable collective of "Russian trimmings" for American onlookers.[123] It is this very intersection between Russian tropes and American culture that will be explored in chapter 2.

Notes

1. Eugenia S. Bumgardner, *Undaunted Exiles* (Staunton, VA: McClure Co., 1925), 115.

2. *Russian Orthodox Church of Christ the Saviour in New York: The Tenth Anniversary Book, 1924–1934* (New York: Rossiya Publishing Company, 1934), pages unnumbered [hereafter cited as *Christ the Savior Tenth Anniversary Book*, English Edition].

3. "*K kontsertu N. Poliakovoi i S. Fullon* [In preparation for the concert of N. Poliakov and S. Fullon]," Unmarked newspaper clipping, Christ the Savior Papers, The Archives of the Orthodox Church in America, Syosset, NY [hereafter cited as Christ the Savior Papers].

4. Richard Taruskin, *Defining Russia Musically: Historical and Hermeneutic Essays* (Princeton, NJ: Princeton University Press, 1997).

5. Robert H. Johnston, *New Mecca, New Babylon: Paris and the Russian Exiles, 1920–1945* (Kingston, ON: McGill-Queen's University Press, 1988), 7; Marc Raeff, *Russia Abroad: A Cultural History of the Russian Emigration, 1919–1939* (New York: Oxford University Press, 1990), 16.

6. Alaina Lemon, *Between Two Fires: Gypsy Performance and Romani Memory from Pushkin to Postsocialism* (Durham, NC: Duke University Press, 2000), 36.

7. Natalia Alexandrovna Rachmaninoff to Alfred and Jane Swan, May 3, 1943, Rachmaninoff Correspondence, Alfred J. Swan Papers, University of Virginia Library, Charlottesville, VA. Natalia Rachmaninoff goes on to write, "When he was leaving for New York and Philadelphia this year, he developed edema of the eye. But, nothing will happen to him because he still must return to Russia . . ." to which she later added, "he did not return!, 1943."

8. Victor Turner, *From Ritual to Theatre: The Human Seriousness of Play* (New York: PAJ Publications, 1982), 107–108.

9. Ibid., 104.

10. Ibid., 107.

11. Thomas Turino, "Introduction: Identity and the Arts in Diaspora Communities," in *Identity and the Arts in Diaspora Communities*, ed. Thomas Turino and James Lea (Warren, MI: Harmonie Park Press, 2004), 10.

12. Waltraud Kokot, Khachig Tölölyan, and Carolin Alfonso, "Introduction," in *Diaspora, Identity and Religion: New Directions in Theory and Research*, ed. Waltraud Kokot, Khachig Tölölyan, and Carolin Alfonso (London: Routledge, 2004), 5.

13. Raeff, *Russia Abroad*, 24. Robert Johnston claims that one million people left Russia between 1918 and 1921 [*New Mecca, New Babylon*, 4], while Michael Glenny and Norman Stone report that estimates of the emigrants are "no less than three million," [*The Other Russia: The Experience of Exile* (New York: Viking Penguin, 1990), xv].

14. Duke, *Passport to Paris*, 75, 71.

15. Bumgardner, *Undaunted Exiles*, 161.

16. Sir John Hope Simpson, *The Refugee Problem: Report of a Survey* (London: Oxford University Press, 1939), 469–470; Raeff, *Russia Abroad*, 17, 23; *Christ the Savior Tenth Anniversary Book*, English Edition, n.p.; *Iubileinyi sbornik Khrama Khrista Spasitelia v N'iu Iorke* [The tenth anniversary booklet of Christ the Savior Church in New York] (New York: Rossiya Pub. Co., 1934), 19 (hereafter cited as *Christ the Savior Tenth Anniversary Booklet*, Russian edition), 19.

17. James E. Hassell, *Russian Refugees in France and the United States Between the World Wars* (Philadelphia: American Philosophical Society, 1991), 57.

18. Duke, *Passport to Paris*, 84.

19. See, for example, "I Played Fiddle for the Czar" (1932), *Tovarich* (1935), and *Balalaika* (1939).

20. *Christ the Savior Tenth Anniversary Booklet*, Russian edition, 19; Raeff, *Russia Abroad*, 17; Simpson, *The Refugee Problem*, 469, 470.

21. *Christ the Savior Tenth Anniversary Booklet*, Russian edition, 20.

22. Mikhail Blizniuk, *Prekrasnaia Marusia Sava: russkaia emigratsiia na kontsertnykh ploshchadkakh i v restoranakh Ameriki* [The Wonderful Marusia Sava: The Russian Emigration on the Concert Stages and Restaurants in America] (Moscow: Russkii Put', 2007), 85–86; Hassell, *Russian Refugees in France and the United States*, 54.

23. The building is no longer standing.

24. Johnston, *New Mecca, New Babylon*, 27.

25. Raeff, *Russia Abroad*, 26.

26. Hassell, *Russian Refugees in France and the United States*, 55.

27. Aside from serving as cultural and spiritual institutions, Orthodox churches in the emigration also stood as literal memorials to the past. In addition to its allusion to the famous Moscow cathedral by name, Christ the Savior included a memorial chapel in

honor of those who perished during the Bolshevik Revolution, Civil War, and First World War. Similarly, in helping to design a new church on the outskirts of Paris, Grand Duchess Marie of Russia approached the project of decorating the chapel as "a memorial for the members of [her] family murdered during the revolution" [Grand Duchess Marie of Russia, *A Princess in Exile* (New York: Viking Press, 1932), 241]. Although beyond the scope of the present study, the idea of Orthodox parishes in the emigration serving as memorial sites to a prerevolutionary past would be a compelling one to pursue.

28. Michel Fokine, *Fokine: Memoirs of a Ballet Master* (Boston: Little, Brown, and Company, 1961), 296.

29. David Chavchavadze, *Crowns and Trenchcoats: A Russian Prince in the CIA* (New York: Atlantic International Publications, 1990), 123.

30. Advertisement in *Rossiya*, April 16, 1933, 6.

31. *Christ the Savior Tenth Anniversary Book*, English edition.

32. Svetlana Zvereva, "*Blogotvoritel'naia deiatel'nost' Sergeia Rakhmaninova v otnoshenii Russkoi Pravoslavnoi Tserkvi* [The philanthropic work of Sergei Rachmaninoff in relation to the Russian Orthodox Church]," in *S. V. Rakhmaninov—Natsional'naia Pamiat' Rossii* [S. V. Rachmaninov—The National Memory of Russia], ed. S. V. Kostiukova (Tambov: Rachmaninovskii Tsentr), 25.

33. Ibid.

34. Simon Morrison, *Lina and Serge: The Love and Wars of Lina Prokofiev* (Boston: Houghton Mifflin Harcourt, 2013), 56.

35. Concert Program featuring Nina Koshetz from February 6, 1932, "East European Fund, Inc. (Ford)" Folder, MS 2, Christ the Savior Papers.

36. On wartime benefit concerts, see Herbertus F. Jahn, *Patriotic Culture in Russia During World War I* (Ithaca, NY: Cornell University Press, 1995), 98, 100–102.

37. Duke, *Passport to Paris*, 85.

38. Fokine, *Memoirs of a Ballet Master*, 281.

39. "Ko vsem russkim muzykantam v Amerike," *Novoe Russkoe Slovo*, October 17, 1925, 3.

40. Within three years of the publication of this letter, Glazunov would permanently leave his Russian homeland for Paris.

41. "Ko vsem russkim muzykantam v Amerike."

42. A. A. Voloshin, *Na putiakh i pereput'iakh: "dosugi vechernye," Evropa-Amerika, 1921–1952* [On Pathways and Crossroads: "Evening Leisure," Europe-America, 1921–1952] (San Francisco: Delos, 1953), 20–21.

43. "Concert of Russian Songs: Mme. Voronzov and Her Friends Entertain Fellow-Refugees," *New York Times*, August 31, 1924.

44. Estrada in prerevolutionary Russia was a production open to all social classes and encompassed many types of entertainment—from folk singing and dancing to operettas and satirical skits. For more on prerevolutionary Estrada, see Jahn, *Patriotic Culture in Russia*, 97–99; Laura J. Olson, *Performing Russia: Folk Revival and Russian Identity* (New York: Routledge Curzon, 2004), 19; Richard Stites, *Russian Popular Culture: Entertainment and Society Since 1900* (Cambridge: Cambridge University Press, 1992), 20.

45. On the porous boundary between rural and urban songs, see Robert A. Rothstein, "Death of the Folksong?" in *Cultures in Flux: Lower-Class Values, Practices, and Resistance in Late Imperial Russia*, ed. Stephen P. Frank and Mark D. Steinberg (Princeton, NJ: Princeton University Press, 1994), 108–120.

46. For more on the trend of composing music in a folklike style, see Rothstein, "Death of the Folksong?", 117–118; Vadim Prokhorov, *Russian Folk Songs: Musical Genres and History*

(Lanham, MD: The Scarecrow Press Inc., 2002), 127–131. Other composers whose songs became central to urbanized folk music repertoire include Alexander Alyabyev ("*Vechernyii zvon*") and Ivan Larionov ("*Kalinka*").

47. For more on the work of Olga and Dimitry Agrenev-Slavianskii, see Olson, *Performing Russia*, 28–31.

48. Concert Program (in Russian), December 26, 1931, "East European Fund, Inc." Folder, MS 2, Christ the Savior Papers; Concert Program (in English), December 26, 1931, "Khor" Folder, MS 2, Christ the Savior Papers.

49. Vladimir de Smitt, "Sergei Victorovich Savitsky," *Prikhodskii listok* [Parish bulletin], No. 24 (March 1951): 31.

50. Ibid., 32.

51. Ibid.

52. Elena Vorontsova, "I Was At a Party," Victor 78079, 78 Recording, 1924 [Recorded Sound Reference Center, Library of Congress, Washington, DC].

53. On the correlation between the balalaika and conceptions of "authentic" Russianness among the Russian elite and middle classes in prerevolutionary Russia, see Olson, *Performing Russia*, 16–19.

54. Compared to other émigré renditions of "*Na piru byla*," Vorontsova's interpretation is quite folksy, despite her more operatic interludes. The daughter of Nina Koshetz, Marina Koshetz, for example, relies completely on an operatic head voice replete with continuous vibrato as she sings the folk song [Marina Koshetz, *Gypsy Airs*, RBA 09520–09522, 78 Recording].

55. For examples of Shield's output of Russian records, see Richard K. Spottswood, *Ethnic Music on Records: A Discography of Ethnic Recordings Produced in the United States, 1893–1942* (Urbana: University of Illinois Press, 1990), 887, 912, 924, 925.

56. "*Kontsert E. V. Vorontsovoi*," *Russkaia Mysl'*, March 14, 1924. As a newspaper founded by Russian émigrés in 1923, the nostalgic and nationalist direction of *Russkaia Mysl'* is furthered not only by the tone and content of its articles but also by the inclusion of both "Old" (Julian) and "New" (Gregorian) style calendar dates, by the paper's extended title ("The Organ of Russian National Thought"), and by the orthography of its title page (a fairytale style reminiscent of Silver Age artwork).

57. "*Kontsert E. V. Vorontsovoi*," *Russkaia Mysl'*, February 14, 1924.

58. A. Aslanov, *Novoe Russkoe Slovo*, January 13, 1929 and January 23, 1929.

59. "*Kontsert N. V. Plevitskoi*," *Novoe Russkoe Slovo*, January 15, 1927, 4. Aside from her renown as a folk music performer, Plevitskaya is also notorious for her indictment in the kidnapping and murder of White Russian General Evgeny Miller (1867–1939), as she and her husband secretly worked for the Soviet government. Plevitskaya allegedly later wrote an apology to the wife of General Miller ("*Plevitskaia v arestantskikh odezhdakh* [Plevitskaya in convict attire]," *Novoe Russkoe Slovo*, June 13, 1939, 2). For more on Plevitskaya, see, V. L. Strongin, *Nadezhda Plevitskaia: velikaia pevitsa i agent razvedki* [Nadezhda Plevitskaya: The Great Singer and Secret Service agent] (Moscow: Ast-Press 2005); Pamela A. Jordan, *Stalin's Singing Spy: The Life and Exile of Nadezhda Plevitskaya* (Lanham, MD: Rowman and Littlefield, 2016).

60. *Novosti* March 14, 1888, quoted in Olson, *Performing Russia*, 19, 23.

61. Ibid., 23.

62. Mikhail Bakhtin, "Forms of Time and of the Chronotope in the Novel," in *The Dialogic Imagination: Four Essays*, ed. Michael Holquist, transl. Caryl Emerson and Michael Holquist (Austin: University of Texas Press, 2006), 84.

63. Ibid.

64. Ibid., 90, 91.

65. Ibid., 225.

66. Ibid.

67. Ibid., 226.

68. Mario Rey, "Sexuality, Imaging, and Gender Construction in the Music of Exile," in *Queering the Popular Pitch*, ed. Sheila Whiteley and Jennifer Rycenga (New York: Routledge, 2006), 116.

69. Ibid., 117.

70. Svetlana Boym, *The Future of Nostalgia* (New York: Basic Books, 2001), xviii.

71. Ibid., 41–48.

72. Ibid., 42.

73. Ibid., 44.

74. Aslanov, *Novoe Russkoe Slovo*, January 23, 1929.

75. Boym, *Future of Nostalgia*, 42.

76. Ibid., 49, 41. For a detailed comparison between restorative and reflective nostalgia, see Boym, xviii, 49–51.

77. Gema R. Guevara, "'La Cuba de Ayer/La Cuba de Hoy': The Politics of Music and Diaspora," in *Musical Migrations: Transnationalism and Cultural Hybridity in Latino/a America*, ed. Frances R. Aparicio and Cándida F. Jáquez (New York: Palgrave, 2003), 35.

78. Ibid.

79. The men appear to be wearing the uniforms of prerevolutionary sacred choral singers [see, for example, the cover of Vladimir Morosan's *Choral Performance in Pre-Revolutionary Russia* (Madison, CT: Musica Russica, 1994)].

80. Olson, *Performing Russia*, 29.

81. The appropriation of peasant dress by upper-class Russians had started as early as the reign of Catherine the Great (1762–1796) [See, for example, Orlando Figes, *Natasha's Dance: A Cultural History of Russia* (New York: Metropolitan Books, 2002), 108, 222]. I explore the connection between traditional costuming and an idealized Russia in further detail in chapter 5.

82. Figes, *Natasha's Dance*, 538, 539.

83. Boym, *Future of Nostalgia*, 43.

84. See, for example, Anna D. Jaroszynska-Kirchmann, *The Exile Mission: The Polish Political Diaspora and Polish America, 1939–1956* (Athens: Ohio University Press, 2004), 14; Adelaida Reyes, *Songs of the Caged, Songs of the Free: Music and the Vietnamese Refugee Experience* (Philadelphia: Temple University Press, 1999), 66–69; María de los Angeles Torres, *In the Land of Mirrors: Cuban Exile Politics in the United States* (Ann Arbor: University of Michigan Press, 1999).

85. Khachig Tölölyan, "Beyond the Homeland: From Exilic Nationalism to Diasporic Transnationalism," in *The Call of the Homeland: Diaspora Nationalisms, Past and Present*, edited by A. S. Leoussi, A. Gal, and A. D. Smith (Leiden, Netherlands: Brill Publishing, 2010), 34.

86. The fractured existence of the émigrés as well as their adaptability and interaction with the American culture (a point which will be taken up in chapter 3), in fact, suggests a more multifaceted relationship to nostalgia than Boym's binary paradigm as it applies to the Russian emigration.

87. Tolstoy cited in Figes, *Natasha's Dance*, xxvi.

88. On the history of Rom in Russia, see Lemon, *Between Two Fires*, 7–9.

89. One of the more prominent estates visited by Rom was that of Leo Tolstoy, whose favorite Russian gypsy song was *"Akh, da ne vecherniaia"* and whose children and grandchildren carried on the musical tradition in the emigration, as relayed, for example, in the introduction of this book.

90. At the time this romance was penned, it was commonly believed in Russia that gypsies had originated in Egypt.

91. Take, for example, the depictions of gypsies in the following works: Alexander Pushkin's *"Tsygani* [The Gypsies]," which served as the basis for Rachmaninoff's *Aleko*; Mikhail Lermontov's *"Tsyganka* [The Gypsy Girl]"; Nikolai Leskov's *Ocharovannyi strannik* [The Enchanted Wanderer]; Anton Chekhov's *Drama na okhote* [The Shooting Party]; and *Zhivoi trup* [The Living Corpse] by Tolstoy.

92. See, for example, Marina Koshetz, *Gypsy Airs*, RBA 09520–09522, 78 Recording; Adia Kuznetsov, *Gypsy Songs of Russia*, RBA 04925–05927, 78 Recording; Fedor Zarkevich, *Russian Caravan*, 17 Continental C-5018, 5019, 5020; Emma Hurok, *Gypsy Songs of Old Russia*, RBA 09644–09646; Nikolai Grushko, *"Chernaia Shal',"* Seva C-2.

93. Gerald Stanton Smith, *Songs to Seven Strings: Russian Guitar Poetry and Soviet "Mass Song"* (Bloomington: Indiana University Press, 1984), 63–64. For a detailed history of the seven-stringed guitar, see Oleg Vitalyevich Timofeyev, "The Golden Age of the Russian Guitar: Repertoire, Performance Practice, and Social Function of the Russian Seven-String Guitar Music, 1800–1850" (PhD diss., Duke University, 1999).

94. Izaly Zemtsovsky, "Russia," In *The Garland Encyclopedia of World Music*, Vol. 8, ed. Timothy Rice (New York: Garland Publishing Inc., 2000), 767; Program notes, "The Alexandra L. Tolstoy Centennial Jubilee," September 23, 1984, Maria Sarandinaki, private collection.

95. Miron Petrovskii, *"Skromnoe obaianie kicha, ili chto est' russkii romans* [The Subtle Charm of Kitsch, or, What Is the Russian Romance]," in *Russkii romans na rubezhe vekov* [The Russian Romance at the Boundary of the Century], ed. Valentina Morderer and Miron Petrovskii (Kiev: Oranta-Press, 1997), 13–14.

96. *Russian and Gypsy Songs*, LP recorded on Reed Farm in Valley Cottage, NY on June 8, 1952, Private collection. A second LP was recorded on August 18, 1963 [Private Collection].

97. Further complicating its history and reception, the song's melody aligns with that of Soviet composer Vadim Kozin (1903–1996)'s *"Biriuzovye kolechki,"* whose music very well may have originated as a Romani song, considering that Kozin's mother had been a Romani musician.

98. The songs composed by members of the Tolstoy family and allegedly adapted by Romani musicians include: "Why I Fell in Love" (Michael L. Tolstoy and Alexandra V. Tolstoy) and "The Distant Light of Stars" (arranged by Anna I. Tolstoy and Ilia I. Tolstoy).

99. Fomeen also took part in Christ the Savior concerts, as evidenced in his participation in the December 3, 1932, fundraiser organized by the church's sisterhood, for which Fomeen played accordion and is referred to by the informal "Vasia" in the program ("Printed Materials—Obshchestvo Special Events" Folder, "Printed Materials" Box, Obshchestvo Pomoshchi Collection, Bakhmeteff Archive, Columbia University).

100. Carol Silverman, "Music, Emotion, and the 'Other': Balkan Roma and the Negotiation of Exoticism," in *Interpreting Emotions and in Russia and Eastern Europe*, ed. Mark D. Steinberg and Valeria Sobol, 224–247 (DeKalb: Northern Illinois University Press, 2011).

101. Vladimir Nabokov, *Speak, Memory: An Autobiography Revisited* (New York: Everyman's Library, 1999), 174–175.

102. The link between a specific performance practice, ideas of "soulfulness," and a static, timeless homeland bound to an idyllic past is common to both fado and Russian gypsy songs and emerges as a significant parallel between the reception of the two genres. On *saudade* in fado, see Lila Ellen Gray, "Memories of Empire, Mythologies of the Soul: Fado Performance and the Shaping of Saudade," *Ethnomusicology* 51, no. 1 (Winter 2007): 106–130. Although not as closely aligned with *toska*, the concept of *duende* in flamenco likewise confers a state of intense emotion [see, for example, Jason Webster, *Duende: A Journey into the Heart of Flamenco* (New York: Broadway Books, 2003)].

103. The association between Russian gypsy music and prerevolutionary Russia was commonplace in Soviet and post-Soviet Russia as well [see Lemon, *Between Two Fires*, 44].

104. Bumgardner, *Undaunted Exiles*, 127.

105. "*K kontsertu N. Poliakovoi i S. Fullon* [In preparation of the concert of N. Poliakov and S. Fullon]," Unmarked newspaper clipping, Christ the Savior Papers. Based on accounts of Poliakov's concert schedule, this particular performance most likely took place in 1935 [See Blizniuk, *Marusia Sava*, 144–148].

106. Eugenie Chavchavadze, granddaughter of Smitt, personal communication, March 25, 2007, Washington, DC.

107. The idea of gypsy music moving its listeners to tears is not limited to the Russian émigré experience, and may have been part of a broader, learned response to the genre [Carol Silverman, "Rom (Gypsy) Music," *Garland Encyclopedia of World Music*, Vol. 8 (accessed March 25, 2009); Silverman, "Music, Emotion, and the 'Other,'" 233].

108. Gray, "Fado and Saudade," 117.

109. To date, I have not been able to determine the primary composer of "*Dve gitary*," although Malcolm Brown attributes the work to Grigor'ev himself [Brown, "Native Song and National Consciousness in Nineteenth-Century Russian Music," in *Art and Culture in Nineteenth-Century Russia*, ed. Theofanis George Stavrou (Bloomington: Indiana University Press, 1983), 75].

110. Lyrics from: *Russkii romans*, ed. Vadim Rabinovich (Moscow: Pravda, 1987), 504 and *Russkie pesni XIX veka* [Russian Songs of the Nineteenth Century], ed. Ivan Rozanov (Moscow: Gosudarstvennoe izdatel'stvo khudozhestvennoi literatury, 1944), 348. The lyrics of "*Dve gitary*" are far from standardized and appear in numerous versions that tend to combine stanzas from two of Grigor'ev's poems, *O, govori khot' ty so mnoi* [Oh, at Least You, Speak to Me], and *Tsyganskaia vengerka* [Gypsy Dance Hongroise]. For the complete texts of Grigor'ev's original poems, see B. O. Kosteliants, ed., *Apollon Grigor'ev: izbrannye proizvedeniia* [Apollon Grigoriev: Selected Works] (Leningrad: Sovetskii pisatel', 1959), 159, 160.

111. Basil Fomeen, "*Spoi mne pesniu tsyganskuiu*," Op. 5, no. 4. The text cited above comes from Kuznetzoff's recording, which differs slightly from the 1940 published score with the words "*liubov'*" (love) instead of "*zhizn'*" (life) and "*zaglushit'*" (to drown) instead of "*pozabyt'*" (to forget).

112. Basil Fomeen, "*Gde zhe ty, milaia tsyganka* [Where Are You, My Dear Gypsy Girl?]" (Op. 21, no. 3). Text source from manuscript, Basil Fomeen Papers, "Fomin Arrangements (Manuscripts) 1 of 1" Box, Library of Congress.

113. For more on the trope of volia as it was projected onto Rom people and music in prerevolutionary Russia, see Lemon, *Between Two Fires*, 35–46.

114. Sybil Milton, *Is there an Exile Art or Only Exile Artists?* (Bonn: Bouvier Verlag, 1990).

115. Benedict Anderson, *Imagined Communities: Reflections on the Origin and Spread of Nationalism* (London: Verso, 1991), 6.

116. David Lowenthal, *The Past Is a Foreign Country* (Cambridge: Cambridge University Press, 2005), 8–9.

117. William Safran, "Diasporas in Modern Societies: Myths of Homeland and Return," *Diaspora* 1, no. 1 (spring 1991): 94, 95; Khachig Tölölyan, "Rethinking Diaspora(s): Stateless Power in the Transnational Moment," *Diaspora* 5, no. 1 (Spring 1996): 14; Waltraud Kokot, Khachig Tölölyan and Carolin Alfonso, "Introduction," in *Diaspora, Identity and Religion*, 5.

118. Lowenthal, *The Past Is a Foreign Country*, 8.

119. Figes, *Natasha's Dance*, 538.

120. As Turner exclaims, "Entertainment! That's a key word," *From Ritual to Theatre*, 121.

121. Turino, "Identity and the Arts," 12.

122. Turner, *From Ritual to Theatre*, 122.

123. Duke, *Passport to Paris*, 233.

2

NEW YORK'S RUSSIAN VOGUE

The Fox-Trotsky and Other
Musical Delights

"To make it more incomprehensible, I will explain." With this non sequitur, Nikita Balieff began the 1922 New York season of his vaudeville show, *Chauve-Souris* (The Bat). Starting as an informal production taking place in Moscow during the off hours of the notorious Moscow Art Theater in 1908 and one of the many variety shows common in Russia in the years preceding World War I, *Chauve-Souris* (or *Letuchaia mysh'*, as it was known in Russian), entailed a mix of skits, parodies, and musical numbers.[1] After fleeing Bolshevik Russia, Balieff soon put his production on in Paris (at which point the show acquired its French name) and London before making his New York debut. Sponsored by the affluent banker and philanthropist Otto Kahn and organized by the Russian-born impresario Morris Gest, the production on Broadway (featured in the newly opened Majestic Theater on Forty-Ninth Street) continued in the style of the opening show, with Balieff appearing on stage each night to announce the evening's entertainment in broken English.

In many respects, the show reminded American critics of the more familiar vaudeville productions, as it was replete with humor and featured a smorgasbord of dances, songs, and skits. Yet from its first Broadway performance, *Chauve-Souris* was noted for several striking distinctions from its American counterpart. For one, the cost of tickets was a then-unheard-of five dollars, compared with the typical dollar-fifty cost of admission for other vaudeville shows.[2] Another surprise for critics was the show's continuous six-month run, consisting of more than four hundred performances of a singular, unchanging program.[3] Featuring skits that were simultaneously lighthearted and tightly polished and played out amid sophisticated visuals created by the Russian artists Nikolai Remisoff and Serge Sudeikin (both of whom had been involved in the modernist World of Art movement in prerevolutionary Russia), the show was difficult to pigeonhole for critics, as it occupied a position somewhere between high and low art.[4]

The most unusual aspect of the Broadway sensation, however, was the fact that the skits of *Chauve-Souris* were conducted in the Russian language. Indeed, aside from Balieff's intentionally mangled linguistic executions, the theatrical and musical numbers of the initial Broadway run were presented in a language that very few audience members could understand.[5] Despite the hefty linguistic barrier between the Russian performers and American audience members, New York was abuzz with talk of the "Great Nikita," and the show's only rival in popularity was the Ziegfeld Follies.[6]

The excitement over the first Broadway season of *Chauve-Souris* was but the starting point of a Russian vogue that swept New York in the 1920s and early 1930s. The trend for things Russian would soon be found in American fashion, films, and Russian-themed nightclubs that mushroomed throughout the city during this time. Although the Russian vogue of this period has been noted within the sphere of the Hollywood and fashion industries as well as by contemporaries of the time, its place within the music world has been overlooked.[7] Exploring sites of music production (specifically sheet music, society balls, jazz numbers, and Russian nightclubs), this chapter examines the Russian vogue as it emerged within Gotham's cultural scene.

What is further surprising about the Russian vogue as it emerged in 1920s New York is that its inauguration coincided with one of the more ethnically exclusionary moments of the twentieth century in the United States. Indeed, following World War I, a heightened idea of Anglo-Saxon and Nordic superiority developed in the United States that only increased in the years following the Red Scare (1918–1920), during which time Russians were viewed as "deranged, violent anarchists."[8] This nativism culminated with the Immigration Act of 1924, whose quota restrictions "favored the 'Nordics' of northern and western Europe over the 'undesirable races' of eastern and southern Europe" among others and whose immediate predecessor, the Emergency Immigration Act (1921), established quotas that would have direct bearing on First Wave Russians.[9] Mathew Frye Jacobson posits 1924 as possibly presenting the "high-water mark of the regime of Anglo-Saxon or Nordic supremacy" in this period.[10]

The years surrounding the Immigration Act, however, simultaneously served as a turning point for the beginning of a gradual melding of whiteness into a single racial category, thereby situating the Russian émigrés at a particularly mutable period in American history with regard to articulations of race and ethnicity. In conjunction with the gradually more inclusive understanding of whiteness that took shape during the 1920s, I argue that the Russian émigrés were able to bypass the xenophobic trend through their affiliation with a lost, romanticized Russia as well as with an upper-classness associated with the former imperial regime. Although trends for things Russian came and went in New York since at least the late nineteenth century, the vogue of the 1920s and early 1930s was informed by the specific circumstances under which the First Wave Russian emigration came into existence.[11] The flight of approximately one and a half million people from Russia following the Bolshevik Revolution (1917) and Russian Civil War (1918–1922) served as the catalyst for this particular *style Russe*, as it was largely driven by the captivation of the West with the prerevolutionary Russia with which the refugees were associated. As Catriona Kelly explains, the Russian vogue that emerged following the émigré exodus rested on the cultural currency gained by prerevolutionary culture through its perceived annihilation by the Bolshevik Revolution.[12] As such, the Russian vogue that developed during this time can be understood as a trend inspired simultaneously by an exoticism (that of Russian Other) and an admiration stemming from a perceived connection between the émigrés and a lost nation. Moreover, the Russian émigrés themselves often mediated these representations, capitalizing on their position as ethnic and cultural outsiders to engage in a deliberate and marketable auto-Orientalism. Indeed, as opposed to many fellow immigrants, the Russians who came to New York City in the early 1920s enjoyed a relatively privileged position that was enabled by expanding definitions of whiteness and leveraged through a class-oriented cultural capital that helped fuel the attraction for things Russian, commodifying both the émigrés and the lost Russia with which they were associated.

To elucidate the Russian vogue as it developed in New York in the 1920s and early 1930s, this chapter focuses on three distinct processes at work within the realm of Russian music production: the diasporic adaptability of the Russian émigrés; the Russian-American intersections that occurred within jazz; and a strategy of auto-Orientalism that underscored émigré efforts at performing an exotic, Eastern otherness. Rather than acting as an impediment, the overt ethnicity on which this music rested emerges as a site of simultaneous (self)-objectification and privilege, offering a means for the post-Bolshevik exiles to shape "Russianness" in ways that resonated with the American public and to help define what it meant to be Russian abroad.

Balieff's Broadway Hit: Katinka and Her Polka

The same year that Balieff's *Chauve-Souris* made its New York debut (enabling audiences "to imagine, if not talk, in Russian"),[13] the Harms sheet music publishing company released a series of songs from the show. These selections included the Russian gypsy standards, "Dark Eyes" and "Two Guitars" (whose iconicity in Russian émigré culture is discussed in chap. 1), as well as songs composed explicitly for the show by Balieff's friend and contemporary Alexei Archangelsky (1846–1924).

Despite the fact that these songs were performed on stage in Russian, their marketing by the New York–based sheet music company suggests that they were published with an American audience in mind and provide a starting point for understanding how the trend for things Russian began to materialize in New York. For one, the printed versions of the songs are all presented in English translation. As a curious inversion of the songs' presentation in Balieff's show, this reversal demonstrates the effectiveness of the cast's theatrical performance as well as the pragmatism of the Harms company. Moreover, the content found on the sheet music covers underscores each song's affiliation with Balieff's show, rather than centering on the title of each song—even for those pieces with which Russian audiences would have been intimately familiar. The subtitle of "Two Guitars," for example, states, "Russian Gypsy Song: Sung in Balieff's 'Chauve-Souris'," and does not refer to the song's position as a staple of the Russian popular music repertoire (see chap. 1). This correlation suggests that the Harms music publishing company marketed its songs primarily for an audience more familiar with Balieff's show than with the songs themselves and capitalized on the show's success with American audiences to sell a new series of songs.

The way in which the *Chauve-Souris* production was presented in the American press offers additional clues about how New York's Russian vogue took shape. Anticipating the American debut of the show, for example, a critic for the *New York Times* described the production as "the hallmark of Russia's quaint, exotic, often half-barbaric art, recalling . . . songs of the Russian

Isba [peasant hut], tinkling melodies of the Balalaika players, dances of the Diaghileff and Pavlowa troupes."[14] Balieff capitalized on this formulaic conception of Russia as his show reinforced what John Bowlt has described as "the public's desired interpretation of Russia as a colorful, barbaric nation consisting of samovars, bears, merchants, and peasants in high leather boots, lovely country maidens, sleighs hastening across the snow, and carousing hussars."[15] Soon enough, the New York production of the *Chauve-Souris* became explicitly associated with a Russian "vogue" and "invasion."[16]

The "quaint" and "exotic" Russia presented in the *Chauve-Souris* show is likewise evident in the songs published by the Harms sheet music company. One of the most famous songs appearing in the show and in sheet music was "Katinka."[17] The Harms version of this song vividly illustrates the "half-barbaric," mythologized Russia touted by American critics. The sheet music cover, for example, presents a Russian peasant couple sitting in front of the prototypical "Isba" mentioned in the *New York Times* review of the same year (see fig. 2.1). The woman in the picture wears a kerchief and long, polka-dotted skirt as she blankly stares ahead, listening to the sounds of the concertina played by her kaftan-clad husband. Emblems of a merry village life surround the couple, including a birdhouse, trees, sunflowers, and an ornately carved hut and fence. Such self-representations of Russians as "colourful Other" were eagerly consumed by the Western public.[18]

This seemingly formulaic image, however, contains a modernist edge that reflects the broader impulse of the *Chauve-Souris*, as the "Katinka" sheet music cover presents a carnivalesque tinge that distorts the figures and objects into rather surreal, grotesque variations. The vantage point of the viewer is likewise skewed and tilted, resulting in a queasy effect. The prominent lettering showcasing Balieff's production, moreover, consists of a striking orange hue and is in a playful font reminiscent of the Art Nouveau style popular in turn-of-the-century Russia.

The stylization marking this folk scene is not surprising, considering that it was drawn by Nicholai Remisoff (1884–1975), the cutting-edge artist who likewise designed many of the sets and costumes of Balieff's productions.[19] Rather than mere mimicry or a romanticized depiction of a Russian folk scene, Remisoff's illustration betrays his modernist sensibilities and, more broadly, reflects the nuance and wit associated with the *Chauve-Souris* production as a whole.

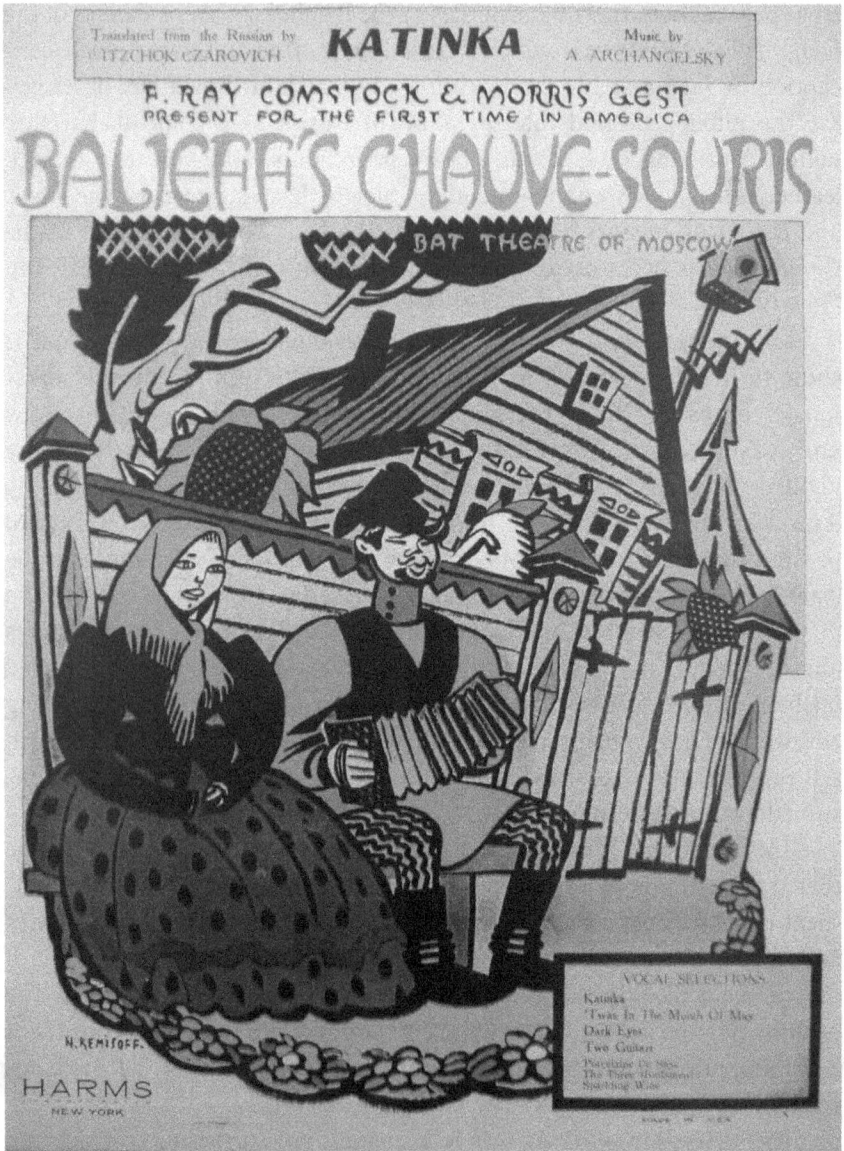

Figure 2.1. Sheet music cover of "Katinka," published by Harms, Inc. (1922). Sam DeVincent Collection of Illustrated American Sheet Music, Archives Center, National Museum of American History, Smithsonian Institution.

The lyrics of "Katinka" as they are presented in the Harms publication further convey an unconventional presentation of village life.[20] Rather than depicting an idyllic village scene, the text relays the story of a young woman (Katinka) who dances the polka.[21] Katinka's parents are shocked by the little vixen who returns from boarding school, dancing a step that they deem "daring" and "much too gay." In this story, the polka is not merely a dance but a symbol of city life and loose morals. To her parents' chagrin, Katinka now flirts with officers, reveals her stockings, and even steals from the family moneybox.[22] Perhaps Katinka's greatest offense, however, is her desire to marry not a "peasant" but a "nobleman."

Katinka's transgressions all stem from her dancing the polka, which is presented as the root of her moral downfall:

K: I've a winning way with the men; The officers flirt with me;
What it is, I can't understand, My dancing it must be.

FATHER: What's that funny dance, Katinka?

K: It's the polka, my dear Papa.

MOTHER: Daring, I should say, Katinka!

K: Very fashionable, dear Mama.

M: Dear, oh dear, how shocking, Your stocking is showing!
I will not have you do it, You'll rue it, if you keep on!

F: Where'd you learn it, my Katinka?

K: At the boarding school, dear Papa.

M: Whom d'you dance it with, Katinka?

K: With the officers, my dear Mama.

M: You're a very bold little girl, A bad little girl, I'll say!
Ladies must be far more discreet, This polka is much too gay.

F: Tell me daughter, whence all this gold?

K: From the money box, please don't scold!

M: Dared you take it without permit?

K: Oh, forgive me, it was just a bit!

K: It isn't very pleasant to go with a peasant;
A nobleman, I'd marry and be in society.

F: I forbid it, my Katinka!

K: Please permit it, oh dear Papa!

M: I'll disown you Katinka!

K: If you do so, I will die, Mama!

F/M: Oh, how distressing, oh, how depressing, Tell me who's to blame, not I! It's up to you now, What shall we do now? Hurry up or else she'll die!

F: What's ailing you, Katinka?

K: Let me marry, oh dear Papa!

M: If you wish it, dear Katinka,

K: Thank you many times my dear Mama.

ALL: What a happy ending, The fates are befriending, And here we all are dancing The polka, ha! ha! ha! ha![23]

Hints of class tension pepper the text, and Katinka's rural parents are shocked by the urban and, by extension, morally questionable actions of their daughter. Nevertheless, Katinka's parents continually address their daughter by the endearing diminutive, "Katinka," rather than by the formal "Ekaterina" (Katherine), reflecting their enduring love despite their daughter's transgressions.

The musical style of "Katinka" adds another playful element to the piece. The song exhibits characteristics typical of polkas, including 2/4 meter, eight-bar phrases, and a repeated sixteenth-note pattern. Further marking the spirited nature of the piece is the recurring motif of a grace note preceding a downward-octave leap, followed by a lower-neighbor gesture (see example 2.1). This repeated figure adds buoyancy to the song and prevents the piece from turning into a heavy admonition, in this way mirroring the lighthearted diminutive of the protagonist's name.

Katinka's "impish polka" made a strong impression on American audiences. By September 1922 (a mere seven months after the opening night of *Chauve-Souris*), the song's composer, Alexei Archangelsky, was featured in the popular *Town and Country* magazine. The headline marking the article—"The Composer of 'Katinka'"—speaks to the popularity of both song and theatrical production. Further attesting to the song's fame, the first lines of the article state: "Of course one knows the Chauve-Souris. Equally, of course, one knows 'Katinka,' which, with 'The March of the Wooden Soldiers' [another *Chauve-Souris* number], runs the danger of being the best known piece of contemporary music at every dinner table."[24] One month following Katinka's appearance in *Town and Country*, a review of the much-anticipated second season of *Chauve-Souris* in the *New York Times*

Example 2.1. "Katinka," measures 17–20, published by Harms, Inc. (1922). Sam DeVincent Collection of Illustrated American Sheet Music, Archives Center, National Museum of American History, Smithsonian Institution.

spoke almost exclusively about Katinka's fate (unveiled as her marriage to a wooden soldier, which her parents protest and consequently face an attack by a brigade of wooden soldiers). The review reports a happy ending, describing the final scene complete with the characters singing the "now universally familiar polka."[25]

Despite the Russian tinge of the first season of *Chauve-Souris*, the "Katinkas" of Balieff's second season, began to take on American per-mutations. This evolution is vividly illustrated by the upbeat "O, Katha-rina." Although "O, Katharina" shares a namesake (Katherine) with her earlier Russian counterpart, the similarities end there. For one thing, the lyrics are no longer based on a translation of an earlier Russian song but are newly composed in English. Moreover, the story relayed is no longer about the pitfalls of the polka; nor does it make any reference to anything Rus-sian. Instead, the lyrics present a narrative about an immigrant couple from Rotterdam whose old-world conventions are challenged by the swinging American culture they encounter: after seeing the Ziegfeld Follies, the hus-band determines that "wifie" is too hefty for American standards of beauty and commands her to lose weight. This sentiment makes up the central thrust of the song as well as the words in the chorus: "O, Katharina, oh, Katharina. To keep my love, you must be leaner."

"O, Katharina" operates on a New World/Old World dichotomy in which American culture trumps its outdated European counterpart. The Old World is marked by such objects as "pig's feet," "sauerkraut," and a "plump" wife. ("At home we thought a girl was fine if she was fat and plumpy, But here a girl must never look a trifle short and dumpy.") By con-trast, the United States holds the key to what is "up to date," including svelte women who wear "less." The adoption of American standards of beauty mirrors the husband's foray into jazz on his (old-world) concertina, which, aside from the shared name of the female protagonist, stands as the only direct remnant of the earlier "Katinka."

The compositional process of "O, Katharina" similarly reflects a shift toward American culture. Instead of involving a fellow member of the White Russian emigration (Archangelsky passed away in 1924), the song's lyrics were created by Tin Pan Alley luminary Louis Wolfe Gilbert (1886–1970), who immigrated to the United States from Russia as an infant with his parents and, by the time he composed "O, Katharina," was already a well-established songwriter within the New York circuit.[26]

The most striking shift from Old World to New, however, is reflected in the music itself. No longer does the song feature an upbeat polka but instead entails the cutting-edge sounds of a fox-trot, composed, in this case, by Richard Fall (1882–1945). Undoubtedly, it was the musical style of "O, Katharina" that caught the attention of theatergoers and now also New York jazz bands. Katharina's fox-trot ignited the jazz world and was soon played by numerous ensembles, including Carl Fenton's Orchestra, Ted Lewis and His Band, the International Novelty Orchestra (one of Victor's house ensembles), Ben Bernie and his Band, and Billy Murray. Collaborating with composer Abel Baer (1893–1976), Gilbert soon wrote an even hotter, more swinging song for *Chauve-Souris*—"I Miss My Swiss Miss"—which was taken up by such notable jazz players as Paul Whiteman, Fletcher Henderson, and Louis Armstrong.

"Katherine's" highly adaptable nature—and, by extension, the nature of the *Chauve-Souris* as a whole—is rooted in the style in which Balieff both introduced and operated his show. Indeed, Balieff's work was predicated on a combination of flexibility and rootedness that enabled its success. As Joseph Horowitz claims in his work on exiled artists in the United States, a "twofold posture of openness and retention" was needed for artists to succeed in the years between the world wars and that "too great an eagerness to fit in [could] vitiate creative possibilities."[27] Providing the case study of George Balanchine as an example par excellence of a Russian émigré artist whose professional transition to the New World proved decidedly successful, Horowitz underscores the choreographer's adaptable nature as the means of his triumph: "Balanchine arrived [to the United States] with a layered identity that easily absorbed additional layers. In his choreography, he chose from these various affinities, or ironically combined them."[28]

Moreover, Balanchine infused much of his work with a sense of play (for example, the ballerinas in his *Western Symphony* who simulated stagecoach horses while en pointe).

These very traits—irony, flexibility, play—are mirrored in New York's earlier émigré sensation. Balieff's onstage play with words, languages, and genres; the swift marketing of Russian songs in translation and the adoption by New York jazz bands; and the easy integration of American originals into the Russian show enabled Balieff's work to remain pertinent and to thrive within its new surroundings. The deliberate combination of New World and Old, which elicits an "ironic wink [that] seals its sophistication and charm," presented a cornerstone for the diasporic adaptability that enabled these artists (and their respective art forms) to succeed.[29] Balieff's show was not a simple continuation of a prerevolutionary artistic production but rather a vibrant example of a continually adapting work whose Russian origins provided merely the roots, rather than anchors, for a playfully mutable diasporic art form.

The Fox-Trotsky and Other (Russian) Jazz Delights

The transition from Balieff's Katinka to a jazz-swinging Katharina reflects a broader trend of a Russian-American intersection that occurred specifically within the sphere of jazz. Not only was this synthesis apparent among the jazz ensembles that played, boomed, and ticked *Chauve-Souris* songs, but it also emerged within the realm of American sheet music. One of the most vivid illustrations of the Russian-American intersection as it was brokered through jazz was the trope of a jazz-dancing Russian she-devil found in Tin Pan Alley songs of the time.

A lively example of this Russian-American amalgamation can be found in the 1926 "Katinka." Written by Ben Russell (lyrics) and Henry Tobias (music), the song presents a modernized reference to the *Chauve-Souris* hit by the same name. Labeled a "Fox-trotsky," the cover depicts an image of a young woman wearing a combination of Russian peasant blouse, printed skirt, boots, and the short-haired bob of the progressive flapper (see fig. 2.2).[30]

On the one hand, Katinka's attire reflects the Russian style that permeated American and Parisian fashion in the early and mid-1920s. Examples of the *style russe* can be found in Leon Bakst's flower-print designs for Lord and Taylor (1924) and in the tunics, furs, and ornate embroidery that defined Coco Chanel's Slavic Period.[31] Indeed, the trend for things Russian within the fashion world in this period elicited émigré composer Vernon

Figure 2.2. Sheet music cover of "Katinka," published by Leo Feist Inc. (1926). Sam DeVincent Collection of Illustrated American Sheet Music, Archives Center, National Museum of American History, Smithsonian Institution.

Duke to proclaim that, "everything Russian was then very popular."[32] Beyond the seemingly frivolous world of fashion and sheet music, however, this fabricated Russianness helped destitute émigrés procure a living, as many émigré women (including Duke's mother) found employment sewing Russianness into garments.[33] We see, then, the threads of transnational imagery at play in dress shops as well as in sheet music, with Russian tropes appearing in both spheres.

The young woman depicted on the sheet music cover, however, presents no conventional Russian maiden, as her posture and foot position immediately signal the thoroughly modern step of the American Charleston. Indeed, the song's visual imagery and lyrics reflect a fluid traversal and ultimate synthesis between Russian and American spheres. In this variation of Balieff's "Katinka," the song's narrative similarly focuses on Katinka's downfall through the devious influence of a social dance (originally the polka and now the Charleston).[34] Instead of causing Katinka to lose favor with her parents, however, the dance now occasions Katinka to abandon her very Russianness—dropping her Slavic beau, Russian dancing, and even her motherland for the hot sound of the Charleston and the love of a Yankee:

> There in Petrograd, lived a Russ who had a Russian maiden who was called "Katinka,"
> Then one day she heard about the Charleston,
> From a Yankee boy she learned to Charleston,
> She left Petrograd, With this Yankee lad, Left her Russian sadly crying:
>
> Who thought Katinka would pack up on me?
> It was that Charlesburg I know,
> She would Kazatsky with me every day,
> But she went nutsky from 'Hey! Hey!' 'Hey! Hey!'
> That hotsky music just led her astray, And I lost Katinka that way.

The rift between Katinka's Russian past and her swinging present is underscored by the words of her forlorn Russian lover, whose naiveté is accentuated by his mispronunciation of the American dance ("Charlesburg") and by his quaint reminiscences of the kazatsky (whether as dance or reference to sexual act).[35]

Despite Katinka's meanderings away from Russian culture, the piece as a whole operates by fusing Russian and American tropes in its narrative and its visual imagery. This amalgamation likewise occurs on a linguistic level, as the lyrics include Russified English words like "nutsky," "hotsky," and the politically oriented "fox-trotsky." Demonstrating a kind of containment of Russian language, this linguistic fusion plays on the audience's lack of familiarity with the language and produces a stereotyped phonology of Russian.

Other examples of Tin Pin Alley songs likewise situate a Russian-American amalgamation within the sphere of jazz. Similar to the 1926 "Katinka," the 1934 "Hotcha Chornia Brown" bases its narrative around the idea of modernizing Russians through jazz. The transformation is instigated in this case by the arrival of Mabel Brown, an American wallflower who leaves her home city of Kokomo, Indiana, to reinvent herself in Russia. This cultural exchange entails a symbiotic relationship in which both sides have something to gain—the Russians are modernized through their encounter with jazz, while Mabel becomes the talk of the town:

> Hotcha Chornia Brown is turning Moscow upside down,
> Hotcha Chornia Brown can make each Cossack "Go to town," . . .
> She's improved on their kozotsky, pepped it up and made it hotsky,
> Each night she does her stuff with a hey, nonny nonny and a Rubinoff,
> When it's twenty-one belowsky, You should see them "Hi-de-hoe-sky"
> They never get enough when she makes hey, hey!

Mabel spices up Russian life through jazz and its thinly veiled allusion to sex, enrapturing Cossacks, Volga boatmen, and even the deceased Grigori Rasputin, who turns in the ground, "shoutin' Hotcha! Hotcha! Hotcha Chornia Brown!" The song is replete with conventional signifiers of Russian culture, including tea rooms, vodka, and Mabel's "private samovar," to which her suitors flock every night.[36]

Another recurring pattern found within jazz-oriented, Russian American–themed sheet music of the time is a subtle satirizing of Bolshevik Russia and of Russian émigrés. Written by Irving Kahal, Sammy Fain, and Irving Mills, for example, the 1925 "Valeska" references the kazatsky and utilizes hip, Russified language in describing the current situation in Russia: "Ev'ry thing is Russian in old Russia, the country's on the bumsky we all know, still I find that I must go to Moscow, to my Valeska I must go." The 1932 "I Played Fiddle for the Czar" explicitly references not only the rift between pre- and postrevolutionary Russia but also the specific subject of the White Russian émigré in New York. The lyrics state:

> My heart is broke, I'm blue and sad I miss my home in Petrograd.
> In the days of old Russia no other days were greater.

In those days that used to be I was known as a Marquis,
But what's a marquis over here a sign on a Theatre.

I was once a member of the Court; Now my life is gloomy,
Now I'm just a member of the Court; When some one wants to sue me.

The amalgamation of Imperial Russia and American jazz is made explicit in the song's chorus:

I played fiddle for the Czar.
When he'd say play something hotsky I would play a hot kasotsky . . .
But I was there, yes I was there with wine and Caviar. . . .
They would all go off their nutka; Sloppin' up a glass of Vodka.

I played fiddle for the czar, When he had a cold I played catarrh
Then came the Revolution and it really got my goat
They didn't ask me questions, They just shoved me on a boat.
And here I am, yes I am, Could ya' let me have a dime.
I played Fiddle for the Czar.

This work in particular attests to the extent to which the "Russian émigré" stereotype has been established by this time and hints to the depictions of destitute Russian aristocrats that would soon appear in Hollywood films.[37]

On one hand, we can approach the Russian-themed sheet music that emerged in the 1920s and early 1930s at face value: a commodity deployed for popular consumption and both based on and actively contributing to collective discourses about the political, racial, and ethnic Other. Allowing its reader to gauge the "common cultural currency"[38] about any number of interchanges, sheet music has reflected and helped generate collective views on geopolitics, ethnic stereotypes, and racial hierarchies.[39] As such, sheet music emerges as a site rich for analyzing collectively recognized symbols of identity that have helped "form the public discourses" about ethnic groups in the United States.[40] Thus, it is not surprising that the symbols defining Russia as a land brimming with vodka, caviar, tea, and balalaikas would endure in sheet music and in the public imaginary for decades to come.

Aside from presenting a largely essentialized reading of Russia, the narratives found in these examples of sheet music also suggest an underlying notion of American cultural superiority and imperialism. Mabel Brown's visit to Russia improves Russian culture as she turns the "kozotsky" into something "hotsky." The kazatsky-trotting Katinka renounces her quaint

Russian ways for the hot steps of the Charleston. In these examples, the modern music of jazz imposes itself onto and transforms its seemingly more traditional, staid neighbor. Indeed, the inclusion of jazz in ethnic-themed sheet music can be seen as a form of subjugating ethnic Others under the ruling thumb (or Charleston-induced heel) of their American cultural colonizers.[41]

Cultural imposition, however, is a somewhat limited paradigm when considering the broader power dynamics of the jazz-mediated Russian-American exchange. Indeed, the Russian-American intersection through jazz can be likewise viewed as a symbiotic relationship, as evidenced in the narratives found in the sheet music as well as in historic manifestations of this cultural transaction. Within the realm of American sheet music, for example, jazz appears to be as much of an equalizer as it is a force of cultural subjugation. Mabel "Hotcha" Brown only gains potency once she leaves her familiar American shores and ventures to Russia. While importing jazz, Mabel simultaneously wears a "Russian smock" that makes her look "more Russian than the czar." Clearly, Mabel does not simply impose American culture onto her Russian companions but rather engages in cross-cultural fusion and exchange. In other examples, American male protagonists fall in love with Russian women and leave behind the comforts of American life to pursue their objects of affection. As a salient microcosm for cross-cultural performance and exchange, sheet music afforded Russian characters the possibility of modernization through jazz, while the buyers of the music could partake in Russianness by engaging with the explicit textual and visual markers, in this way allowing American consumers to experience the Russian Other within the familiar space of the jazz idiom.

The jazz rage that swept the Soviet Union beginning in the mid-1920s further disrupts the idea of unidirectional cultural imposition and demonstrates that the narrative of jazz-crazed Russians was not merely a Tin Pan Alley construction but an actual trend that occurred in Soviet Russia. Although Russians had eagerly embraced the American phenomenon of ragtime starting in 1910, it was not until 1922 (a handful of years after the jazz boom in Europe) that jazz reached Russian shores.[42] The first jazz band to play in Russia was not an American import, however, but the brainchild of futurist poet Valentin Parnakh (1891–1951), who had the means to assemble a jazz ensemble and the smarts to convince the communist regime to tolerate this new music.[43] Russian sheet music publishers soon tried to keep up with the high demand for fox-trot tunes (many of which were composed by native Russians), and jazz was heard in the accompaniments for silent Hollywood films (performed, for example, by a young Dimitry Shostakovich).[44] In 1926, prominent Russian musician Leopold Teplitsky received permission to visit the United States, where he studied with Paul Whiteman and returned to Russia to play at numerous restaurants and clubs.[45] And Russian dancer Lydia Iver astounded Russian audiences with her spirited dancing, bobbed hair, and flapper attire.[46]

These and other examples suggest that, far from a simple cultural invasion, as the narratives in American sheet music tend to present, Russians were active agents in embracing and acclimating jazz to suit their tastes. Paralleling the narrative of Mabel Brown, the influx of American jazz resulted in a Soviet jazz craze that did indeed turn Russia "upside down"— a movement that lasted until the tail end of the Cultural Revolution (1928– 1930), only to be followed by a "red jazz age" (1932–1936).[47] With tunes like Vadim Kozin's "Lyuba" and the music featured in films like *Veselye Rebiata* (Jolly Fellows), a genuine indigenization of jazz had taken place that made the music no longer a mere import but an inherent part of Russian culture.[48]

Jazz likewise presented a site for integrating Russian elements into American culture. The many Russian songs played by New York jazz bands discussed earlier in this chapter present one salient example of this Russian-American intersection. Within the realm of dance, the Americanized version of the Russian *kazachek*, referred to by its playfully anglicized name of the "kazatsky," presents another vivid illustration. The dance was introduced to New York audiences in the World War I era by African-American tap dancer Ida Forsyne (1883–1936).[49] Enamored with the traditional Russian dancing she saw performed by a Russian dance troupe on Broadway in 1905 and then on a trip to Russia soon thereafter, Forsyne began incorporating elements of the *kazachek* into her tap routine and reconfigured the traditional male dance into a "swinging blend of tap and acrobatics."[50] Since Forsyne instigated this seemingly unlikely union, American tap has regularly incorporated elements of Russian dancing, which appealed to Forsyne for both aesthetic and pragmatic reasons.[51] Although Russian-style dancing lost favor among New York's black audiences in the 1920s, it was at that moment that white audiences were captivated by the form, of which they received a "concentrated taste" in Balieff's *Chauve-Souris* production.[52] As such, we may consider the extent to which Balieff was playing off American preconceptions of Russianness by incorporating the "kazatsky" into his show. Since this period, the kazatsky appeared not only on stage, but in sheet music, cartoons, and to this day emerges within the wider American lexicon on Russianness.[53]

Finally, jazz was a central part of the Russian émigré scene in New York. The "Russian Evenings" at Harlem's Russian Club (examined in chap. 1), for example, frequently featured the sounds of a jazz band to round off a night of Russian folk and gypsy music. The Russian-American jazz connection took on a literal dimension as well with the Russian roots of numerous American Jewish musicians and composers, including Irving Berlin and the Gershwin brothers.[54] The Russian-American jazz union was only furthered by the collaboration, friendship, and intermarriage among members of this prewar immigration and the postrevolutionary émigrés.[55] Perhaps the best known of such alliances was that between George Gershwin and Vernon Duke (Vladimir Dukelsky), who composed the music for the all-black Broadway musical, *Cabin in the Sky* (choreographed by fellow émigré George Balanchine) and penned numerous American standards, including "April in Paris."[56]

Predating the US-Soviet cultural diplomacy efforts of the 1950s and 1960s, the cultural sharing that occurred three decades earlier points to the possibility of Russian-American dialogue through the swinging beats of jazz.[57] This exchange, however, was not a strategic government tactic to export American culture in order to conquer the hearts and minds of a people under communist rule, as it was during the Cold War. Instead, the Russian-American jazz synthesis of the late 1920s and early 1930s presents an example of a more spontaneous and bilateral cultural exchange: American jazz bands playing Russian tunes, Russian band leaders bringing the sounds of jazz to eager Russian audiences, and Russian immigrants climbing to the top of the American popular music world. In local contexts, as in geopolitics, jazz emerges as a facilitator for cultural exchange and interaction. As a revolutionary musical form that was perceived to embody lighthearted pursuits, sex, laxity, emancipation, individual freedom, and a general "liberation of the human body," jazz served as a cultural leveler celebrated by an entire generation of American and Russians following the ravages of war.[58]

Russian Gypsies Meet Krazy Kat: The Dark Eyes Phenomenon

It is clear that the Russian vogue that swept New York's music culture in the 1920s was informed from both outside (for example, in Tin Pan Alley numbers) and inside (Balieff's *Chauve-Souris*) the realm of Russian émigré cultural production. Yet the saliency of this vogue as a diasporic phenom-enon lay in the intersection between Russian and American forces inform-ing its development. An especially rich example of such an intersection can be found in the trajectory taken by the Russian gypsy song, "Dark Eyes" within the New York cultural circuit.

Here, I wish to return to the swinging sheet music example of "Hotcha Chornia Brown," for within the song's title is embedded a cultural trend that would make a significant mark on the American popular music land-scape. At first glance, the protagonist's newfound name of "Hotcha Chor-nia" brings to mind nothing short of a hip, albeit somewhat odd name. Mabel's moniker simultaneously evokes a physicality ("hot") and an imme-diacy ("gotcha")—an amalgamation suiting her fresh persona.[59]

When taken within the context of the Russian vogue, however, "Hotcha Chornia" immediately warrants a different reading. Rather than a peculiar, Russified name, "Hotcha Chornia" presents a swinging, anglicized refer-ence to the notorious Russian gypsy song, "*Ochi chernye* [Dark Eyes]." The shift from Russian to American pronunciation echoes the song's passage through the folds of American culture that would include sheet music, car-toons, and performances by singers whose styles were as varied as those of Chet Atkins and Louis Armstrong.

The song's idiosyncratic trajectory through the American music scene mirrors its complex roots and earlier appropriations. Although "Dark Eyes" was written by Ukrainian Evgeny Grebenka (1812–1848) and initially had nothing to do with the Russian gypsy genre, it became a staple of the rep-ertoire in prerevolutionary Russia (see example 2.2). The "gypsy" song was enthusiastically performed in cabarets throughout the diaspora, including by musicians within the Russian enclave in Harlem. Many renowned émi-gré concert musicians likewise embraced "Dark Eyes."[60]

By the mid-1920s, "Dark Eyes" continued its haphazard course, break-ing out of the domain of the émigré house concert and into the realm of the American music industry. Along with other songs featured in Balieff's *Chauve-Souris*, for example, "Dark Eyes" began circulating as sheet music in translation as a Harms Company publication. By the late 1920s, the sheet music market had numerous renditions of "Dark Eyes" and was published by multiple New York sheet music companies, including Carl Fischer (1928, 1935), George F. Briegel (1928), J+J Kammen (1929), Edward B. Marks Music Company (1929, 1932, 1934), F. B. Haviland Publishing Company (1929), Belwin (1931), Robbins Music Corporation (1932), and G. Schirmer (1933).

Example 2.2. Opening of "Dark Eyes" (Melody transcribed by author from Don Cossacks Choir, *Folk Songs and Romances*, Hymns of the Russian Orthodox Church and Folk Songs, Disc 3).

By this time, "Dark Eyes" no longer needed to rely on its association with Balieff's show and had gained enough notoriety to be referred to simply as "the famous Russian Gypsy Air."[61]

"Dark Eyes" soon emerged in American films, jazz recordings, and animated cartoons. The song was featured, for example, in the films *My Man Godfrey* (1936), *Shall We Dance* (1937), and *The Wonder Bar* (1934), in which it is performed by Russian-born American jazz singer Al Jolson. Considering the fate of other Russian songs that circulated in the form of sheet music, it is not surprising that "Dark Eyes" was also adopted by American jazz ensembles. In 1938, the song was performed by jazz vocalist Maxine Sullivan, whose interpretation includes verses sung in Russian and in English, as well as a musical quotation of Rachmaninoff's Prelude in C-Sharp Minor (Op. 3, no. 2). The inclusion of the Russian language as well as an excerpt from a Russian piano classic serve as an aural nod to the song's roots. Later renditions include an upbeat, swinging version by Louis Armstrong (1954), and a playful adaptation by Spike Jones (1942), who incorporates the opening strands of the "Volga Boatmen" (with humorous, responsorial grunts) and a balalaika solo within an otherwise conventional jazz lineup.[62] The name of the Spike Jones version, "Hotcha Cornia," immediately recalls that of the earlier sheet music vixen.

An excellent testament to the evolution of "Dark Eyes" within the American cultural circuit can be found in a 1933 episode of the cartoon, *Krazy Kat*. Entitled, "Russian Dressing," the cartoon is replete with stereotypical images found in Russian-themed sheet music of the era. Musically, the cartoon opens with a Russian male choir, singing indiscernible, garbled words and whose babble linguistically and sonically signifies the

Russian Other. The action begins with Krazy Kat sitting behind a horse-drawn sleigh and playing an upbeat tune on his balalaika. Krazy Kat's playing propels the action in the clip, including inciting his horse to stand on its hind legs to merrily dance the by-now-familiar kazatsky. As Krazy Kat approaches his sweetheart's hut, the mood quickly shifts to a romantic one as our hero whole-heartedly breaks out into a rendition of "Dark Eyes." The song is performed in Russian with no trace of an accent, suggesting that it was likely sung by a recent Russian émigré. (The singer is not credited in the cartoon.) Importantly, the fact that the piece is performed in Russian rather than in translation suggests that the audience would have been familiar enough with the melody not to need an Anglophone reference. The Russian text adds yet another layer of exoticism to the already colorful scene.

Although "Russian Dressing" is based on seemingly conventional visual and sonic symbols of Russianness, a certain degree of sensory mix-up is also at play. For example, although Krazy Kat and his accompanying choir of long-bearded, kaftan-clad Cossacks are shown playing the balalaika during the strands of "Dark Eyes," it is the accordion that is actually sounded. In this way, the cartoon presents a sonic-visual conflation of Russian tropes that collapses the idea of "Russia" into a hodgepodge of sensory-mixed stereotypes: the ear hears not what the eye sees. Like the Spike Jones song that would be released a year later, Krazy Kat's version of "Dark Eyes" also includes an interjection of "Volga Boatmen," which further underscores the codification of musical emblems of "Russia." The cartoon continues in this vein, replete with the stereotypical images of Russia found in earlier sheet music examples: a heavy-drinking Cossack with beard and large hat, a kazatsky-dancing Krazy Kat, oodles of balalaikas (albeit playing to the sounds of an accordion), and an element of revolutionary danger. Similar to sheet music, music in cartoons has often similarly been used as "fodder for social commentary," hence presenting a reflection of the dominant ways Russianness was conceived and constructed within American popular culture.[63]

"A Certain Exotic Aperitif Flavor": A Strategy of Auto-Orientalism

The inclusion of "Dark Eyes" in the worlds of jazz, sheet music, and animated cartoons demonstrates the song's ubiquity within American culture. The "Dark Eyes" phenomenon simultaneously reflects an exoticism that was both imposed from the outside and instigated from within Russian émigré circles, in this way creating a type of feedback loop that helped New York Russians take advantage of their position as ethnic Others.

For one, Russian-themed sheet music, including various publications of "Dark Eyes," became a central site for framing and further exoticizing the Russian Other. For example, "Dark Eyes" is labeled simultaneously as both a "Russian folk song" and a "Russian gypsy air." Such interchangeable labeling suggests a reciprocal, even shared, Russian-Romani otherness within the sphere of American culture. This conflation is likewise evident in the overlapping imagery found in sheet music. Many of the "Dark Eyes" sheet music covers, for example, feature sultry women with ornate sashes, unbuttoned blouses, and heads of bountiful curls. Similar imagery is presented on the covers of other Russian-themed sheet music, suggesting a further elision between Russian and Romani women into a single exotic Other.

In other examples, the Russian woman is cast more generally as Eastern Other. "Natacha, My Star of Love" (1931), for example, depicts "Natacha," a dark-haired, red-lipped beauty with large, gold hooped earrings, amid mysterious, exotic towers. Typical of Orientalist fantasies, Natacha is a lusty, sexy, free-spirited woman who has given herself to the presumably unmarked (i.e., Anglo-Saxon/Western) male narrator: "Natacha, my star of love, You came as tho a blessing, caressing me from above; The night was dark you made it splendid, All unhappiness was ended."[64] Natacha's fingers suggestively and elegantly close her cape, which drapes down far enough to reveal her white bosom, the color of which is emphasized against the bright red hue of her jacket and hair (see fig. 2.3). Natacha casts a knowing, perhaps even longing, glance at the exotic towers behind her, as such, framing the cover with a circular line and signaling her deep connection to her Eastern roots. Natacha's otherness is likewise underscored with an emphasis on her "dusky eyes," within which the narrator finds "a story of Paradise." As such, "Natacha" frames Russianness through an Orientalalist lens, replete with non-Western signifiers.

The amalgamation between "Russian" and "Gypsy" occurred not only within the realm of sheet music but also was undertaken by Russian émigrés themselves. This self-positioning as Gypsy Other is made evident in the Russian-themed nightclubs that featured "gypsy" choirs (which, although often featuring Romani singers, were made up mostly of ethnic Russians); "Gypsy" costume balls organized by Russian émigrés; and on LP covers with Russian singers in the same "gypsy" costumes that had been featured in thethe earlier sheet music and society balls.[65]

Figure 2.3. Sheet music cover of "Natacha" published by Song Hit Guild, Inc. (1931). Sam DeVincent Collection of Illustrated American Sheet Music, Archives Center, National Museum of American History, Smithsonian Institution.

Figure 2.4. Club Petroushka Interior (mural by Nicolas Remisoff). Box 16, Folder 3, Nicolas Remisoff papers, Collection no. 0199, Special Collections, University of Southern California Libraries.

The Russian-themed nightclubs included Nicolai Remisoff's and Theodore Bauer's Club Petroushka (50 E. Fiftieth Street, between Park and Madison Avenues). Opened in 1923, the club featured a "gypsy" choir, waiters in exotic dress, and Russian food, and was enthusiastically frequented by such figures as the Gershwin brothers, Harpo Marx, and Rudolph Valentino.[66] Similar to his work for the *Chauve-Souris* productions, Remisoff applied his whimsical taste to the club's decor and ambience, as he painted murals of Russian tavern scenes, served Russian delicacies, and organized a "gypsy" choir (headed by fellow émigré and Romani singer, Anna Shishkina) (see fig. 2.4). The third floor even featured a so-called "Gypsy Room," which was "fancifully decorated to simulate a gypsy tent with tapestries and brilliant hangings covering the walls."[67]

The "gypsy"-themed costume balls organized by Russian émigrés likewise held great appeal to New York society. Part of the broader trend of Russian costume balls that was inaugurated by the émigrés in 1922, these balls featured costume-clad guests, lively decorations ranging from cherry orchards to gypsy camps, and the participation of both the émigré and New York elite, including society ladies Mrs. Theodore Roosevelt Pell and Mrs. Cornelius Vanderbilt, as well as members of the Russian nobility.[68] Musically, these balls featured "gypsy" choirs, balalaika orchestras, and well-known émigré performers like Nadezhda Plevitskaya, Basil Fomeen, and Sergei Rachmaninoff.

The collapse between Russian and Romani subjects as well as the broader performance of exotic Other suggests a deliberate strategy of auto-Orientalism deployed by the émigrés in New York. Unlike Edward Said's model of Orientalism, in which Eastern Others serve as objects of the Western imagination, auto-Orientalism engages a deliberate projection of the exotic self. This kind of "self-stereotyping" enables nonhegemonic Others to temporarily invert conventional power dynamics by enticing members of the status quo into a constructed, untamed world.[69] In this way, auto-Orientalism offers a strategy of empowerment and a site of agency for Eastern Others, even if the images evoked play off of essentialized conceptions of the Others in question.[70] For First Wave émigrés in New York, this strategy entailed a careful traversal between titillating Other and cosmopolitan insider, as it operated on an underlying objectification of the "high-class" émigré while engaging long held ideas of the Eastern Other.

The performance of Gypsy Other specifically within the primarily non-Rom emigration, however, presents a complex positioning. On the one hand, the trope of "gypsy" as it had developed among Russian and Rom performers in nineteenth-century Russia presented an established model for the recent refugees. As a phenomenon that "offered an opening to a gypsy world that promised the possibility of excitement and escape to many segments of Russian elite society," Russian gypsy music culture in prerevolutionary Russia became associated with entry into an exotic realm.[71] With this correlation firmly entrenched in the Russian imaginary, Russians in the emigration adopted the gypsy trope to evoke an exoticism far-removed from their quotidian existence in New York and to offer "excitement and escape" for themselves and for their American spectators. A central part of the tsyganshchina ("gypsy mania") that dominated Russian culture through the end of the nineteenth century and that was triggered by the popularity of Count Alexei Orloff's (1737–1807) choir of Romani singers, so-called Russian gypsy music was a deeply ingrained aspect of prerevolutionary Russian culture whose valorization was only strengthened for émigrés through nostalgia. The performance of Russian gypsy music by First Wave émigrés hence presents a foreseeable means of upholding the culture the émigrés had embraced in their homeland. (The specific musical and textual qualities that were identified as being especially conducive to fostering feelings of nostalgia is a point I explore in detail in chap. 1.)

The Russians playing gypsy in the diaspora, however, were no closer to being Romani than they had been in prerevolutionary Russia. Indeed, the Russian émigrés in New York engaged in auto-Orientalism from a position of power, while Romani performers in prerevolutionary Russia ultimately belonged to a disempowered social category.[72] From this perspective, the Russian-Romani amalgamation in the restaurants and society balls of New York can be seen as one of cultural cooption—an opportunist move to position the Russian self as a played-up Other for the pleasure of the American public.

Specific examples of auto-Orientalism undertaken by New York Russians through a performance of Gypsy Other can be observed among a number of émigrés, including Vernon Duke. One of Duke's first means of employment after arriving in New York City entailed singing Russian gypsy songs at a Russian restaurant. Duke's candid description of his loathsome job underscores the performative nature of his work:

> So, back to synthetic gypsies I went, as accompanist to one of the tribe in a pseudo-Russian midtown night spot... one evening when I was about to charge into the obnoxious "*Otchi Tchornya*," who should walk in but the impeccably clad Karol Szymanovski, a half-dozen composers in tow. . . . Words cannot describe my pain and mortification. Here were my senior contemporaries, proudly practicing their craft—nay, *my* craft!—and here was I, a young fellow composer, about to prostitute myself publicly. I closed my eyes, raced through the hateful "*Otchi*" at breakneck speed, causing the gypsy diva intense discomfort and annoyance, then excused myself and buttonholed [Lazare] Saminsky. . . . The "*Otchi Tchornya*" interlude proved to be an epilogue, and never again did I have to don a red silk blouse and black dress trousers (part of a dinner suit, purchased on Eighth Avenue for seven dollars) to entertain hiccuping customers.[73]

Although Duke's response in part reflects his longstanding conflict between working as a composer of art music and as a thrall of popular entertainment, it also shows the utterly self-aware and shrewd nature of his performance of Gypsy Other.[74] Duke's choice of wording, including his description of "synthetic" gypsies, a "pseudo-Russian" nightclub, and the "obnoxious" and "hateful" "*Otchi chernye*" points to the consciously crafted nature of the episode. In this example, Duke is literally donning the "gypsy," as he clothes himself in the stereotypical male "gypsy" dress and enacts the exotic Other for tipsy customers. Further reflecting the entangled connection between Romani and Russian cultures that occurred in the emigration is the presentation of the restaurant itself—a "Russian" restaurant featuring "gypsy" entertainment—which was but one of numerous such establishments.[75]

Yet another example of Russian émigré cooption of the gypsy trope can be observed in the behavior of the Russian émigré cum Hollywood actor Yul Brynner (1920–1985). Born in Vladivostok, Brynner spent his early years in the Russian émigré center of Harbin with his mother and sister until the family moved to Paris in the early 1930s. It was in Paris that Brynner became intimately close with the renowned Russian Romani family, the Dimitrievitches. During this time, Brynner learned the Romani language and a wealth of Russian gypsy romances from the celebrated family of Rom musicians, with whom he would often perform.[76] Gradually, Brynner came to adopt a "gypsy" persona and began to present himself as someone of Romani descent. By the time he married Hollywood starlet Virginia Gilmore in 1944 (Brynner had immigrated to the United States in 1940), Brynner's alleged Romani roots had become common knowledge, a point that is reflected in his wedding announcement where he is referenced as "some Gypsy [Gilmore] met in New York."[77]

Although beyond the scope of the time frame in question, a vivid presentation of Brynner's gypsy enactment can be observed on a 1967 Ed Sullivan broadcast, demonstrating both the salience and longevity of the Russo-Romani collapse in the American imaginary. The broadcast presents Brynner and his close friend Aliosha Dimitrievitch (member of the celebrated Rom family), singing Russian gypsy romances.[78] In their performance of "Dve gitari [Two Guitars]," Brynner and Dimitrievitch make an ethnolinguistic swap, as Brynner sings in Romani and Dimitrievitch answers in Russian. Meanwhile, Brynner looks fixedly at his friend, suggesting a strong carnal energy that complements the seemingly spontaneous yelps and cries produced by both singers. Immediately following the spirited performance, Ed Sullivan approaches Brynner with the question, "Didn't you tell me there was a strain of Gypsy blood in your family?" to which Brynner answers, "Oh yes, there is a lot of Gypsy blood in me." As if to cover his tracks, however, Brynner quickly turns to the audience and adds, "And, I hope there is a lot of Gypsy in everybody and that they like our music."[79]

Perhaps inevitably, Brynner's auto-Orientalist strategy was occasionally sniffed out, as reflected in Melville Shavelson's *How to Make a Jewish Movie*:

> Whether Mr. Brynner is Jewish or not, I don't know. That he is a devout gypsy is true. Or as true as anything about Mr. Brynner can ever be. He has, on various occasions, admitted to being born in Bulgaria, Yugoslavia, China, Russia, The Bronx, Japan, and Outer Mongolia. He speaks the mysterious gypsy language, Romany, which has never been written down and forms an international bond. Yul Brynner can walk into any gypsy caravan in the world and have his palm read free. He can sing strange melodies all night long in strange languages no one can understand.[80]

Even in such a potentially damning exposé, however, Brynner is still cast as having an insider's status and knowledge of the "strange" and "mysterious" "gypsy" culture, which reflects both Brynner's legitimate and longstanding ties with various Rom musicians as well as his vigorous performance of "devout gypsy." Moreover, Shavelson's choice of wording, including "devout," "mysterious," and Brynner's ability to partake in "strange melodies" suggests an almost metaphysical connection between Brynner and the Romani culture, thereby furthering Brynner's positioning vis-à-vis his enigmatic past as well as the cultural stereotypes on which these discourses rested.

In other instances, Russian émigrés took advantage of the wide-sweeping otherness projected onto them by adopting a guise of multiple ethnicities. The ethnic roles of Hollywood actor Akim Tamiroff (1899–1972), for example, included playing not only Russian, but also, Greek, Chinese, French, Balinese, Polish, Mexican, Indian, Hungarian, and Spanish. Tamiroff's capitalization of a generic otherness is reflected in his assessment that his foreign accent had become his "golden goose," claiming that "everybody says my accent is worth a million dollars."[81] Meanwhile, Mischa Auer's (1905–1967) acting roles ranged from Russian ballet master (*You Can't Take It With You*, 1938) to pseudo-Russian ethnic Other ("Carlo" in *My Man Godfrey*, 1936). Émigré bandleader and accordionist Basil Fomeen (1902–1983), likewise took on a non-Russian ethnic identity, marketing himself as "Don Basilio Fomeen" in the 1950s during his Latin phase.[82] Fomeen's publishing agent, moreover, recognized the selling potential of the artist's Russian background in particular by noting the appeal of Fomeen's autobiography in having a "certain exotic aperitif flavor."[83]

To further unpack the layers of signification of ethnic Other at play within the Russian émigré sphere, it is useful to identify such auto-Orientalist moves "within the webs of power in which they are located," rather than simply accept them "at face value."[84] In part, the Russian émigré web consisted of the dollar-paying public demanding an exoticized Other to which émigrés, including Tamiroff, Duke, and Brynner, responded. Indeed, one cannot help but wonder the extent to which Russian émigré performers would have promoted this otherness had it not been popular with American audiences. These webs of power also entail the long-held Russian subsumption of Romani culture as a means of both asserting power over and identifying with Romani people as fellow outsiders to the West. As Alaina Lemon writes, "here lies a subtle difference between Russian and Western nostalgia about Gypsies. Likewise not 'normal,' Russians simultaneously expel Gypsy *from* civilization into nature, and identify *with* them against the 'coldness' of the West."[85] In this way, the Russian cooption of gypsiness demonstrates a conscious play of *svoi-chuzhoi* (self-other) that rests on what Simon Morrison describes in his work on Nikolai Rimsky-Korsakov's *Sadko* as a "representation of sameness as otherness and otherness as sameness."[86] The notion of outsiders to the West in particular reflects the long-held duality informing discourses of Russian national identity as being located somewhere between "East" and "West."[87]

Conclusion

The Russian-themed music culture that flourished in New York in the 1920s and early 1930s reflects a dialectic process that involved internal and external representations of the Russian émigré Other. In his work on the role of the arts within diasporic communities, Thomas Turino underscores the significance of art in enabling diasporans to establish new subject positions as he states, "whether for a new nation, a new sub-culture or an emerging diasporic cultural position, artistic forms can be used to make the imaginings of what the new subject position might look like, sound like, and feel like through a concrete, coherently constituted perceivable form."[88] In the case of First Wave émigrés in New York, this subject position constituted exotic, yet simultaneously cosmopolitan, cultural brokers.

As the musical acts of *Chauve-Souris* and Vernon Duke transmuted into American commodities, émigré artists themselves increasingly entered the New York cultural circuit, hence developing economic and social capital and allowing exile to operate as an "opportunity for renewal" rather than stagnation.[89] Yet these permutations did not equate with the abandonment of the Russian culture in which these forms were rooted. Indeed, the "Russianness" that framed this music emerges as a selling point and a source of exoticism that helped inform American discourses about Russia and about the émigrés themselves. In the case of Russian-themed sheet music focusing on jazz, the narratives that permeated this music reflect actual Russian-Soviet exchanges that occurred through the hopping musical medium. Finally, the auto-Orientalism surrounding the performance of much of this music allowed Russians to underscore a strategic otherness that helped delineate the parameters of being a Russian émigré in New York City, even as this performance at times rested on the cooption of other ethnic tropes, such as the "Russian Gypsy."

This promotion of ethnic Other among First Wave émigrés in New York is especially significant considering the xenophobic atmosphere of the early to mid-1920s. It was at this time that America's open-door policy on immigration began to close, culminating in the Immigration Quota of 1924 that severely limited the entry of most ethnic groups to the United States, including Russians. Considering that the early 1920s saw the concept of race extend to ethnicity, nationality, class, and language, not to mention the only recent formal cessation of the Red Scare (1919–1920), the Russian émigrés might have fared poorly.[90] Instead, coupled with the gradually increasing scope of "whiteness," the émigrés ultimately presented a desired commodity predicated on a myth of aristocracy and of an exotic past replete with tsars, gypsies, and samovars—a point that offered social collateral to the otherwise largely economically impoverished group. Ultimately, Russian-themed music in New York presented a venue for enacting and reinforcing recognizable symbols around which the émigrés could solidify collective representations of Russianness, while simultaneously presenting a desired commodity, that of the Russian Other, to the American public.

Notes

1. On the formation of Balieff's *Chauve Souris*, see Alma Law, "Nikita Balieff and the Chauve-Souris," in *Wandering Stars: Russian Émigré Theatre, 1905–1940*, ed. Lawrence Senelick (Iowa City: University of Iowa Press, 1992), 19–20.

2. Norman E. Saul, *Friends or Foes?: The United States and Soviet Russia, 1921–1941* (Lawrence: The University Press of Kansas, 2006), 144.

3. Merian C. Cooper, "From a Cellar in Moscow to a Roof in New York," *New York Times*, June 4, 1922, 48.

4. See, for example, Alexander Woollcott, "Second Thoughts on First Nights," *New York Times*, February 12, 1922, 68; H. I. Brock, "Russia in Broadway's New Mood Shop," *New York Times*, March 19, 1922, 52.

5. "Gay 'Chauve-Souris' Welcomed Back," *New York Times*, September 4, 1923, 12.

6. Saul, *Friends or Foes?*, 144.

7. See, for example, Oksana Bulgakowa, "The 'Russian Vogue' in Europe and Hollywood: The Transformation of Russian Stereotypes through the 1920s," *Russian Review* 64, no. 2 (April 2005): 211–235; Olga Matich, "The White Emigration Goes Hollywood," *Russian Review* 64, no. 2 (April 2005): 187–210; Steven G. Marks, *How Russia Shaped the Modern World: From Art to Anti-Semitism, Ballet to Bolshevism* (Princeton, NJ: Princeton University Press, 2003), 198.

8. Valleri J. Hohman, *Russian Culture and Theatrical Performance in America, 1891–1933* (New York: Palgrave Macmillan, 2011), 16. For more on nativism in the post-World War I period, see, for example, Matthew Frye Jacobson, *Whiteness of a Different Color: European Immigrants and the Alchemy of Race* (Cambridge, MA: Harvard University Press, 1998), 93; John Lescott-Leszczynski, *History of the United States Ethnic Policy and Its Impact on European Ethnics* (Boulder, CO: Westview Press, 1984), 24; Matthew Pratt Guterl, *The Color of Race in America, 1900–1940* (Cambridge, MA: Harvard University Press, 2001), 42–43.

9. Mae M. Ngai, "The Architecture of Race in American Immigration Law: A Reexamination of the Immigration Act of 1924," *The Journal of American History* 86, no. 1 (June 1999): 69. In his unpublished memoir, for example, accordionist Basil Fomeen noted that his was the last ship allowed entry to the United States that was not affected by the quota system ("Part 3: 1922–1930" Folder, "Autobiography 2 of 3" Box, Basil Fomeen Collection, Library of Congress Music Division). Fomeen's observation is but one example of a much broader trend that would impact Russia's post-Bolshevik exiles (see, for example, "6,000 Aliens due for Dec. 1 Quotas . . . Russian Quota Is Filled for the Year and Fifty More Surplus Immigrants Will Go Back," *New York Times*, November 29, 1923, 14; "Vladivostok Refugees Make Plea," *New York Times*, August 14, 1923, 9).

10. Jacobson, *Whiteness of a Different Color*, 93.

11. For earlier examples of American interest in things Russian, see "Cloths New and Old," *New York Times*, September 25, 1892, 10, whose opening line states, "Things Russian still prevail," and continues to describe the Russian fashions then in style; Anne Rittenhouse, "What the Well-Dressed Women Are Wearing," *New York Times*, October 24, 1909, X4, which aligns the tours of the Russian Imperial Ballet featuring Anna Pavlova with the fact that "the whole world has gone Russian mad." It appears that these earlier Russian trends were more closely aligned with fashion than with the more wide-ranging vogue of the 1920s.

12. Catriona Kelly, "Russian Culture and Emigration, 1921–1953," in *Russian Cultural Studies: An Introduction*, ed. Catriona Kelly and David Shepherd (New York: Oxford University Press, 1998), 301.

13. "Meet Mr. Archangelsky," *New York Times*, July 16, 1922, X2.

14. William B. Chase, "The Last Laugh Out of Russia," *New York Times*, January 15, 1922, 43.

15. John Bowlt, "Introduction," in *The Salon Album of Vera Sudeikin-Stravinsky*, ed. and transl. John Bowlt (Princeton, NJ: Princeton University Press, 1995), xiii.

16. Brock, "Russia in Broadway's New Mood Shop," 52.

17. For a vivid account of Balieff's earlier Parisian run, as well as Igor Stravinsky's personal introduction to "Katinka," see Richard Taruskin, *Stravinsky and the Russian Traditions: A Biography of the Works through Mavra* (Berkeley: University of California Press, 1996), 1,539–1,549.

18. Kelly, "Russian Culture and Emigration," 303.

19. Remisoff's cutting-edge position is reflected in his involvement in both the Russian modernist *Mir Iskusstva* movement and in the prerevolutionary Russian magazine *Satiricon*, which featured his caricatures of political and cultural figures. For more on Remisoff, see, "Biographical Note" (Finding Aid for the Nicolas Remisoff Papers, University of Southern California, accessed October 17, 2014, http://www.usc.edu/libraries/finding_aids/records /finding_aid.php?fa=0199#id430939).

20. Further situating the sheet music as being intended for an English-speaking audience, the first page of "Katinka" offers an explanation of how to pronounce the title of the song (including the accent placement on the first syllable).

21. According to *Chauve-Souris* programs, "Katinka" stems from a Russian polka of the 1860s.

22. The trope of a loose, flirtatious woman by the name of Katherine is not uncommon in Russian culture and can be seen, for example, in such wide-ranging examples as Alexander Blok's poem, "The Twelve" (1918) and in discourses surrounding Empress Catherine the Great (1729–1796).

23. Itzchok Czarovich (translator of the lyrics) and Alexei Archangelsky (music), "Katinka," Harms Inc., 1922. The playful pseudonym of the translator suggests that the work might have been undertaken by a member of Balieff's production.

24. *Town and Country*, Volume 79, September 1, 1922, 23. Katinka's popularity did not stop within the musical realm, and even extended into Manhattan's restaurant circuit, with entrepreneurs banking on the recognition among the general public to open such establishments as "Katinka" (109 W. Forty-Ninth Street) and "Chauve Souris Tavern" (231 W. Fifty-Fourth Street) in late 1924 and early 1925, respectively.

25. "Katinka Marries the Wooden Soldier: Her 'Unexpected Romance' One of the Features of New Program of Balieff's Chauve-Souris," *New York Times*, October 11, 1922, 29.

26. Gilbert's involvement in the *Chauve-Souris* undertaking stands as one example of collaboration between prewar and postrevolutionary émigrés from Russia.

27. Joseph Horowitz, *Artists in Exile: How Refugees from Twentieth-Century War and Revolution Transformed the American Performing Arts* (New York: HarperCollins Publishers, 2008), 19.

28. Ibid., 38.

29. Ibid., 40.

30. The clever allusion to Leon Trotsky in "Fox-trotsky" had been used before the publication of Russell and Tobias's song. See, for example, the cartoon in *Literary Digest*, June 19, 1920, 20.

31. Janet Wallach, *Chanel: Her Style and Her Life* (New York: Doubleday, 1998), 50–53. Chanel's Slavic Period was allegedly inspired by her romantic encounter with Russian émigré Grand Duke Dimitry, whose sister, Grand Duchess Marie, opened a boutique (Kitmir) that sold its goods to Chanel and who created the mid-1920s sensation of the crocheted chenille hat (Wallach, 49).

32. Vernon Duke, *Passport to Paris* (Boston: Little, Brown and Company, 1955), 170.

33. See, for example, Wallach, *Chanel: Her Style and Her Life*, 50–53.

34. Like the earlier Katharina, this Russian maiden was also picked up by jazz bands, including by George Olsen and His Music and The Six Hayseeds.

35. The kazatsky is an American reference to a physically demanding dance for men that involves holding oneself up on bent knees while alternating outstretched legs. I discuss the emergence of the kazatsky within the American cultural sphere in greater detail in this chapter.

36. The correlation between lascivious behavior and Mabel's (or "Masha's") samovar may be a reference to the earlier foxtrot, *U samovara ia i moia Masha* [At the samovar, it's me and my Masha] (1931) written by Russian émigré Fanny Gordon and covered by fellow émigré Pyotr Leschenko (1933) and Soviet jazz star Leonid Utyosov (1934).

37. See, for example, *Roberta* (1935), *The Chocolate Soldier* (1941), and *His Butler's Sister* (1943).

38. William H. A. Williams, *'Twas Only an Irishman's Dream: The Image of Ireland and the Irish in American Popular Song Lyrics, 1800–1920* (Urbana: University of Illinois Press, 1996), 6.

39. Alfred Lemmon, "New Orleans Popular Sheet Music Imprints: The Latin Tinge Prior to 1900," *The Southern Quarterly* 27, no. 2 (Winter 1989): 41–57; Judy Tsou, "Gendering Race: Stereotypes of Chinese Americans in Popular Sheet Music," *repercussions* 6, no. 2 (Fall 1997): 25–62.

40. Williams, *'Twas Only an Irishman's Dream*, 6.

41. In the case of Chinese-themed sheet music, for example, jazz has been mapped onto the figure of an erotic, loose "Oriental" woman (Tsou, "Gendering Race," 46). In the case of Russia, this cultural assertion became especially evident in the Cold War propagation of jazz as a means of spreading democracy [Stephen A. Crist, "Jazz as Democracy?: Dave Brubeck and Cold War Politics," *Journal of Musicology* 26, no. 2 (Spring 2009): 133–174].

42. The delayed arrival of jazz in Russia can be explained by a wide-ranging number of factors, including the civil war, the new nation's disastrous economic situation, a certain isolationism, a striving for ideological appropriateness, and, most essentially, a lack of saxophones. For more on the early dearth of jazz in Russia, see S. Frederick Starr, *Red and Hot: The Fate of Jazz in the Soviet Union, 1917–1980* (New York: Limelight Editions, 1985), 39–43.

43. Starr, *Red and Hot*, 43–46.

44. Saul, *Friends or Foes?*, 172; Starr, *Red and Hot*, 59.

45. Saul, *Friends or Foes?*, 173; Starr, *Red and Hot*, 66–70.

46. Starr, *Red and Hot*, 61.

47. Richard Stites, *Russian Popular Culture: Entertainment and Society Since 1900* (Cambridge, MA: Cambridge University Press, 1992), 74.

48. This swinging Soviet culture continued at full steam until Stalin's purges of the mid-1930s, which instigated an era of hard repression that would stifle the production of jazz in Russia until after the Second World War.

49. Marshall and Dean Stearns, *Jazz Dance: The Story of American Vernacular Dance* (New York: Macmillan, 1968), 248.

50. Stearns, *Jazz Dance*, 248; Constance Vallis Hill, *Tap Dancing America: A Cultural History* (New York: Oxford University Press, 2010), 79.

51. Brenda Bufalino, "Russia: A Warm Tap Welcome After the Cold War," *On Tap* 13, no. 2 (Fall 2002): 11.

52. Stearns, *Jazz Dance*, 248–249.

53. While attending the 2012 Metropolitan Opera production of *Khovanshchina*, for example, I had the pleasure of sitting beside two energetic elderly women. Although they were regular Met attendees, the women were struck by the overt Russian elements of the opera, exclaiming with sarcasm at one point, "What next, the kazatsky?"

54. Perhaps the most vivid example and personification of the Russian-Jewish-jazz intersection is Al Jolson's performance in *The Jazz Singer* (1927).

55. Though not dealing with jazz, other examples of prewar and First Wave interactions include the outreach and invitation of Russian-born Morris Gest to numerous First Wave artists to the United States and the marriage between impresario Sol Hurok and First Wave émigré singer Emma Rybkina (Hurok).

56. I explore Vernon Duke's relationship with George Gershwin in further detail in chapter 4.

57. For more on jazz in Cold War relations, see Lisa E. Davenport, *Jazz Diplomacy: Promoting America in the Cold War Era* (Jackson: University Press of Mississippi, 2009); Penny M. Von Eschen, *Satchmo Blows Up the World: Jazz Ambassadors Play the Cold War* (Cambridge, MA: Harvard University Press, 2004).

58. Starr, *Red and Hot*, 11, 9. In his work on Soviet jazz, Starr positions jazz as the genre solving the "great conundrum" of social theory and "romantic aesthetics" of the nineteenth century, as it "reconciled the individual and society, giving each a new freedom and direction that was inconceivable even to the most utopian dreamers of the world that had died" (*Red and Hot*, 10).

59. The term, "Hot cha!" likewise entered the African American lexicon in the 1930s and may refer to an oath given during a game of craps [*Juba to Jive: A Dictionary of African-American Slang*, ed. Clarence Major (New York: Penguin Books, 1994), 242].

60. For an account of Sergei Rachmaninoff and Feodor Chalipin performing "Dark Eyes" in Rachmaninoff's New Jersey home, see, Sergei Bertensson and Jay Leyda, *Sergei Rachmaninoff: A Lifetime in Music* (Bloomington: Indiana University Press, 2001), 233.

61. See, for example, Gregory Stone, "Dark Eyes: Otchi tchornyia: pharaphrase on the famous Russian gypsy air" (New York: Prelude Music Co., 1934).

62. The performance of "*Ochi chernye*" by African American musicians, including Armstrong and Sullivan, takes on a racial level of signification and presents a rich site for further analysis.

63. Daniel Goldmark, *Tunes for 'toons: Music and the Hollywood Cartoon* (Berkeley: University of California Press, 2005), 8.

64. On Orientalist fantasies focusing on the Russian Gypsy, see Alaina Lemon, *Between Two Fires: Gypsy Performance and Romani Memory From Pushkin to Postsocialism* (Durham, NC: Duke University Press, 2000), 37. It is quite possible that the lyrics for the song were based on those of the earlier Russian romance, "*Gori, gori moia zvezda* [Shine, Shine My Star]."

65. See for example, the cover of Vera Brynner's *Russian Gypsy Folk Songs*, Kapp KL1116, LP recording, 1958.

66. "Biographical Note," *Finding Aid for the Nicolas Remisoff Papers*, University of Southern California, accessed October 17, 2014, http://www.usc.edu/libraries/finding_aids /records/finding_aid.php?fa=0199#ref8.

67. "Owner and Wife Die in Restaurant Fire," *New York Times*, February 1, 1924, 1.

68. See, for example, "Taking Part in a Colorful Annual Ball: 'A Night With Russian Gypsies,'" *New York Times*, November 13, 1938. I explore New York's Russian balls in further detail in chapter 5.

69. Carol Silverman, *Romani Routes: Cultural Politics and Balkan Music in Diaspora* (New York: Oxford University Press, 2012), 257.

70. Aihwa Ong, "Chinese Modernities: Narratives of Nation and of Capitalism," in *Undergrounded Empires: The Cultural Politics of Modern Chinese Transnationalism*, edited by Aihwa Ong and Donald Nonini (London: Routledge, 1997), 195; Erik R. Scott, "The Nineteenth-Century Russian Gypsy Choir and the Performance of Otherness," Berkeley Program in Eurasian and East European Studies Working Paper (2008), 51n2.

71. Scott, "The Nineteenth-Century Russian Gypsy Choir," 2. For an excellent analysis of the interplay between Romani stereotypes and enactments within the Russian context, see Lemon, *Between Two Fires*, and Scott, "The Nineteenth Century Russian Gypsy Choir."

72. For a detailed account of the history of Roma in Russia, see David M. Crowe, *A History of the Gypsies of Eastern Europe and Russia*, second edition (New York: Palgrave Macmillan, 2007), 151–194.

73. Duke, *Passport to Paris*, 92.

74. For more on Vladimir Dukelsky's professional conflict, see Scott Holden, "The 'Adventures and Battles' of Vladimir Dukelsky (a.k.a. Vernon Duke)," *American Music* 28, no. 3 (Fall 2010): 297–319.

75. For other accounts of Russian gypsy music entertainment in the emigration, see, for example, Eugenia Bumgardner, *Undaunted Exiles* (Staunton, VA: McClure Co., 1925); Joseph Kiblitsky, E. N. Petrova, and Juan Allende-Blin, *Russkii Parizh, 1910–1960* (Saint Petersburg: Palace Editions, 2003).

76. Rock Brynner, *Empire and Odyssey: The Brynners in Far East Russia and Beyond* (Hanover, NH: Steerforth Press, 2006), 137–139.

77. Louella Parsons, cited in Brynner, *Empire and Odyssey*, 154.

78. For a live clip of Brynner's broadcast (September 17, 1967), see https://www.youtube .com/watch?v=zoJ_1-sf504&list=RDuWI_VijGVLg&index=4 [accessed December 30, 2014]. Jim Morrison and the Doors also perform on this show, reflecting an especially rich and idiosyncratic cultural moment.

79. Brynner's most notorious Orientalist role was, of course, as the king of Siam in *The King and I*.

80. Melville Shavelson, *How to Make a Jewish Movie* (Englewood Cliffs, NJ: Prentice-Hall, 1971), 56.

81. "Tamiroff Calls Accent Key to His Success," *Paterson Call*, December 21, 1965, cited in Harlow Robinson, *Russians in Hollywood, Hollywood's Russians: A Biography of an Image* (Lebanon, NH: Northeastern University Press, 2007), 74.

82. See, for example, the cover of Fomeen's "Esperanza Tango," on which he is shown playing the accordion and is referred to throughout as "Don Basilio Fomin" ("Music By Basil Fomeen: Esperanza" Folder, Printed Music Composed by B. F., Box 6, Basil Fomeen Collection, Library of Congress Music Division).

83. Letter from George T. Bye to Basil Fomeen, March 12, 1937 ("George T Bye and Co. Folder; Correspondence, Box 1, Basil Fomeen Collection, Library of Congress Music Division). Bye also worked with Grand Duchess Marie of Russia in publishing her autobiography.

84. Silverman, *Romani Routes*, 258.

85. Lemon, *Between Two Fires*, 46.

86. Simon Morrison, "Semiotics of Symmetry, or Rimsky-Korsakov's Operatic History Lesson," *Cambridge Opera Journal* 13, no. 3 (November 2001): 268, 285.

87. See chapter 5 for a more extensive exploration of this duality.

88. Thomas Turino, "Introduction: Identity and the Arts in Diaspora Communities," in *Identity and the Arts in Diaspora Communities*, ed. Thomas Turino and James Lea (Warren, MI: Harmonie Park Press, 2004), 11.

89. Horowitz, *Artists in Exile*, 28.

90. Douglas, *Terrible Honesty*, 305.

3

EMIGRATION AT THE BOUNDARY

Russian DPs, Second Generation Émigrés, and Soviet Song in the World War II Era

IN 1956, THE FOLLOWING WORDS APPEARED ON THE jacket notes of the Mercury label recording, *Balalaika: Music and Songs of White Russia*: "While contemporary political leaders of the U.S.S.R. have frowned on vestiges of the culture that was Czarist Russia, this music will never die, for Russia, long before Lenin and Trotsky, had contributed immeasurably to the international development of music."[1]

Framing the musicians whose sounds were featured within its grooves as carriers of the condemned Tsarist traditions, these words reflect one of the main principles underlying Russian émigré ideology: the task of the diaspora to preserve prerevolutionary Russian culture from its annihilation in the Soviet Union. By the time these words appeared on the American-produced album, the idea that Russian émigrés were the bearers of the "real 'Russia,'" one that was dying under the hands of the Bolsheviks, had become standard in émigré speeches, letters, and other forums of public discourse.[2] As early as 1924, writer Ivan Bunin (1870–1953) stood in front of his fellow émigrés in Paris and expressed the urgency of the diaspora's "mission" to reject "Lenin's cities, Lenin's commandments," drawing a stringent line between the Russia "enslaved" by exile and that which "sold Christ for thirty pieces of silver."[3] In 1931, the usually reserved Sergei Rachmaninoff (1873–1943) published a letter in the *New York Times* with two fellow exiles, openly criticizing the Soviet regime under which "all Russia is groaning."[4] The notion that the Bolsheviks had usurped Russia politically and culturally permeated all strata of émigré culture, ranging from high poetry (Marina Tsvetaeva's 1918 eulogy to her homeland: "And the wind blows along the steppe: Russia! Martyr! Rest in Peace!"), to more prosaic forms of art (the iconic émigré romance, *"Zamelo tebia snegom Rossiia"* [Snow Has Covered You, Russia]), to such borderline novelty items as *Balalaika: Songs of White Russia*. By the end of the World War II, the idea that "we [i.e., members of the Russian diaspora] and only we are the sole keepers and guides of the Russian creative force" was a regular part of émigré discourse.[5] The growing stability of the émigrés' quotidian existence abroad, enabled by regular work and permanent places of residence, afforded the possibility for the former refugees to focus their efforts on the task of cultural preservation rather than on mere survival.

The emphasis on preserving prerevolutionary Russian culture, coupled with the Soviet-Russian binary upon which the émigré mission was based in no small part, was a response to the circumstances under which the First Wave Russian diaspora came into existence. A movement that sought to "sweep away the memory of a hated past," the Bolshevik Revolution was typical of such deliberate and comprehensive takeovers.[6] As a means of revolutionizing their country, the Bolsheviks destroyed many aspects of the former way of life, which became a rallying point for those who fled the Bolshevik regime. As Richard Stites writes, "Sovdepia—as the Whites contemptuously called the Bolshevik ruled territory during the Civil War—was swathed in red, a new universe largely denuded of the old symbols and adorned with the new."[7] This strategy of cleaning house perhaps was most vividly marked by the 1923 deportation of Russia's top philosophers—including religious mystic and thinker Nikolai Berdyaev (1874–1948) and theologian Sergei Bulgakov (1871–1944). The Philosophy Steamer, as it was known, literally dissipated prerevolutionary Russian thought, as its boats shipped those deemed too subversive to the new ideology far from Russia's shores.[8]

As a result of the systematic annihilation of the old values and way of life, Russians in the diaspora quickly adopted a mission to preserve the assaulted culture and to reject the Soviet regime they saw responsible for its eradication. This preservationist impulse based on an oppositional binary of authentic/prerevolutionary and inauthentic/communist would become typical of other exile groups fleeing communist regimes. Members of the Vietnamese diaspora, for example, would later unify themselves around anticommunist sentiment, sharing a conviction that they were "protectors of the 'true' Vietnamese culture."[9] Polish exiles fleeing communism after the World War II placed the preservation of "Polish high culture" as their top priority.[10] The anticommunist sentiment that informed Cuban Miami was so strong that a return to Castro's Cuba was deemed an "act of treason."[11]

Upon closer examination, however, the seemingly impenetrable boundary between Soviet and Russian émigré spheres emerges as being more porous than it is often presented. This nuance comes into sharp focus in the period surrounding World War II. A moment of transition in the history of the Russian emigration, the wartime era involved several key changes that would affect the First Wave Russian diaspora: the children of the First Wave, the second generation of émigrés, was coming of age; an entirely new group of Russians (the "Second Wave") fled the Soviet Union and joined the ranks of the now-aging First Wave; and, as a result of the dispersal from war-torn Europe, the United States became the new center of the Russian emigration, with New York City supplanting Paris as its cultural capital. The complexity surrounding the integration of the Second Wave into the Russian diaspora was compounded by the concurrent flight of First Wave Russians from Eastern Europe (most notably from Yugoslavia, Poland, and Czechoslovakia) during World War II. The two groups initially encountered one another in the displaced persons (DP) camps that dotted the landscape of Central Europe after the war. It was in the DP camps that these exiles first exchanged horrific tales of flight, memories of two very different Russias—prerevolutionary and Soviet—and, most notable for this project, music banned in the Soviet Union for its associations with the prerevolutionary regime and also that which was newly created in the Soviet state.[12] For the First Wave Russian émigrés already living in the United States, their exposure to Soviet music would fluctuate with the erraticism that defined US-Soviet relations (and subsequently trade) throughout the 1930s and 1940s.

An overlooked aspect of Russian émigré history, the introduction of popular songs from the Soviet Union to the anticommunist Russian diaspora during the years surrounding World War II illuminates the complex dynamics of boundary maintenance fueled by discourses of authenticity informed through music. Specifically, this chapter presents an in-depth exploration of what Marc Gidal calls *musical boundary-work*, scrutinizing the ways music is used to draw, negotiate, and dissolve boundaries between and around groups of people.[13] A study of the Russian emigration in the period surrounding World War II offers an especially salient point of inquiry for music's role in mediating boundaries, as it involves the introduction of a new emigration wave and the coming of age of the second generation of émigrés, thus presenting a case study of musical-boundary work as it engages inner-diaspora politics. Indeed, such critical times of change present heightened moments of boundary maintenance and nego-tiation, revealing the ways that people "guard or transform symbolic, social, and spiritual boundaries."[14] The present study of the émigré music scene in the period surrounding World War II demonstrates how songs from the Soviet Union were deployed as discursive, auditory, and social sites for asserting and shifting ideas of "True Russia" so prevalent in émigré dis-course, both affirming and ultimately transcending differences between Us and Them applied to prerevolutionary and Soviet Russia.

Russian Harlem: A Waning Community?

From the time of its founding in 1923 through the early 1930s, Harlem's Rus-sian enclave had transformed itself from a little-known group of destitute refugees into an active hub of cultural activity, with the impressive Christ the Savior Cathedral on 121st Street at its center. Perhaps most notable were the weekly evenings that took place in the adjacent parish house that revolved around echoes of Russia's prerevolutionary past, which included declamations of Pushkin's lyrical verses, impassioned performances of Russian gypsy songs, and festive recitals of folk music (see chap. 1). The American public relished the idea of reliving Russia's Imperial past in the company of former aristocrats and placed Christ the Savior Church at the center of White Russian New York. Meanwhile, the former refugees were settling into a comfortable life, a point that is reflected in the increas-ing financial success of the weekly parish gatherings.[15]

This self-proclaimed "Golden Page" in the community's history, how-ever, came to a temporary halt beginning in late 1929.[16] Recent immigrants were no more immune to the devastating effects of the Great Depression than were established American citizens.[17] Coupled with financial diffi-culties, Harlem's Russian community deteriorated further, as many of its younger families began attending Russian Orthodox churches whose ser-vices were held in English, while others left the vicinity of Harlem for sub-urbs and farms. Attracted by the fresh air, good schools, and then-cheap real estate of Long Island, for example, many Russians relocated to Sea Cliff, which affectionately became known as a "Russian Nest."[18]

Perhaps more telling with regard to the assimilation of the Russian émi-grés than the movement of some families to Anglophone churches were the more than one hundred parishioners who enlisted in the United States Armed Forces during World War II.[19] The enlistments had a direct impact not only on the parish as a whole but specifically on the choir, which dwindled in number from its peak of thirty-four people in the late 1930s to an all-women's choir of sixteen in 1945.[20] Recalling the wartime period in the history of the parish, longtime choir conductor Serge Savitsky (1886–1951) reflected that, "the Russian settlement of Harlem was melting, and with it melted the choir and the school!"[21] Coupled with the social volatility that marked New York's Russian émigré community in the 1930s and 1940s, the enclave likewise encountered a period of cultural transition, for it was at this time that Soviet songs began to permeate the folds of émigré culture.

Soviet Songs in New York City

Although the United States did not formally recognize the Soviet Union until 1933, the two nations began engaging in commercial trade in the mid-1920s. One of the outcomes of this relationship was the regular, though scant, importation of Soviet popular music starting around 1935, when Amkniga Corporation (most likely a verbal amalgamation of "American" and "*kniga*" [book]) began to distribute Soviet recordings to the New York public. The company, which was located at 258 Fifth Avenue, stressed the unique nature of its goods, exclaiming that its services presented "A Rare Opportunity to Acquire Russian Books and Music."[22]

The overly enthusiastic tone describing such products as books on Russia's Five-Year Plan and *The U.S.S.R. in Construction* might have been a tipoff that Amkniga was run by Soviet agents. Nevertheless, the company continued to operate steadily through the 1930s, altering its name whenever it encountered trouble.[23] By 1939, American federal agents sniffed a rat, and the owners of Amkniga were indicted for failing to register as agents of a foreign state, a requirement that resulted from the passing of the Foreign Agents Registration Act of 1938. In its place, a new organization, the Am-Rus Music Corporation, became the primary distributor of Soviet music in New York, a position it would occupy until the end of World War II. Plugging itself as the "exclusive distributors of Soviet music in America," the Am-Rus Music Corporation made a point to stress its importance and legitimacy by the tone of its advertisements and by the novelty of its services. In 1942, for example, the company flaunted the fact that it had received the score of Dmitri Shostakovich's Seventh Symphony by way of microfilm—a highly unusual means of delivering a score at the time.[24] The reputation of Am-Rus was bolstered further by its acceptance in 1943 into the American Society for Composers, Authors, and Publishers (ASCAP), which made Soviet music available to more than 850 American radio stations.[25]

Although enthusiastic in tone, the descriptions and advertisements for Am-Rus Music in the American press lack any specifics regarding the popular music it sold, suggesting that the music's origin in Soviet Russia held more appeal than did its content for the average American consumer.[26] This level of specificity was left to the market that was more likely to be interested in such details: New York Russians. Hence, advertisements for Soviet music in the Russian-American press foreground not only the music's origins in the Soviet Union, but also the individual song titles comprising the songbooks and recordings for sale. Although these songbooks and recordings contained material with which the Russian émigrés were already familiar, including well-established Russian folk songs like "*Kalinka*" and "*Vo pole bereza stoiala* [In the field stood a birch tree]," *chastushki* (rhyming ditties), and art music selections, they also featured a new genre of music that came out of Stalinist Russia: the mass song. Conspicuously absent from these advertisements are Russian romances and gypsy songs, a trend reflecting the strict policy of Stalin's early years against remnants of "bourgeois" culture.[27]

In place of the condemned bourgeois genres, songwriters in 1930s Russia concentrated their efforts on developing an explicitly Soviet form of popular music that could embody the official values of the state.[28] This new "mass song" grew out of the cultural project of Socialist Realism, whose promoters strove for "ideologically remoulding and training the laboring people in the spirit of socialism."[29] The mass song contributed to this ideological remolding by articulating and sounding official state values. With straightforward harmonies, simple duple meter, and catchy melodies, mass songs convey a rousing optimism that celebrates the triumph of the collective over the individual, a timeless, ahistorical patriotism, and a promise of the "glorious future of socialism."[30] Although the song lyrics range in content, they tend toward several themes, including that of the "positive hero," the Motherland, motherhood, and a bucolic landscape whose idyllic imagery is remarkably similar to that found in stylized Russian folk songs.[31] Mass songs allegedly manifested the "spirit of socialism" in both sound and word, while the means to acquiring this spirit was through the very act of singing (and listening). As the opening song to the 1934 classic film, *Veselye rebiata* [Jolly Fellows], maintains: "And whoever goes through life singing shall never lose his way."

An integral part of the 1930s-era Soviet film, mass songs reinforced the positive plots, providing sonic verification of the unfailingly happy ending. Aside from recordings in which mass songs were featured individually, films were another primary venue in which Russians in New York were exposed to this music. The handful of theaters in New York that showed Soviet films in the late 1930s and early 1940s included the Miami Play House, the Stanley Theater, and the Central Theater. Like the recordings and songbooks containing Soviet popular songs, these films made their way to the United States thanks to yet another arm of the Soviet propaganda machine, Amkino.[32] Although these films drew only small audiences of communist sympathizers among Americans, members of the emigration enjoyed these films as a welcomed piece of Russophone culture.[33] The granddaughter of the founder of New York's Christ the Savior Church, for example, was taken by her mother to the Stanley Theater on her name day (commemoration of the Christian saint after whom she was named).[34] Meanwhile across the ocean, children of Russian émigrés living in Eastern Europe relished these films, which they found delightfully humorous and unquestionably attractive because they were in the Russian language.

By way of songbooks, recordings, and films, Russian émigrés in New York heard mass songs like "*Pesnia o rodine* [Song of the Motherland]" (from the 1936 film *Circus*), "*Marsh* [March]" (from the 1934 film *Jolly Fellows*), and "*Esli zavtra voina* [If Tomorrow Brings War]" (from the 1938 film of the same title). These songs eventually made their way into the Russian school program of Christ the Savior Church in Harlem. On a curricular level, mass songs were printed in the Russian grammar books that the parish received from the Soviet consulate and used in the weekly Russian school classes. On one hand, there is a certain level of irony underlying the dissemination of Stalinist culture among an anticommunist group whose motivation in obtaining these books was the maintenance of prerevolutionary Russian culture. Any pro-Soviet lyrics, however, were typically crossed out with black markers and replaced with ones deemed more acceptable by the teachers (such as "*vesna, vesna* [spring, spring]" for "Moskva, Moskva").[35] The children of the First Wave émigrés also incorporated this music into Russian school pageants. At the 1950 Christmas pageant, for example, a young George Kalbouss, future professor and founder of the much-beloved Russian Culture course at the Ohio State University, sang the lighthearted, humorous "*Vodovoz* [Water Carrier]" from the 1938 film *Volga, Volga*. Expressing the plight of the water carrier, the song centers around a playful philosophy: without water, one is neither here nor there.

The ensemble most often presented on early Soviet recordings of mass songs and one that is particularly emblematic of the Soviet Union is the Alexandrov Ensemble, otherwise known as the Red Army Choir. Formed in 1928 to entertain troops under the leadership of Moscow Conservatory graduate Alexander Alexandrov (1883–1946), the Red Army Choir initially performed Soviet military and revolutionary songs and hymns to the Soviet Union, later adding Russian folk songs and selections from operas to its repertoire as it started touring internationally.[36] By the time recordings of the Red Army Choir were featured in the Russian-American press in the late 1930s, the choir's repertoire encompassed a range of prerevolutionary folk songs as well as overtly pro-Soviet mass songs, including "*Esli zavtra voina*," "*Partizanskii marsh* [Partisan's March]," and "*Krasnnaia armiia vsekh sil'nei* [The Red Army is the Strongest]." As the Soviet military chorus par excellence, the Red Army Choir stood as a "metaphor for official [Soviet] culture."[37]

Despite the explicit Soviet patriotism depicted in the group's repertoire, its standard army uniform attire, and its name, the Red Army Choir was popular among second-generation Russian émigrés. When asked about the possible contradiction of members of an anticommunist diaspora supporting an ensemble whose very name references White Russia's antagonist, consultants interviewed for this project responded with a variety of explanations, ranging, for those living in the United States before World War II, from the wartime Soviet-American alliance to the easy, likeable style of the choir.

Aside from records, songbooks, and films in local theaters, another critical conduit for introducing Soviet music to New York Russians was the 1939 World's Fair, which infused the air of Flushing Meadows with an excitement inspired by the impressive architectural structures, range of international cultures on display, and by the fair's theme, "Building the World of Tomorrow." The massive Soviet pavilion, made with eight hundred pounds of marble and lined with stones from the Ural Mountains, was designed by Russia's leading Socialist Realist architects and inspired awe among its visitors.[38] Like the mass songs that were sold on 78s in the pavilion's souvenir shop, the exhibit was to elicit a "supposedly typical Soviet mood of 'joyfulness, cheerfulness, and optimism.'"[39] It was at the World's Fair that many White Russians living in New York first heard Soviet music. A fifteen-year-old David Chavchavadze (direct descendant of the royal Romanov family) visited the fair daily, spending hours at the Soviet pavilion watching classic Stalin-era films like *Chapaev* "over and over again" until he could "fully understand the soundtrack."[40]

Aside from catchy tunes from Soviet films (many of which were attacked later by Soviet critics for lacking a "clear ideological line") and folk-like songs, some overtly political songs were also featured in the World's Fair output as well as on the recordings advertised in the Russian-American press.[41] Much of the explicitly political repertoire, however, was not popular among First Wave Russians. Mass songs like the 1935 classic "*Pesnia o rodine*," for example, were disliked and even ridiculed by members of the emigration. Written by the renowned mass song duo of Vasily Lebedev-Kumach (text) and Isaac Dunaevsky (music), the song exalts the Soviet Union, glorifying both the physical landscape and the ideals embodied by the government. The refrain, for example, exemplifies these traits, stating:

Shirkoka strana moia rodnaia,	How spacious is my motherland,
Mnogo v nei lesov, polei i rek.	How many forests, fields, and rivers.
Ia drugoi takoi strany ne znaiu	I know of no other country,
Gde tak vol'no dyshit chelovek!	Where one can breathe so freely!

The most overtly political moment occurs in the penultimate stanza, as the text glorifies both Stalin and the policies for which he stands. ("With golden letters we write the nationwide law of Stalin.") The song's pro-Stalinist implications were only furthered when the piece became the radio signal for Radio Moscow in 1939.[42] A second-generation émigré recalled singing "*Pesnia o rodine*" as a youth simply to poke fun of the overtly propagandist nature of the piece, while another consultant continuously chuckled when mentioning the farm-themed songs she heard on the recordings from the 1939 World's Fair.[43]

DPs and Soviet Music in the Flesh

The warm-cold reception of mass songs among the émigrés was mirrored by the ambivalent relationship between the United States and the Soviet Union throughout the 1930s. Any underlying hostility between the two nations, which reached a peak following the Molotov-Ribbentrop Pact in August 1939, however, was temporarily and tepidly placated after the

German invasion of the Soviet Union and the subsequent US-Soviet wartime alliance.

World War II would alter not only US-Soviet relations but would make a deep impact on the White Russian diaspora as its members encountered for the first time their Soviet compatriots en masse. Comprised of people either fleeing the Soviet Union or brought to the West by force as German laborers, this Second Wave of emigration came crashing into Russia Abroad as the 7.2 million people who left the USSR during World War II.[44] Complicating this classification were the First Wave émigrés who escaped Eastern Europe during this time, many of whom ended up in displaced persons camps alongside their Second Wave counterparts. Whether in DP camps or, later on, in New York City, members of the Second Wave became a major source of current Soviet culture for First Wave Russians. Indeed, the years immediately following World War II engendered exchanges completely radical in the diaspora: Soviet culture was no longer transmitted by proxy but by the mouths of the very Soviet Other(s) of whom the émigrés were trying to make sense.

The Truman Acts of 1948 and 1952 enabled many of the First and Second Wave Russians who had lived in DP camps after the war to enter the United States, a change that occurred in the New York émigré community seemingly overnight.[45] The presence of the DPs reinvigorated New York's waning Russian émigré community, with 1949 emerging as a turning point in the cultural life of Russian New York. This revitalization is illustrated by the Christmas pageants that took place that year throughout the city and its vicinity, including at the Russian Orthodox parishes in Harlem, the East Village (Second Street), and at the Tolstoy Farm in Valley Cottage (New York) (see fig. 3.1). These pageants abounded with energy, filling parish halls to capacity (so much so that many feared that the floor of Harlem's Russian Club would collapse under the weight of so many feet).[46] And by November 1951, half of Christ the Savior's parish would be made up of DP families.[47]

Harlem's Russian Christmas pageant from 1949 featured popular selections of prerevolutionary culture, including Russian gypsy songs and skits from Nikita Balieff's *Chauve-Souris*.[48] Instead of members of Balieff's cast, however, now it was the children and grandchildren of those who had originally enjoyed *Chauve-Souris* in Russia reenacting pages from Russia's past (see fig. 3.2 and 3.3). The fifty-one participating children also sang the Russian folk standard, "*Vo pole bereza stoiala*," and, by request of the adolescent

Figure 3.1. Nicholas Afonsky conducting a children's choir at a Christmas pageant at the Orthodox Cathedral of the Holy Virgin Protection (Second Street), c. 1952. Nicholas Afonsky Papers, The Archives of the Orthodox Church of America.

participants, *Tsyganskii tabor* [The Gypsy Camp], a medley of Russian gypsy songs.

The discourse surrounding the pageants that took place in Russian Orthodox parishes throughout New York in 1949 serves as testimony to the emphasis placed on transmitting prerevolutionary Russian culture to the next generation. At the conclusion of Harlem's Russian pageant, for example, the head of the parish expressed his thanks to "the grandmothers, grandfathers, mothers and fathers who so unanimously contributed to the success of this wonderful performance, which promotes a love and knowledge of our Russia, our Russian language, our Russian music and songs among our parishioners."[49] Similarly, the pageant taking place at the Tolstoy Farm included several teenagers who had been born to émigré parents in Austria, Germany, and Czechoslovakia declaiming accounts from Russian history in "brilliant Russian" and inciting in listeners "memories of our dear, former nation of great Russia."[50]

Finally, the description of that year's pageant taking place in the East Village likewise underscores the weight of the past in defining these events:

Figure 3.2. George Kalbouss at a Christmas pageant (Christ the Savior Cathedral, Harlem), c. 1949. Courtesy of George Kalbouss.

Figure 3.3. Eugenie de Smitt and George Kalbouss at a Christmas pageant (Christ the Savior Cathedral, Harlem), c. 1949. Courtesy of George Kalbouss.

"it was a joy to see how many families work with their children to remain faithful to the old, dear traditions."[51] The hope placed onto the second generation at times took on literal dimensions as well, as it was etched into a sign that hung over the stage at the Second Street cathedral's parish hall. Stating, "Children: Our hope, our future. Your duty is to tell us about the former majesty of Rus'," the sign underscores the emphasis placed on the second generation in maintaining not only Russian culture but of upholding an idea of "Rus'," a medieval, even archetypal, Russia.

Although seemingly cordial and based around a shared discourse of cultural preservation, relations between the First Wave Russians already living in New York and the recent arrivals were often strained. In part, the tension between the two groups was informed by the contrasting ways each group related to Russia. These differences existed between the First and Second Waves and also between second-generation First Wave émigrés from Eastern Europe and those who grew up in the United States. Many of the second-generation Russians raised in New York, for example, spoke Russian with difficulty, if at all, and, although participating in various cultural events affiliated with Christ the Savior parish, identified as American. Regarding the Americanization that occurred within her own family, the grand-daughter of the primary founder of Christ the Savior church notes: "[after arriving in the United States, my grandfather] became a very, very loyal American—very patriotic—my whole family was. And we never considered ourselves 'Russian-American,' we were 'American.' We were not hyphen-ated. Although we kept our culture, language, and Church—everything—our loyalties were completely to America."[52] Other second-generation First Wave émigrés who were raised in New York and interviewed for this project likewise consistently self-identified as American.

In contrast, children of First Wave émigrés who came to the United States from Eastern Europe tended to self-identify as Russian, despite the fact that they had never stepped foot in Russia. This unwavering commit-ment was not only expressed in interviews taken for this project but can also be found in songs and poems written by members of this group. The following song, for example, which circulated among the youth in an Aus-trian DP camp, relays a steadfast commitment to the unknown but loved Russian homeland:

Amidst the Austrian Alps we've gathered, as a friendly scout family,
Although we were born abroad, Russia is pulling us homeward.

We grow, we sing, we bring good fortune to our homeland,
We call forth the youth as we sing,
Onward, friends, our homeland is waiting,
Our motto is "be prepared" and the response is "always prepared!"

As we sit by the fire we remember, the struggle of our fathers;
And at night we often could not sleep, awaiting the ambush of the enemies.

And we hardened ourselves, preparing for the great struggle,
We gave our word to our homeland, to topple the regime that She hates.[53]

Several reasons account for this striking difference in the self-conception between European- and American-born children of the First Wave émigrés. For one, many of the émigrés who came to New York in the 1920s had come to terms with settling in the United States and not returning to Russia. In contrast, many of the émigrés who came to the United States only after World War II stayed in close proximity to Russia with the hope of return-ing, settling in such countries as Yugoslavia, Poland, and Czechoslovakia. During World War II, many postwar émigrés fled again, relocating several times between their host countries, DP camps, and finally to the United

States, and thus had little occasion or will to assimilate into any single country. With their Russian classical high schools (gymnasiums), newspapers, and active parishes, the Russian émigré communities in Eastern Europe in many ways resemble the exiled Armenian community in Lebanon, which maintained a level of autonomy to such an extent that "pressure to assimilate was not great."[54] Moreover, the fractured nature of the postwar Russian émigré community in New York likewise mirrors the Armenian case (this time in California), whose very lexicon signals a differentiation within the community based on migratory routes.[55]

The differences in identity and migratory pasts between the First Wave Russians resulted in a wall of social prejudice between the two groups of émigrés. Amid their American patriotism, pre-War World II First Wave émigrés condemned the DPs for not fully appreciating the United States, while postwar émigrés criticized their prewar counterparts for becoming Americanized and for directing toward them what they saw to be supercilious superiority. A similar dynamic existed between other DPs and their American counterparts. Polish Americans, for example, acted in "dismissive and patronizing ways" toward Polish DPs, while the recent refugees accused their fellow Poles of "political inactivity, cultural backwardness, and advanced Americanization."[56] DPs more broadly were treated with condescension, especially in postwar Europe. As Mark Wyman writes, "in Europe the letters *DP* themselves seemed pejorative, an epithet. Applied to Polish refugees, 'dipisi' was equated with the German word *Untermensch*, or subhuman, and they felt they were at the bottom of postwar European society."[57]

The tension between European and American First Wave émigrés, however, paled in comparison to that found between First and Second Wave Russians. As literary scholar John Glad asserts, the encounter between the two groups was "not an altogether congenial one," as there existed a perceived "social-class gap" between First and Second Wave émigrés.[58] This idea has been echoed directly by members of the two waves. A woman whose father had fought in the White Army but was unable to leave Russia after the Civil War describes the interaction between the children of First and Second Wave Russians in New York, to which her family immigrated in 1949: "[the children of First Wave Russians] felt that they came from the better class. But I think that many of them were blue blood. The second emigration, I think, was looked on more as the working class. Yes, absolutely people who abhorred communism and ran from communism, but, you know, 'OK, you're from a different class.'"[59]

A man from the Second Wave, now in his seventies, recalled being rejected for a position of altar boy in a New Jersey Russian Orthodox Church, as the parish priest deemed him to be "too Soviet."[60] A descendent of First Wave émigrés who grew up in Cleveland in the 1950s notes that the members of the "old emigration" (i.e., First Wave) stuck together in her home parish and that "there was really a wall, in most cases, between the first emigration and the second emigration."[61]

A marked difference between the First and Second Waves was also articulated by second-generation First Wave émigrés. A second-generation Russian who was born in New York described the arrival of the DPs after the war as "stressful" due to the great cultural and perceived class difference between the two waves. Another second-generation New York Russian relayed the different approaches in such mundane practices as eating dinner between herself and her future husband, who had fled Soviet Russia: "Well, manners, for one thing. Yura thought—and it was part of it, because they were starving [in the Soviet Union]—he thought that dinner was strictly for eating, and for us it was dining, socializing. That's just one little thing." These accounts reflect a broader trend of differentiation that can occur between waves of immigrants based on such factors as perceived distinctions of class, education level, and reason for leaving the homeland. Indeed, such distinction has been noted as occurring among a wide range of ethnic Americans, including the Poles, Arabs, Chinese, Koreans, and Cubans.[62]

Asserting Boundaries Musically

The division between Soviet and émigré spheres noted among members of First and Second Waves was likewise articulated in spheres of cultural production. Music, specifically, was mobilized as a potent forum for asserting these differences. The divisive rhetoric found on albums produced commercially in the diaspora spanned the gamut from subtle to blatant, yet in many cases a line was underscored between the Soviet Union and prerevolutionary Russia.

One such album that marks a division between pre- and postrevolutionary Russia is *Old Russian Romances and Songs*. The album features Boris Evtushenko, a First Wave émigré who had fought in the White Army and then followed a path typical of many émigrés between Turkey, Czechoslovakia, and Germany before settling in the United States in 1948. Similar to other recordings featuring White Russian émigrés, the jacket notes position the Bolshevik Revolution as an endpoint to the development of "true" Russian culture and, by extension, the role of émigrés like Evtushenko in maintaining this tradition. Emphasizing the negative impact on the development of Russian popular music by the Soviet regime, the album notes of *Old Russian Romances and Songs* immediately set up a division between Soviet Russia and an idyllic, golden age, when such music reigned supreme:

> In the second half of the nineteenth century and up to the time of the Russian revolution, life in the Russian cities was gay and happy. . . . The large restaurants often located on the outskirts of the cities[,] such as the "Yar" outside of Moscow, were a popular rendezvous for entertainment and romance. . . . The Russian revolution changed the mode of life entirely and new ideas influenced the development of music, so that while the romances started to fall into oblivion in Russia, they spread and became more popular not only in Europe, but all over the world.[63]

Despite the reference to Moscow's premiere prerevolutionary gypsy restaurant, the album presents salon romances as the musical means of keeping Russian life "gay and happy." The album includes such standards as Varlamov's "*Na zare ee ne budi* [Don't Wake Her at Dawn]," "*Zabyty nezhnye lobzan'ia* [Forgotten Gentle Kisses]," and "*Ia pomniu val'sa zvuk prelesnyii* [I Remember the Glorious Sounds of the Waltz]." The latter two songs themselves serve as eulogies to days gone by, contrasting happy days in spring to those of solemn winter. The notes go on to assert that it is up to émigré musicians like Evtushenko to carry on the proverbial "old-fashioned waltz" in the form of song.

Such rhetoric of cessation has also been expressed by other anticommunist groups, including Cuban exiles in Miami. Symbolized by songs like Billo Frometa's "El Son Se Fue de Cuba [The Son Has Left Cuba]," this rhetoric suggests both a halt of the production of "authentic" homeland music—whether in the form of Russian romances or the Cuban *son*—after the revolution and the subsequent responsibility of émigrés for preserving and ultimately returning to the homeland "its musical heritage."[64] In both cases, the émigrés are positioned as keepers and arbiters of an "authentic" homeland culture, a stance that is given voice through the music produced in the diaspora.

An even clearer case of delineation is evident with *Balalaika: Songs of White Russia.*[65] The album's title instantly politicizes the recording by placing its repertoire and performers within the realm of White Russia, the cultural, political, and ideological space opposed to communist Red Russia.

The notes on the album jacket do not shy away from a political reading, highlighting the fact that the performers (singers "Pierre" and Vladimir Svetlanoff and balalaika player Sania Poustylnikoff) fled Russia as a result of the Bolshevik Revolution and are now "in exile." The commitment of the players to their art, moreover, is underscored, as the notes explain that the "only luggage" Poustylnikoff was required to take by his parents when fleeing Russia was his balalaika. The notes repeatedly use the word "authentic" in describing this music, asserting ultimately that the music on the album is "true Russian folk music."

Perhaps most instructive for understanding the musical boundary work engaged in this example, the notes present an entire section labeled "The Music of White Russia," delineating the musical parameters of the exiled, anticommunist diaspora. Similar to the previous example, the music belonging to White Russia is defined as that of "Czarist" Russia, with "true" Russian folk music serving as its basis. The repertoire encapsulating White Russia, in this case, includes the romance "*Tol'ko raz* [Only Once]"; the rousing march of the Fifth Imperial Army brigade of the Aleksandrian Hussars, "*Aleksandriiskia gusary*"; and the Russian gypsy standards, "*Tam bubna zvon* [The Jingle of the Tambourine]", "Two Guitars" and "Dark Eyes" (the latter two of which are explored in chap. 1 and 2). Finally, the political agenda of the recording is underscored in the last lines of the notes, which state: "Along with Borodin, Rimsky-Korsakov, Glinka[,] modernists like Shostakovich and Stravinsky keep alive the fundamentals of true Russian folk music prior to the Communist takeover." Such rhetoric only reveals an attempt to place "true Russian folk music" within the domain of precommunist Russia, even when dealing with a living Soviet composer like Shostakovich.

Three overlapping themes predominate in these examples: the perceived authenticity of the culture from prerevolutionary Russia; the disappearance of this culture from Soviet Russia; and the safeguarding of this culture by the émigrés. In these examples, music is presented as a discursive (as album) and auditory (as repertoire) means for asserting a boundary between the Soviet Union and the émigré diaspora. Weaving its way through these assertions is an underlying claim of ownership—the diaspora as being custodian of authentic Russian music, and, by extension, of the true Russia.

To a certain extent, Soviet policies helped further the idea that some music would be destined for censure under the Soviet state, as many genres (most notably, Russian gypsy music, jazz, and folk music) were formally condemned during the Cultural Revolution of the late 1920s and early 1930s, in favor for music that promoted "industrial construction and collectivization."[66] Regarding the impetus behind Stalin's policies on gypsy music specifically, Richard Stites writes that critics "wanted to upturn the world once again and for the last time, to silence the noisy purloiners of vulgarity, to drown out the sickly whimpers of the gypsy violins with the shrill factory whistle."[67] Although all three genres made a speedy return at the conclusion of the Cultural Revolution, the fear-ridden climate of the great purges in the late 1930s once again threw into confusion what genres were to be tolerated and which were to be dismissed as remnants of a decadent past. This fluctuating relationship between Soviet critics and music from Russia's prerevolutionary past politicized these genres and helped frame them as signifiers of an authentic homeland culture within the emigration.

The mobilization of music to demarcate boundaries of authenticity is not unique to the Russian case and emerges as a common strategy of delineation among other groups of exiles. In her study on the Vietnamese diaspora, for example, Adelaida Reyes has shown the extent to which music has been used to demarcate pre- and postcommunist Vietnam, a division that served as "indicator of what constituted the truly Vietnamese in the realm of human relations, art, music, politics and social life in general."[68] Music emerged as a particularly potent symbol and means to assert this boundary, with the act of demarcation through song holding tangible consequences.

In her fieldwork, Reyes found, for example, that a young man who performed a piece from communist Vietnam was ostracized by the community, while another man shot the researcher an "almost hostile glare" when asked if he knew any "post-1975" songs.[69] Similar to the First Wave Russian emigration, the discourse of authenticity as structured around the pre- and postcommunist takeover signaled in these instances through the performance of a particular body of musical repertoire, served as indicator of "what constituted the truly Vietnamese" and permeated all aspects of the refugee existence.[70] Reyes's study presents particularly poignant illustrations of music's symbolic capacity to draw boundaries, including the moment when her placement of two stylistically similar songs (one of which was composed before and the other after the communist takeover) into a single category left her consultants incensed. In this instance, the formal qualities of the music bore little impact on their legitimacy, a point that did not diminish their power in demarcating what was "truly Vietnamese."

In her work on the Armenian diaspora, Sylvia Alajaji has likewise shown the efficacy of music in delineating what is and what is not considered to be Armenian. "True" Armenian music, as epitomized by the music associated with Komitas Vartabed, the early-twentieth-century musicologist who sought an authentic Armenian sound in folk music and was later killed in the Armenian genocide, has been a salient forum for developing collective narratives of the Armenian Self. The folk songs resurrected by Komitas in particular have served as symbolic sites in which boundaries between us and them (Armenians/Turks) have been drawn. Such "oppositional identifications" underlying these narratives of the (persecuted) diasporic Self parallel the prerevolutionary/Soviet binary permeating Russian émigré discourse.[71]

Yet, as Alajaji points out, the very stringency that defines the boundary between authentic and inauthentic brings into sharper focus the multitude of Selves underlying the seeming unity of the diaspora. Alajaji states: "On the surface, there is a sense of clarity: a known Self, a known Other. Underneath, however, the picture becomes far murkier. Here, Self and Other are intricately intertwined."[72] Although Alajaji applies this line of reasoning to explain the multiplicity underlying the Armenian community in California, one can also consider the great potential for dissolving boundaries between Self and Other harbored within this diversity. Music specifically has been mobilized as an effective equalizer, dissolving the "oppositional identifications" permeating exilic discourse.

Evidence of this dissolution can be found on recordings displaying even the most pronounced articulations of difference. Despite its assertion of presenting only "true" Russian music that "contemporary political leaders of the U.S.S.R. have frowned on," for example, *Balalaika: Songs of White Russia* includes the popular Soviet song "Moscow Nights" alongside the otherwise-typical émigré repertoire. Considering the overtly political message of this recording and the implication of its repertoire as belonging to the realm of White Russia, the inclusion of this song, which is made further peculiar by its translation into English as "Lily Time," marks a definitive break from the traditional prerevolutionary mold. The inclusion of state-sanctioned Soviet songs on albums recorded by émigré artists calls to attention the potential of music in muddying the Soviet-prerevolutionary binary dictating émigré discourse.

"The People's Soul": A Singular Russia

Perhaps no musical group serves to better illustrate the playing out and mediation of the juxtaposition between Soviet and émigré realms than the Don Cossack Choir. An overt symbol of anticommunist White Russia, the group was founded in 1921 by Sergei Jarov (1896–1985) in a refugee

Figure 3.4. The Don Cossack Choir, Serge Jarov in front. Private Collection, Courtesy of Tatiana Kamendrowsky.

camp outside of Constantinople and was made up of former members of the White Army. Although the group began by singing Orthodox services, it soon incorporated secular music into its repertoire, performing Russian folk songs as well as a range of prerevolutionary Russian and gypsy romances. By the midtwenties, the choir had gained international renown and in 1930 embarked on its first tour of the United States, during which it performed at the Metropolitan Opera House and at Carnegie Hall.[73]

Like the Red Army Choir, the Don Cossack Choir became a musical embodiment of its collective idea of Russia and a mirror image of its counterpart: former soldiers of the White Army donning uniforms and singing folk songs alongside Imperial Russian and Orthodox hymns (see fig. 3.4). The two groups overlapped in their performance of Russian folk songs and in their style of singing, which was marked by tight ensemble work, an abundance of rubato, frequent alternations between showy soloists and loud choirs, and sudden changes in dynamics. The dramatic execution of traditional Russian songs by men dressed in military uniforms, furthermore, staged an exaggerated masculinity fueled by a flamboyant nationalism.[74]

Besides pieces that were emblematic of Russia Abroad, the Don Cossack Choir also included Soviet tunes in its repertoire. Although this repertoire did not feature overtly Stalinist works, the group performed pieces like the jazzy tango "*Serdtse* [Heart]," from the 1934 Soviet film, *Veselye rebiata* [Jolly Fellows] and the notorious "*Podmoskovnye vechera* [Evenings outside of Moscow]," also known as, "Moscow Nights."[75] Aside from merely including this repertoire and thereby legitimizing music from the Soviet Union, the Don Cossack Choir marketed these songs under such labels as *Dark Eyes, Moscow Nights, Two Guitars and Other Russian Songs*. The collectivity implied by "other Russian songs" underscores a single Russian repertoire not divided by the Revolution, thereby blurring the pre-/postcommunist boundary that otherwise frames the Don Cossack Choir.

A unified repertoire is likewise presented on *Russian Gypsy Folk Songs* (1958) featuring émigré artist Vera Brynner (1916–1967).[76] A second-generation First Wave émigré and sister of singer and Hollywood star Yul Brynner (1920–1985), Vera Brynner presents repertoire that was commonly sung in the emigration, including "*Chto nam gore* [The Heck with Heartache]" and "*Kalitka* [Little Gate]." Yet alongside these standard selections, Brynner performs "*Serdtse*" and the 1938 "*Katiusha*," a folklike mass song describing a young woman singing on the riverbank to her beloved, who is away protecting the Russian border.

By the time Brynner's album was released, "*Katiusha*" was renowned both for its folksy sound as well as for its "unabashed militarism," epitomized by the adoption of the song's name for a Soviet rocket launcher during World War II.[77] Instead of differentiating the pieces by periods, by political camps, or even by genre, however, Brynner's album presents the music under the single label of "Russian Gypsy Folk" songs. Placing these stylistically and temporally disparate pieces under the category of music that was most enjoyed in the emigration gives them an instantaneous commonality, authenticity, and rootless past, and facilitates the consolidation of the music into a single, timeless, and nonpolitical category.

The description of the music in the liner notes of *Russian Gypsy Folk Songs* goes beyond the idea of a single repertoire to suggest an inherent expression of this music coming effortlessly from the hearts of a single, unified people: "These are the soulful stories of a people—their sadness, their loves . . . and their simple joys, expressed in their quaintly wistful, deeply poetic folksongs. The messages are close to the hearts of the people and the soil on which they live. Here are the stories as expressed in song by Vera Brynner."[78]

The notes emphasize an intrinsic connectedness among the Russian people, their native soil, and these songs, thereby presenting them as a natural extension of an inherent Russianness. Whether nineteenth-century gypsy romances or wartime expressions of Soviet patriotism, the songs on the album are presented as embodying and representing the plight of a collective Russian people, who are unified in their shared experiences and emotions.

Although albums like Brynner's *Russian Gypsy Folk Songs* allay divisions between Soviet and émigré spheres, it is difficult to assess the extent to which they reflect the views held by the émigrés themselves, since they were produced by record companies with which Russians had little, if any, interaction.[79] From this perspective, an example of recordings assembled by émigrés in New York would be useful in assessing the ways this music was marketed by and for Russians in the emigration. The case of Universal Records presents such a study, as it was founded by émigrés and presents an enterprise rooted in collaboration between members of the First and Second Waves. The company was founded in the 1960s by Second Wave Russian Georgii Kraimov (dates unknown), who paired up with illustrator Mikhail Lermontov (1925–2008), a distant relative of the nineteenth-century Russian author and son of First Wave émigrés from Yugoslavia.[80] Both Kraimov and Lermontov immigrated to the United States following World War II. Universal Records operated in a capacity similar to many of its earlier New York–based record companies: after selecting their favorite songs from recordings already produced in the Soviet Union, Kraimov and Lermontov compiled these pieces onto new albums under their own label, the cover art of which Lermontov illustrated. The LP records were then sold by mail order and in Russian stores throughout New York City and its vicinity.

Although infringing on modern-day copyright sensibilities, the Kraimov-Lermontov enterprise presents a concrete example of music as social act (as commercial undertaking) and as discursive site in its capacity to dissolve social boundaries. As discursive site, a number of the Universal albums mirror Brynner's recording in their focus on verbal and visual evocations of a singular, idyllic Russia. One of the more explicit examples of a Universal record that depicts an idealized, Old Russia is, "*Rossiia* [Russia]."[81] In this example, Lermontov represents Russia with a boyar couple, whose dress mirrors the stylized costumes that have continued to be worn as signs of "Russianness" within the diaspora to the present day (see chap. 1 and 5). The man carries what can either be a palace or an Orthodox church on a

Figure 3.5. Jacket Cover of *Russia* (Universal Records NM 104). Private Collection.

platter, and the entire scene is framed by a border and old-fashioned lettering akin to the Bilibinesque Russian fairytale illustrations of the early twentieth century (see fig. 3.5). The image of an ahistorical, archetypal Russian scene may, at first glance, contrast with the music on the album, which includes songs celebrating the Soviet navy ("The Sevastopol Waltz") and the technological wonders of the Soviet Union ("From the Volga to the Don"). Yet the ways in which these songs are framed by the title of the album and by a visual image of a timeless Russia allows Soviet and Old Russia to be conflated and presented as a single entity.

Having been born outside of Russia, Lermontov's illustrations presents a secondhand view of the Russian homeland, yet one for which he and his Yugoslav-born friends "yearned exceedingly."[82] Akin to hand-drawn cover art found in other forms of ethnic American music, the medium of drawing can stand as the "standard iconographic choice for archetypal imagery," for it has the potential to display, more than any photograph, a perfected object as it is conceived in the imagination of its creator.[83]

The notion of a collective Russian people bound to an idyllic nation suggests a commonality that far exceeds politics. Indeed, the authenticity projected onto the songs on these albums rests on the idea that this music serves as conduit to the emotions of a collective people (relaying their "soulful stories")—an inversion to the earlier albums that frame their music's authenticity as being correlated to prerevolutionary Russia and, by extension, to the diaspora. As music has been shown to blur such seemingly unwavering lines as those often found between immigrant and host land populations as well as within religious denominations, so too, in these examples, does music serve to dissolve exilic boundaries.[84] These "inclusive processes" challenge otherwise stringent lines of demarcation, in this case between diaspora and the (new) homeland, in their "hiding, blurring, combining, influencing, shifting, and expanding" of boundaries.[85] The trope of an essential Russia and its collective people on which this dissolution rested was utilized in the diaspora and, beginning in the wartime era, in the Soviet Union—a point that may be read either as an ultimate expression of commonality or as a contested point of ownership.

The Soviet Wartime Romance

On June 22, 1941, German troops invaded the Soviet Union. The invasion shocked and devastated the Russian people, a national sentiment that would be compounded by the horrific losses that Russia suffered in the course of World War II. To help bolster morale and rally the people, officials turned to staid symbols of Russianness—the land, the Tsarist past, and the once-anathema Orthodox Church. This shift in official culture made room for nuance of feeling not found in the relentless optimism of the 1930s.

This new level of honesty and "deep emotional authenticity" crossed into the musical sphere.[86] The wartime years produced music that engendered an intimacy, lyricism, and focus on "individual feelings" absent from the earlier mass songs.[87] Rather than the rousing marches that stamped out individualism with their sharp duple meter, the new repertoire focused on the inner self, projecting an ambiguity of emotion that markedly contrasted with the compulsory optimism of the earlier repertoire. Both in music and lyrics, this intimacy is found in such wartime standards as "*Sinii platochik*

[Blue Kerchief]" (1940); "*V zemlianke* [In the Dugout]" (1942); "*Temnaia noch'* [Dark Is the Night]" (1943); and "*Ekh dorogi* [The Roads]" (1945).

The folklike "*Ekh, dorogi,*" for example, paints a haunting picture of a soldier's life on the front. Presenting a stark contrast to the ever-confident mass songs ("And whoever goes through life singing shall never lose his way"), "*Ekh, dorogi*" relays the volatility of war, as the path of war promises only sorrow and difficulty: "But the road continues endlessly, with its clouds of dust ever-blowing; And all around the earth is smoldering, in this alien land." Like the chorus of a Greek tragedy, the apocalyptic verses are augmented with the gloomy lines of the refrain ("Oh, those roads. With but dust and mist, cold, angst, and the tall grass of the steppe; One's lot can never be known, Perhaps you will fold your wings in the middle of the steppe"), whose words offer no consolation and contribute to the bleak undercurrent of the song.

The earlier "*Temnaia noch'*" offers a more sensual, although no less radical, look at the front. Told from the viewpoint of a soldier, the lyrics relay the soldier's musings on death and his wistful longing for his wife:

Temnaia noch'	Dark is the night,
Tol'ko puli svistiat po stepi,	only bullets whistle through the steppe,
Tol'ko veter gudit v provodakh,	Only the wind sounds through the wires,
Tusklo zvezdy mertsaiut	and the stars shine dimly.
V temnuiu noch',	In the dark night,
Ty, liubimaia, znaiu, ne spish	I know that you, my beloved, are not sleeping
I u detskoi krovatki taikom	And that you wipe a tear
Ty slezu utiraesh.	As you sit at the child's cradle.

The soldier's solitude is enhanced by its juxtaposition against the warm and safe image of a mother at the cradle. Throughout the piece, the predominant theme of the night both unites and divides, a paradox that lies at the heart of the emotional estrangement that is so central to the song. The juxtaposition between warfront and cradle coupled with the sensual undertone of the soldier's desire to press his lips against the "gentle" eyes of his wife sets up a *danse macabre,* as, in the final verse, death once again shows herself ("I do not fear death, we have met more than once on the steppe, And now again, she hovers above me"). Indeed, in this final verse, the comforting mother/lover is temporarily displaced by bitter death, a juxtaposition made even more effective by the feminine pronoun shared by the words "mother" and "death" in Russian.

Example 3.1. "*Temnaia noch'*" (opening phrase), from *A Russian Song Book*, edited by Rose N. Rubin and Michael Stillman (Mineola, NY: Dover Publications, Inc., 1989), with slight modification based on the performance by Mark Bernes in *Dva boitsa*.

The musical language of "*Temnaia noch'*" reinforces the romantic temperament and exposition of loneliness suggested by the text. The song is set in a minor key with a slow tempo, alternating mainly between the tonic and subdominant chords. The melody gradually descends the range of an octave, which also contributes to the subdued feel of the piece (see example 3.1). The progression of seventh chords and the major key of the middle section of the song present a somewhat jazzy and uplifting respite in the midst of an otherwise subdued piece.

The iconic performance of "*Temnaia noch'*" by Mark Bernes in the 1943 film *Dva boitsa*—the version included on recordings in the diaspora like those made by Universal Records—only furthers the melancholic quality of the piece. Singing in a mezzo piano dynamic, Bernes delivers the text in a practically monotone speaking voice. The restrained manner of his singing suggests a no-frills emotion—this is not the decadent nostalgia of prerevolutionary gypsy romances but the thoughts of a man as he numbly faces death, like so many of his comrades in arms. Only the music betrays any hint of feeling, as Bernes's stone-cold delivery of even the most sensual line in the song ("How I wish to press onto your eyes with my lips at this moment") merely hints to something resembling warm-blooded desire by the climbing tune of the melody.[88]

The onscreen projection of a soldier contemplating life and death not only resonated among audiences in wartime Russia but, most likely unbeknownst to Soviet songwriters and filmmakers, made a deep impression on young émigrés. Comparing wartime romances to earlier Soviet songs, a second-generation émigré born in Yugoslavia stated, "[the songs] were likeable. When you sing them, they say something important. These are not simply empty songs, but these are songs about something significant."[89] In part, the appeal of these songs stems from their emotional and topical engagement with the war, which resonated with Russians in Europe who lived through the conflict west of Russia's border. Experiencing World War II firsthand gave a direct reference point to these songs, as the young émigrés could "identify themselves" with this music as they "understood what suffering meant."[90] Hearing this music in DP camps, moreover, helped humanize the Soviet refugees from whom the émigrés first heard this music: "We understood these songs . . . these words—imbedded in them was human desire. We knew the Soviet Union—how people lived there, how they experienced horrendous persecution. As young people, we felt a deep compassion for all of this."[91]

Even among the second generation of First Wave émigrés in New York, a group that as a whole was spared the experience of World War II, did the Soviet wartime romance make a deep impression. David Chavchavadze, for example, greatly enjoyed the songs, which he saw as having become "sort of free of propaganda."[92] Unlike his fellow New York Russians, Chavchavadze first heard these songs directly from the Soviet soldiers with whom he was working as an interpreter in Alaska as part of the Lend Lease Program during the war. Upon returning to New York and singing songs like "*Katiusha*" and "*Ekh dorogi*" at parties, Chavchavadze became "quite a hit." As a young girl, Zhenia Chavchavadze similarly remembers "absolutely ador[ing]" wartime romances like "*Temnaia noch'*," claiming that the song sounds "very romantic" if one does not listen to it as a war piece.[93] Chavchavadze's statement underscores the significance of music's sonic properties for resonating with members of the emigration. Indeed, beyond serving as a discursive and social site for bridging differences between Soviet and émigré cultures, music also functioned as auditory object in dissolving this boundary.

Generational Divisions

The positive reception of Soviet wartime romances among children of Russian émigrés suggests a broader division among generational lines over culture from the Soviet Union. Consider, for example, the response among first-generation émigrés to David Chavchavadze's performances of Soviet romances: "I was probably the first person in New York to sing the latest Soviet wartime songs, so free of the pre-war propaganda. This led to arguments with some of the older generation. The old, 'right-wing dinosaurs,' as I called them, accused me of being pro-Communist."[94]

The vehement response to music from the Soviet homeland among the older Russians parallels those of other anticommunist diasporas described earlier and speaks to the strategic positioning of music that can occur along political lines among different factions of an émigré community.[95] As Paula Savaglio has noted in her work on the music scene in Polish Detroit, "subgroups within the ethnic group associate musical style with a variety of in-group distinctions and accord them relative value."[96] Thus, the very music that in one context is positioned as being part of a greater Russian repertoire, undivided by Soviet-émigré politics, in another is viewed as a tool for promoting leftist ideals.

The division along generational lines signals not only a general openness to Soviet music among the second generation but, more broadly, a keen interest in the contemporary culture of the Soviet Union. A second-generation Russian who was born in Yugoslavia to Russian exiles in 1932 and who immigrated to New York in 1950, describes the ardent curiosity with which he and his friends first heard wartime Soviet songs in an Austrian DP camp: "We were interested in listening to these songs because there was very little that was known about [contemporary] Russia. There were very few that had ever been to [contemporary] Russia. . . . And many, especially the youth, were very interested in all of this, these new songs. Everyone knew the old, antediluvian Russian songs—romances—and everyone was tired of them. Here, there was nothing new, and suddenly, out of Russia, emerge new songs."[97]

For this particular consultant, the "antediluvian" songs were epitomized by the "sweet" music of prerevolutionary cabaret icon Alexander Vertinsky (1889–1957), whose dreamy, sometimes whimsical songs like "*Vashy pal'tsy pakhnut ladanom* [Your Fingers Smell of Incense]" and "*Jamais (Popugai Flober)* [Jamais (Parrot Flaubert)]," reflected the "unpractical," "wistful," and "naïve" mentality of his parents' generation.

The interest among the second generation in culture from the communist homeland also is evident within groups of other anticommunist exiles. Unlike their parents, second-generation Cubans, for example, were open to the émigrés who came to Miami in the late 1980s, as the young people were "thirsty for island culture."[98] María de los Angeles Torres explains this phenomenon in her book on Cubans in the United States: "Undoubtedly, the *exploration of home country and culture* is a central concern of this [second] generation. And, while this does not translate to support for the Cuban government, it does suggest a *more open attitude toward island culture*"[99] (italics my own).

The possibility of simultaneously partaking in homeland culture without betraying the diasporic cause lies at the root of the ability of second-generation émigrés to reconcile their position as members of the emigration with their interest in the Soviet Union. The sustained interest in anything relating to the homeland (communist or not) suggests a degree of nostalgia at work and the influence of the very émigré mission of cultural preservation that likewise prohibited a full embracing of the Soviet homeland. Unlike the nostalgia motivating the first generation of Russian exiles (see chap. 1), the nostalgia shared by the children of this group was for a place they had never seen. Similar to the repercussion of interwave contact among second-generation Cuban exiles, which engendered a longing that "sought a meaningful connection in the present," the exposure to Soviet culture for children of First Wave Russians simultaneously sparked and satiated a desire to know the homeland as a place existing as part of and beyond the stories of their parents—Russia as a living entity.[100]

It is helpful to approach the nostalgia driving the second generation not as a force of stasis, but rather as a process harboring great constructive potential. In her work on immigrants, nostalgia, and identity, Andreea Deciu Ritivoi posits that it is precisely nostalgia's rootedness and position as an acceptable constant that gives immigrants (and anyone, for that matter, who leaves the archetypal space of home) the freedom to change, without betraying their core selves.[101] Ritivoi states, "I see nostalgia as a defense mechanism designed to maintain a stable identity by providing continuity among various stages in a person's life."[102] While the first period of the Russian emigration revolved around a commitment to maintain an idea of the past, the subsequent period of the World War II era allowed this nostalgia to work as an anchor that permitted change. Central to Ritivoi's reading of nostalgia is her assertion that change is not necessarily opposed to the perpetuation of a group identity: "To value sameness or stability is not tantamount to rejecting difference or resisting adjustment."[103] In other words, within certain limits, one can embrace change without transgressing the boundaries of community that keep a group intact.

Ritivoi's emphasis on nostalgia and boundary construction as it relates to the Russian emigration is further elucidated by the work of Fredrik Barth. In his seminal work on communal boundaries, Barth asserts that to maintain an ethnic group, it is the boundary differentiating one group from another that must remain intact, rather than the common culture the group supposedly embraces.[104] For Barth, it is the notion of insider and outsider that lies at the basis of this boundary construction.[105] Based on Barth's writings, one may assert that, although the content of the musical culture of the Russian diaspora changed, there still remained a boundary between insider and outsider that would serve to define the First Wave community. Barth, however, also points to the possibility of "osmosis" of people across this boundary, without its dissolution.[106] Barth's theory, then, explains how the notion of Russia Abroad could remain intact despite the integration of culture and, ultimately, people from this other Russia, for the boundary between Soviet and émigré Russia would persist as long as there was another Russia(n) with which to compare that represented by the diaspora. Thus, Russians abroad could incorporate Soviet culture without annihilating the boundary between Us and Them—as long as the Soviet Union continued to exist.

Conclusion: A New Cultural Identity

The period surrounding World War II highlights the boundary production at work in the Russian emigration. This moment of change, however, points to a more complex process than one of simple demarcation between groups. Indeed, the boundary, as both social and semiotic space, offers immense potential for forging new cultural identities. In his work on culture and semiotics, Yuri Lotman illustrates the constructive power of the boundary, explaining that the boundary presents an especially fertile site for the (re)creation of meaning, as one of its borders is "always turned to the outside."[107]

An especially potent moment in the history of the Russian émigré diaspora, the years surrounding World War II presented new music and a new group of Russian emigrants, with whom First Wave émigrés negotiated the makeup of Russian homeland, identity, and culture. Aligning with Lotman's theory of periphery-center movement, in which that which lies at the fringes of the boundary gradually gravitates toward the center of the semiosphere, many of the songs that were once deemed controversial because of their Soviet origins eventually became emblematic of diasporic culture. Indeed, the reception of Soviet songs in the years surrounding World War II presents a particularly vivid illustration of what Greta Slobin has labeled *triangulation*, the process by which members of the Russian emigration navigated three "points of orientation" in figuring out how to create a "distinct national legacy."[108] Comprised of prerevolutionary Russia, the Soviet Union, and the specific host countries in which émigrés found themselves, these three points were often "in contradiction" with one another, offering differing angles by which émigrés could position and inform their diasporic culture.[109]

The sphere of music production in the wartime era offers a particularly rich site for examining the traversal of émigré, Soviet, and, in this case, American points of orientation, for, in conjunction with the migratory and social changes permeating the emigration, it was during this period that popular music from the Soviet homeland was first introduced to Russians living in the diaspora. Released in songbooks, recordings, and eventually from the lips of those fleeing the Soviet Union, music from Soviet Russia forced émigrés to face the question of whether culture condoned by the Soviet regime could be accepted by the anti-Soviet diaspora and presented another field in the debate over whether the center of Russian cultural life was to be "'there' or 'here.'"[110]

Rather than an "act of otherness, an act of betrayal" because of the "dichotomized identity" informing émigré discourse, listening to music from the communist homeland served to complicate this oppositional impulse.[111] The continued uncertainty regarding the Soviet Union, moreover, shows that the "intense polemics" over émigré identity that had been an "implicit issue in all exchanges" early on in the diaspora's existence had not been resolved several decades later, pointing to the saliency of the homeland-diaspora question.[112] Ultimately, the integration of Soviet popular music into First Wave culture during the postwar period made room for a broader idea of Russianness than that defined by a Soviet/non-Soviet binary, which resulted in this music becoming an authentic representation of Russia Abroad, rather than a byproduct of an inauthentic homeland, and bringing new life to the waning émigré community in New York.

Notes

1. Sania Poustylnikoff and the Brothers Svetlanoff, *Balalaika: Music and Songs of White Russia*, Mercury Records SR 60877/MG 20877, LP recording, 1956–1957.

2. David R. Jones and Boris Raymond, *The Russian Diaspora, 1917–1941* (Lanham, MD: Scarecrow Press, 2000), 10.

3. *Ivan Bunin: From the Other Shore, 1920–1933: A Portrait from Letters, Diaries, and Fiction*, ed. Thomas Gaiton Marullo (Chicago: Ivan R. Dee, Inc.), 126, 127.

4. Iwan I. Ostromislensky, Sergei Rachmaninoff, and Count Ilya L. Tolstoy, "Tagore on Russia. The 'Circle of Russian Culture' Challenges Some of His Statements," *New York Times*, January 15, 1931, 22.

5. "*Ko dniu Russkoi kul'tury* [Preparing for the Day of Russian Culture]," *Rossiia*, May 28, 1949.

6. Richard Stites, "Iconoclastic Currents in the Russian Revolution: Destroying and Preserving the Past," in *Bolshevik Culture: Experiment and Order in the Russian Revolution*, edited by Abbott Gleason, Peter Kenez, and Richard Stites (Bloomington: Indiana University Press, 1985), 1.

7. Ibid., 16.

8. For more on the expulsion of Russia's intelligentsia in the early part of the Bolshevik rule, see Lesley Chamberlain, *The Philosophy Steamer: Lenin and the Exile of the Intelligentsia* (London: Atlantic Books, 2006).

9. Adelaida Reyes, *Songs of the Caged, Songs of the Free: Music and the Vietnamese Refugee Experience* (Philadelphia: Temple University Press, 1999), 69.

10. Anna D. Jaroszynska-Kirchmann, *The Exile Mission: The Polish Political Diaspora and Polish America, 1939–1956* (Athens: Ohio University Press, 2004), 13–15.

11. María de los Angeles Torres, *In the Land of Mirrors: Cuban Exile Politics in the United States* (Ann Arbor: University of Michigan Press, 1999), 186.

12. The cultural scene among Russian émigrés in DP camps remains a vast and rich topic for further inquiry. For a firsthand account of the Russian DP experience, see, for example, Asta Aristova, *Chto sokhranila pamiat': vospominania o zhizni v Germanii, 1945–1949* [What Memory Has Preserved: Memoirs of Life in Germany, 1945–1949], (n.p., 2003).

13. Marc Gidal, *Spirit Song: Afro-Brazilian Religious Music and Boundaries* (New York: Oxford University Press, 2015); Gidal, "Musical Boundary-Work: Ethnomusicology, Symbolic Boundary Studies, and Music in the Afro-Gaucho Community of Southern Brazil," *Ethnomusicology* 58, no. 1 (Winter 2014): 83–109.

14. Gidal, "Musical Boundary-Work," 84.

15. Despite making zero proceeds for the first two years of the parish's existence, these evenings produced \$267 in 1927, which more than tripled to \$840 the following year and peaked at \$1,065 in 1929. Financial records covering September 1924 to December 1934 [Archives of the Orthodox Church of America, Christ the Savior Papers, Manuscript Box 2, "Klub i priemy" Folder].

16. *Iubileinyi sbornik sobornavo Khrama Khrista Spasitelia v N'iu-Iorke, 1924–1949* [The Twenty-Fifth-Year Anniversary Booklet of Christ the Savior Cathedral in New York, 1924–1949], (n.p., n.d.), 131. Hereafter "Christ the Savior Twenty-Fifth Anniversary Book."

17. For an account of the impact of the Great Depression on the Polish-American community, for example, see, Jaroszynska-Kirchmann, *The Exile Mission*, 11.

18. Sea Cliff continues to be the site of a thriving community of Russian émigré descendants, complete with an active social life surrounding the local parish. While conducting field and archival research there, I was struck by the number of Russians I encountered while taking walks around the neighborhood in which I was staying.

19. Christ the Savior Twenty-Fifth Anniversary Book, 117–118; Serge Savitsky, "*Khor khrama* [The Parish's Choir]," *Parish Bulletin of Christ the Savior*, no. 5 (December, 1945): 27.

20. Savitsky, "*Khor khrama*," 26.

21. Ibid., 27.

22. Advertisement from the *New York Times*, June 2, 1935, BR16.

23. Amkniga had grown out of the infamous Amtorg Trading Corporation, which focused on industrial espionage. For more on early Soviet espionage as it occurred within the realm of trade, see Katherine A. S. Sibley, *Red Spies in America: Stolen Secrets and the Dawn of the Cold War* (Lawrence: University of Kansas, 2004), 13–52.

24. "Asides of the Concert and Opera World: Delivering a Score on Microfilm from Soviet Union by Air," *New York Times*, June 21, 1942, X7.

25. "Concerts and Opera Asides: Am-Rus Joins ASCAP, Making Large Catalogue of Soviet Music Available to American Broadcasters," *New York Times*, August 29, 1943, X5.

26. An intriguing counterexample of an American seemingly obsessed with acquiring a recording of a specific song ("March" from the 1938 Soviet film *Tsyrk*) is recounted in Virginia Lash, "Sail Away Music," *The North American Review* 252, no. 1 (January 1967): 36–39. The great lengths to which Lash goes in her attempts to procure this album and the trouble she encounters along the way, however, suggest the unusual nature of the undertaking.

27. Richard Stites, "The Ways of Russian Popular Music to 1953," in *Soviet Music and Society Under Lenin and Stalin: The Baton and Sickle*, ed. Neil Edmunds (New York: Routledge, 2004), 24.

28. Gerald Stanton Smith, *Songs to Seven Strings: Russian Guitar Poetry and Soviet "Mass Song"* (Bloomington: Indiana University Press, 1984), 12; S. Frederick Starr, *Red and Hot: The Fate of Jazz in the Soviet Union, 1917–1980* (New York: Oxford University Press, 1983), 172.

29. Statute of the Union of Soviet Writers (1934), cited in Stanton Smith, *Songs to Seven Strings*, 11.

30. Starr, *Red and Hot*, 172.

31. Stanton Smith, *Songs to Seven Strings*, 14–30.

32. For more on the political dealings of Amkino, see Thomas Doherty, *Hollywood and Hitler, 1933–1939* (New York: Columbia University Press, 2013), 186–187.

33. Ibid., 187.

34. Eugenie Chavchavadze, interview by author, Washington, DC, October 7, 2007.

35. Eugenie Chavchavadze, interview by author, Washington, DC, May 31, 2006.

36. Willy Wenger, Notes to *The Best of The Red Army Choir*, SBMC SILKD 6034, CD, 2002.

37. Richard Stites, *Russian Popular Culture: Entertainment and Society Since 1900* (Cambridge: Cambridge University Press, 1992), 78.

38. Anthony Swift, "The Soviet World of Tomorrow at the New York World's Fair, 1939," *Russian Review* 57, no. 3 (July 1998): 377, 374.

39. Ibid., 368.

40. David Chavchavadze, *Crowns and Trenchcoats: A Russian Prince in the CIA* (New York: Atlantic International Publications, 1990), 110. By contrast, the cinema in the Soviet pavilion was not of interest to the average American visitor (Swift, "The Soviet World of Tomorrow," 374).

41. Peter Kupfer, "Volga-Volga: 'The Story of a Song,' Vernacular Modernism, and the Realization of Soviet Music," *The Journal of Musicology* 30, no. 4 (Fall 2013): 530.

42. Stites, *Russian Popular Culture*, 90.

43. Mikhail Lermontov, telephone interview by author, December 21, 2007; Eugenie Chavchavadze, interview with author, Washington, DC, May 31, 2007.

44. Catherine Evtuhov and Richard Stites, *A History of Russia: Peoples, Legends, Events, Forces* (Boston, MA: Houghton Mifflin Company, 2003), 20, 521.

45. Eugenie de Smitt, for example, remembers coming home from school to her apartment on the Upper West Side one day to a large curtain hanging in her living room, which served to divide the room into equal sections for two First Wave families from Yugoslavia who had come through the DP camps [Eugenie Chavchavadze, interview by author, Washington, DC, February 15, 2007].

46. Kalbouss, telephone interview, December 11, 2015.

47. Memorandum, November 15, 1951, Christ the Savior Papers, The Archives of the Orthodox Church in America.

48. "*Elka v prikhode Khrama Khrista Spasitelia* [The Christmas Pageant at Christ the Savior Church]," *Rossiia*, January 12, 1949.

49. "*Elka v prikhode.*"

50. "*Elka na Russkoi ferme* [The Christmas Pageant at the Russian Farm]," *Rossiia*, January 19, 1949, 4.

51. "*Sobornaia elka* [The Parish Pageant]," *Rossiia*, January 19, 1949, 3.

52. Eugenie Chavchavadze, interview with author, Washington, DC, May 31, 2007.

53. Handwritten songbook, 1948, 32, Personal copy of Alexey Zacharin.

54. Sylvia Angelique Alajaji, *Music and the Armenian Diaspora: Searching for Home in Exile* (Bloomington: Indiana University Press, 2015), 8.

55. As Alajaji explains, "*Menk* ('us') became the Armenian community from which the speaker came, and *eerenk* ('them') the various other Armenian communites," *Music and the Armenian Diaspora*, 139.

56. Jaroszynska-Kirchmann, *The Exile Mission*, 15.

57. Mark Wyman, *DPs: Europe's Displaced Persons, 1945–1951* (Ithaca: Cornell University Press, 1989), 207.

58. John Glad, *Russia Abroad: Writers, History, Politics* (Washington, DC: Birchbark Press, 1999), 361–362.

59. Interview with author, Arlington, VA, December 17, 2006.

60. Interview with author, Washington, DC, September 14, 2008.

61. Interview with author, Bethesda, MD, February 19, 2007.

62. See, for example, Stanislaus A. Blejwas, "Old and New Polonias: Tensions Within an Ethnic Community," *Polish American Studies* XXXVIII, no. 2 (Autumn 1981): 55–83; Randa A. Kayyali, *The Arab Americans*, The New Americans series, Ronald H. Bayor, ed. (Westport, CT: Greenwood Press, 2006), 27–32; Nazli Kibria, *Becoming Asian American: Second-Generation Chinese and Korean American Identities* (Baltimore: Johns Hopkins University Press, 2002), 50; Silvia Pedraza-Bailey, "Cuba's Exiles: Portrait of a Refugee Migration," *International Migration Review*, 19, no. 1 (spring 1985): 4–34.

63. Boris Evtushenko, *Old Russian Romances and Songs*, Gamut Records C-202, LP Recording, 1970s.

64. Gema R. Guevara, "'La Cuba de Ayer/La Cuba de Hoy': The Politics of Music and Diaspora," in *Musical Migrations: Transnationalism and Cultural Hybridity in Latino/a America*, edited by Frances R. Aparicio and Cándida F. Jáquez (New York: Palgrave, 2003), 40–41.

65. Sania Poustylnikoff and the Brothers Svetlanoff, *Balalaika: Music and Songs of White Russia*, Mercury Records SR 60877/MG 20877, LP recording, 1956–1957.

66. Stites, "The Ways of Russian Popular Music," 24.

67. Stites, *Russian Popular Culture*, 64.

68. Reyes, *Songs of the Caged*, 64.

69. Ibid., 65.

70. Ibid., 64.

71. Alajaji, *Music and the Armenian Diaspora*, 137.

72. Ibid., 138.

73. Andrei Dyakonov, Notes to *The Choir of the Don Cossacks Conducted By Sergei Zharov*, Traditsiia Pravoslavnovo Penia, vol. 143.0, CD, 2005.

74. For a discussion of Soviet and post-Soviet Cossack choruses and masculinity, see Laura J. Olson, *Performing Russia: Folk Revival and Russian Identity* (New York: Routledge Curzon, 2004), 138–159.

75. Serge Jaroff, *Kasakenlierd vom Don*, Polydor 46829, LP recording, 1960s; Serge Jaroff, *Dark Eyes, Moscow Nights, Two Guitars and Other Russian Songs*, Deutsche Grammophon Gesellschaft 63–409, LP recording, 1963.

76. Vera Brynner, *Russian Gypsy Folk Songs*, Kapp KL1116, LP recording, 1958.

77. *Mass Culture in Soviet Russia: Tales, Poems, Songs, Movies, Plays, and Folklore, 1917–1953*, edited by James von Geldern and Richard Stites (Bloomington: Indiana University Press, 1995), 315.

78. Brynner's status as both a First Wave émigré and, borrowing Mark Slobin's terminology, a "star," lend further legitimacy and credibility to the music on the album [Slobin, "Icons of Ethnicity: Pictorial Themes in Commercial Euro-American Music," *Imago Musicae* 5 (1988): 132–134].

79. The rupture between the ideas relayed in liner notes and cover art and those held by musicians featured on an album do not always overlap—a disjunction that Mark Slobin has shown is not uncommon to ethnic music production in the United States [Ibid., 137n15, 137, 138].

80. Mikhail Lermontov, telephone interview with author, December 21, 2007; *Russkie v Servernoi Amerike: biograficheskii slovar'* [Russians in North America: A Biographical Dictionary], ed. E. A. Aleksandrov (Hamden, CT: 2005), s. v. "Lermontov, Mikhail Aleksandrovich."

81. *Rossiia*, Universal Records NM 104, LP recording, 1960s.

82. Lermontov, telephone interview, December 21, 2007.

83. Slobin, "Icons of Ethnicity," 139, 132.

84. See, for example, Alajaji, *Music and the Armenian Diaspora*, 125–127; Gidal, "Musical Boundary-Work," 94–95.

85. Gidal, "Musical Boundary-Work," 93.

86. Stites, *Russian Popular Culture*, 100.

87. Robert A. Rothstein, "Homeland, Home Town, and Battlefield: The Popular Song," in *Culture and Entertainment in Wartime Russia*, ed. Richard Stites (Bloomington: Indiana University Press, 1995), 89.

88. Even the restrained, though emotionally charged, *"Temnaia noch'"* ultimately could not escape Stalin's suspicion, and was condemned after the war for its "escapism and tavern melancholy" (Geldern and Stites, *Mass Culture in Soviet Russia*, 377).

89. Alexey Zacharin, interview with author. Silver Spring, MD. December 19, 2006.

90. Ibid.

91. Ibid.

92. Chavchavadze, interview with author, Washington, DC, October 7, 2007.

93. Ibid.

94. David Chavchavadze, *Crowns and Trenchcoats*, 123.

95. See, for example, Reyes, *Songs of the Caged*, 7–8, 35.

96. Paula Savaglio, *Negotiating Ethnic Boundaries: Polish American Music in Detroit* (Warren, MI: Harmonie Park Press, 2004), 7.

97. Zacharin, interview.

98. Torres, *In the Land of Mirrors*, 161. Later-generation Vietnamese émigrés also tended to have a flexible political stance toward the communist homeland as they were not "bound to the strictures imposed on musical and social life by pre- and post-1975 evocations of Vietnam" (Reyes, *Songs of the Caged*, 69).

99. Torres, *In the Land of Mirrors*, 160.

100. Ibid., 187.

101. Andreea Deciu Ritivoi, *Yesterday's Self: Nostalgia and the Immigrant Identity* (Lanham: Rowman and Littlefield Publishers, Inc., 2002), 6–10.

102. Ibid., 9.

103. Ibid., 10.

104. Fredrik Barth, "Introduction," in *Ethnic Groups and Boundaries: The Social Organization of Culture Difference* (Boston: Little, Brown and Company, 1969), 14–15.

105. Ibid., 14.

106. Ibid., 21.

107. Yuri M. Lotman, *Universe of the Mind: A Semiotic Theory of Culture*, trans. Ann Shukman (Bloomington: Indiana University Press, 1990), 136–7, 142.

108. Greta N. Slobin, *Russians Abroad: Literary and Cultural Politics of Diaspora (1919–1939)* (Brighton, MA: Academic Studies Plus, 2013), 14.

109. Ibid.

110. Ibid., 25.

111. Torres, *In the Land of Mirrors*, 186.

112. Slobin, *Russians Abroad*, 25.

4

RADIO LIBERTY, VERNON DUKE, AND THE "INTERNAL" ÉMIGRÉ VOICE IN COLD WAR BROADCASTING

On July 8, 1964, Radio Liberty beamed another scratchy broadcast from its towers in Spain through the nominally impermeable Iron Curtain and straight into the heart of its primary political adversary. The program began as it always did—with the majestic sounds of Alexander Gretchaninoff's "Hymn to a Free Russia," the musical theme of Radio Liberty since its first broadcasts in 1953. One of the hymns proposed as a replacement for the Russian Imperial Anthem after the abdication of Tsar Nicholas II in March 1917, Gretchaninoff's piece stood as an audible link to the liberal February Revolution of 1917 and reflected the ultimate goal of Radio Liberty: to provide its Soviet listeners with evidence of the existence of an alternative path for Russia and subsequently rousing them to topple the communist regime. Featuring the disembodied voices of fellow countrymen and women carrying on their creative activities in the West, Radio Liberty strove to demonstrate the presence of another Russia. In this way, Radio Liberty offered an alternative to its Cold War counterparts, the Voice of America and BBC, whose programs focused on showcasing the culture of their respective nations as a means of winning over the hearts and minds of listeners found behind the Iron Curtain.

By 1964, America's focus on the Cold War was firmly established, and the anticommunism that informed Russian émigré ideology was now being deployed for pragmatic purposes. As Cold War programs proliferated, so too did professional opportunities for First and Second Wave Russians, whose language skills and political views presented an ideal combination for American recruiters. One need not look far to locate examples of

Russian émigré musicians capitalizing on their craft in the name of freedom and democracy. Desperate to make a living after immigrating to New York in 1940, then little-known Yul Brynner (1920–1985) served as a broadcaster for the US Office of War Information after working various odds-and-ends jobs, including posing as a nude model.[1] New York–based choir conductor Nicholas Afonsky (1894–1971) made no qualms about his choir's connections to the Voice of America, as the choir was advertised as "penetrat[ing] behind the Iron Curtain in a determined effort to portray the mode of living of a free nation."[2] Big band leader Basil Fomeen (1902–1983) applied several times for a job with the US Department of Defense, underscoring and later vehemently disavowing his work with the "anti-Bolshevist" White Army, depending on the nature of the US-USSR relationship. Even Nicolas Nabokov (1903–1978), the most notorious cold warrior among Russian émigré musicians, only became head of the Congress for Cultural Freedom in 1951 after requesting to return to Soviet Russia and after having been rejected in 1942, 1944, and 1948 to work for the US government.[3] One must wonder the extent to which Nabokov's commitment to the American cause was directly correlated to the question that plagued his life: "Can a 'gifted and striving' young composer make a living as a composer?"[4] Without contradicting the anticommunism that undoubtedly informed the Russian diaspora and US Cold War efforts, these examples demonstrate the role of personal gain in actions that may otherwise be framed as driven solely by ideology.

It is within this context that we once again encounter Vladimir Dukelsky, whose days as a struggling musician wandering the streets of Manhattan in wide-eyed awe were far behind him. By 1964, Dukelsky had achieved fame as Vernon Duke, the Broadway show-tunist, had married Kay McCracken, an American singer, and was living a comfortable life, albeit lacking in regular musical acclaim, in the Pacific Palisades neighborhood of Los Angeles. It was also at this time that Duke began working for Radio Liberty, which provided a much-desired musical and managerial outlet for the composer, as he organized and recorded live performances of Russian émigré musicians and poets that were then sent to New York for editing and airing. The July 8, 1964 Radio Liberty broadcast was the final product of but one such evening and featured Duke as composer and performer, accompanying his wife on piano. From the poetry written and declaimed by Los Angeles–based Russian émigrés to the pieces composed and performed by Vernon Duke, the program squarely fulfilled Radio Liberty's agenda of sending the émigré voice into the Soviet ether and presenting listeners with evidence of a culturally vibrant alternative to the Soviet Union, a Russia existing beyond the borders.

Beneath the veneer of a seamless gathering of Russian émigrés, however, lay an intricate web of negotiations and agendas informing the July broadcast. On a fundamental level, the structuring element influencing these agendas rested on Radio Liberty's primary mission of propagandizing to the Russian people to reflect on, question, and eventually to overthrow the Soviet government. Thus, one of the seemingly more lighthearted of Duke's songs included in the program was not merely meant to entertain, but, as shall be examined, was to incite the Russian people to pressure the Soviet government into easing the draconian travel restrictions then in place. Beyond the formal agenda driving the Radio Liberty program, however, lay another level of negotiations far more prosaic, though no less significant to the final outcome of the broadcast. In the case of Duke's broadcasts for Radio Liberty, these negotiations ranged from choosing between singers with personal connections (such as his Anglophone wife) or those with clean Russian diction, to balancing Duke's ardent quest for recognition with the propagandist success of the broadcasts.

Examining the four-year correspondence (1964–1968) between Vernon Duke and Radio Liberty producer Joe Valerio reveals the intricate series of negotiations underlying the seemingly straightforward Cold War broadcasts organized by Duke. Often undetectable in the final product, the agendas revealed by such private exchanges can offer a more nuanced and complete picture of the impulses propelling and ultimately shaping Cold War cultural programs. Examining diplomatic reports from the US government's Cultural Presentations program, for example, Danielle Fosler-Lussier has shown the complex negotiations that took place with regard to America's musical diplomacy, from sending the Cleveland Orchestra to Poland to mend hurt feelings over being passed over by the Boston Symphony Orchestra, to the pride expressed by Uruguayans over a visit by Louis Armstrong.[5] Thus, private exchanges can offer information that expands our understanding of musical diplomacy beyond the musical performance itself to include the series of "negotiations about priorities that surround these performances."[6]

Most useful for the present study is Peter Schmelz's framework of an "intimate history" of the Cold War, one that entails not only a microhistory in which minute examples illuminate broader historical trends, but a history that touches on "hidden corners" of public life by entering the inner world of the individual through the realm of personal exchanges. Whether hidden corners of Soviet musical life (as in Schmelz's study) or Cold War radio programming, such disclosure from exchanges between individuals can offer a counterpart to "grander public histories."[7]

Focusing on the correspondence surrounding the major musical projects Duke undertook for Radio Liberty, including composing a pop song ("*Pora domoi* [Time to Return Home]"), writing an atonal song cycle to the poetry of Mikhail Lermontov (1814–1841), and setting more than sixty Broadway show tunes into Russian, this chapter relays such an intimate history of Cold War radio, offering an important yet unexplored aspect of Duke's life and presenting an example of the involvement of Russian émigré musicians in America's Cold War efforts. Unlike most studies of America's Cold War programs, this chapter specifically scrutinizes an *internal voice* of Cold War cultural production. Indeed, only recently have historians begun to devote more than passing mention of Russian émigré involvement in Western intelligence, while music scholars have all but overlooked this aspect of Cold War studies.[8]

Thus, we return to Vernon Duke—former aristocrat, Broadway composer, and cold warrior? Where does Duke's position as an aspiring composer in the United States intersect with his task as a Russian émigré? What prompted a composer known best for his Broadway show tunes to become involved in American Cold War efforts? By exploring these questions, this chapter seeks to sweep out some of the "hidden corners" of Cold War radio broadcasting, locating the Russian émigré voice as sonic and discursive site in America's Cold War musical programming and demonstrating the tension that often existed between Cold War institutions like Radio Liberty and the individuals implementing their programs.

Becoming Vernon Duke: Or Tales from the New World

Had Vladimir Dukelsky (1903–1969) been born ten years earlier, he might have made it as a composer of classical music. Instead, Dukelsky did not finish his formal music schooling at the Kiev Conservatory, nor did he have the opportunity of establishing himself as a musician as did the slightly older Serge Prokofiev and Sergei Rachmaninoff (born 1890 and 1893 respectively) before the Bolshevik takeover of 1917 forced him to flee Russia. Instead of receiving a diploma, Dukelsky found himself aboard an old cargo ship that carried him to the shores of Turkey, far from the chaos of the Russian Civil War and seemingly even further from his chances of becoming a recognized composer of classical music.

It was in Constantinople that Dukelsky experienced a number of firsts: his first inebriated evening, his first taste of hashish, and his first exposure to the hot rhythms of jazz. Helping to support his brother and mother by playing piano at restaurants and film houses throughout the city, Dukelsky quickly responded to the public's growing demand for the jazz genre by purchasing the sheet music to "Hindustan," "Till We Meet Again," and the latest hits of Irving Berlin.[9] It was also in Constantinople that Dukelsky and his close friend Nicolas Slonimsky (1894–1995) began composing pieces in the jazz idiom, including Slonimsky's Turkish foxtrot, "*Yok, yok effendi* (No, No, Sir)" and songs that Dukelsky signed with the playful pseudonym "Ivan, Ivin."[10]

Here we must pause, for Dukelsky's foray into the world of popular music seems to have been at once fraught with pleasure and resistance. Whether merely appearing in retrospect as described in his 1955 autobiography or occurring at the time, Dukelsky describes his jazz interest with simultaneous enthusiasm and careful qualification. Noting his early sheet music purchases, for example, Dukelsky states that it was not Berlin's music or the "anonymous and crude" tempered New Orleans jazz that caught his attention. Instead, it was the music of a "Geo. Gershwin"—with its "bold sweep of the tune, its rhythmic freshness, and, especially, its syncopated gait"—that turned him into a jazz "fiend." Describing his intensive attempt to understand and compose music a la Gershwin, Dukelsky likens his sudden shift to jazz to "playing golf, after reading too much Schopenhauer."[11] Dukelsky's rhetoric at once situates him as an eager neophyte and distances him from a genre that would become his primary collateral—both economic and social (though, as he would forever sigh, never cultural).[12]

Regardless of the nature of his feelings toward jazz, Dukelsky's professional endeavors in Constantinople initiated what would become a lifelong career in the genre. Duke soon left Turkey for New York, where he conducted the pit ensemble for the burlesque show *Jazz Babies*. Despite the regular pay, Dukelsky belittled the enterprise, noting: "the spectacle of all the unsavory flesh pounding the runway over my head, twenty bare legs strutting lasciviously in a heady cloud of cheap talcum powder and sweat, proved too unnerving."[13] Dukelsky also attempted to peddle his songs to the bustling Tin Pan Alley, albeit unsuccessfully, as his songs, as he would later describe, were neither "good" nor "in the idiom of the street."[14]

Alongside these more ephemeral episodes, Dukelsky's first stay in New York also entailed an encounter that would have a profound effect on his personal and professional life. For it was after a concert of his art songs that Dukelsky was approached by the young George Gershwin (1898–1937), a meeting that would blossom into a close friendship between the two until Gershwin's death in 1937. Perhaps because of Gershwin's status or because of the genuine camaraderie that developed between the two, Dukelsky took to heart Gershwin's advice of composing popular tunes. "Don't be scared about going lowbrow," Gershwin told the Russian, whom he affectionately called Dukie, "[The songs] will open you up!"[15] Although it would be several years until "Vernon Duke" would publish his first piece, his initial interaction with Gershwin made a strong impression on Dukelsky, allegedly opening him up to the possibility of composing within the more accessible medium of popular song.

Along with his initial foray into New York's show tune culture, it was also in the 1920s that Dukelsky made considerable strides in the world of classical music. In 1924, Dukelsky left New York for Paris at the suggestion of Artur Rubinstein, who, upon hearing Dukelsky's piano concerto, urged the aspiring composer to travel to Paris to promote his music.[16] Rubinstein's advice served Dukelsky well, for it was in Paris that Dukelsky's greatest triumphs as a composer of classical music occurred, thanks to a handful of fortuitous encounters within the world of Russian Paris. Dukelsky received the regular and fastidious input of Serge Prokofiev, who spent numerous afternoons with the young composer, critiquing his works. Dukelsky was promoted by Serge Koussevitzky, who commissioned from him a symphony and offered the twenty-one-year-old a life contract with his publishing firm, Éditions Russes de Musique. It was also in Paris that Dukelsky won the favor of Sergei Diaghilev, artistic director, cultural dictator, and overseer of the Ballets Russes. Diaghilev commissioned from the young émigré a ballet, *Zephyr and Flora*, which was to infuse classicism with just a touch of Russianness—"tutus with *kokoshniks* . . . minus the samovars."[17] The young émigré also continued his high-end carousing, sipping wine with Poulenc, boating with Cocteau, whose outings he describes as being "rather like drinking verveine tea with a snake charmer in a hothouse," and dining with members of the French gentry.[18] By all accounts, Dukelsky was riding on the coattails of fame, on the cusp of recognition.

Whether Dukelsky's early success as classical composer was thwarted, as he professes, by his less-than-stellar work ethic, by his immediate need for financing his carousing lifestyle, or by the more altruistic intention of helping his mother, soon after finishing *Zephyr and Flora*, Dukelsky turned to the less prestigious but more lucrative business of composing works for the theatrical stage. Returning to New York in 1929, Dukelsky put his effort into show tunes, while still maintaining the hope of succeeding as a composer of serious music. Getting a job as a tune-master for Paramount and soon after for Broadway, "Vernon Duke" soon emerged triumphant, with a string of hits that included "April in Paris," "Autumn in New York," and "Taking a Chance on Love." Collaborating with Ira Gershwin, Yip Harburg, and Ogden Nash, among a string of notable lyricists, Duke's contribution to Broadway, and to the great American songbook more generally, is indisputable.

Despite Duke's Broadway success, which arguably reached its zenith with his score for *Cabin in the Sky* (1940), Duke continued trying to push Dukelsky's compositions into the classical repertoire, haggling conductors, writing countless letters, and publishing a series of diatribes (the most notorious of which was the forty-page invective against Stravinsky that he included in his book, *Listen Here!*). In 1947, Dukelsky founded the Society for Forgotten Music, which sought to promote unknown musical pieces and whose primary founding impetus was "neglect of the living composer."[19] Whether or not this was a self-serving strategy (Dukelsky was among those "forgotten"), his work for the Society in many ways parallels his later work at Radio Liberty. If Dukelsky was unsuccessful in promoting his music in more conventional venues, then he would use what Scott Holden has described as his "boundless" energy to carve out new channels.[20]

Here we turn to Dukelsky's collaboration with Radio Liberty for, to make sense of his work for the organization, one must understand his ceaseless striving for recognition, his contribution to American popular music, and his vacillation between Duke the "wage earner" and Dukelsky the "would-be composer."[21] It is this unique combination of interests and talents that would attract program directors at Radio Liberty and would inform Dukelsky's work throughout his time with the radio station.

Radio Liberty: The Voice of Diaspora

In 1955, one of Radio Liberty's first employees, Victoria Monditch, interviewed Vladimir Dukelsky for a broadcast feature. Although preceding Dukelsky's formal work with the program by nearly a decade, the 1955 interview entails Dukelsky's first encounter with Radio Liberty and exemplifies the organization's aim of presenting its Soviet listeners with a glimpse of émigré life. The interview was meant to showcase the successful career of a Russian émigré musician in the United States. From the interview's location in Marlon Brando's Midtown New York apartment to integrating the sweeping sounds of Duke's "April in Paris," the episode conveys the story of a cosmopolitan bon vivant who has retained a deep sense of Russianness. During the interview, Dukelsky relays his musical studies with Gliere, his friendship with Prokofiev, and his solicitation by Diaghilev, while noting his close relationship with Gershwin and the American public's supposed confusion over his race when first hearing *Cabin in the Sky*.[22] Completed in beautiful Russian, the interview succeeded in conveying what Radio Liberty producer Joe Valerio would call the "knowledgeable-guest-in-the-living-room" style for which the organization strove.[23]

The idea of a radio station utilizing recent émigrés from Eastern Europe and the Soviet Union was conceived shortly after World War II by George Kennan and Frank Wisner as part of a broader effort of Soviet containment.[24] Radio Liberty (or "Radio Liberation," as it was known until 1959) emerged from the CIA-funded Amcomlib, which attempted to rally different political groups within the Russian emigration into a single communist-fighting entity. The discord existing among the groups eventually resulted in the termination of the initial project and changed the policy to one of using individuals in the service of the United States government instead. Amcomlib soon turned its focus toward realizing one of its primary goals: to establish an émigré-led radio station akin to Radio Free Europe, yet one that would broadcast to the more ideologically established Soviet Union, rather than to recently communized Eastern Europe.[25]

The fundamental idea behind Radio Liberty was that its programs would be aired by and from the perspective of émigrés from Russia and the Soviet Union (First and Second Waves, respectively). Unlike their counterparts at the Voice of America, Radio Liberty's broadcasters were to speak in "pure, unaccented, contemporary Russian" and express "their genuine aspirations for lasting peace, freedom of expression, and a higher standard of living."[26] Presenting Radio Liberty employees as Russian insiders and free agents not bound to the American propaganda machine was a central part of the organization's image and means of influencing its listeners. Contrasting this specific approach to cruder propaganda, the head of the New York Program Section, Boris Shub, wrote: "the listener says to himself—'Aha . . . These aren't simply paid émigré employees of an American operation or propagandists. These are people who have brains of their own, careers that amount to something, and they think Radio Liberation is worth the trouble to talk over.'"[27]

In this regard, Radio Liberty positioned itself as a sort of "surrogate" radio station, offering information not broadcast on official Soviet news channels through the voice of (former) Soviet and First Wave conationals.[28] Organizers hoped that this internal voice would lend Radio Liberty greater credibility and subsequently more success in influencing people within the Soviet Union than that offered by formal American news sources.[29] Moreover, the idea of a single diaspora made up of both First and Second Wave émigrés and unified by an anticommunism, on which Radio Liberty rested, presents yet another example of the post–World War II dissolution of boundaries that occurred between the Waves (see chap. 3 with regard to music's role in this process).

A literal and symbolic contrast to the Voice(s) of America, Radio Liberty's positioning as the voice of the diaspora was to present a potent means of deconstructing Soviet claims of being the sole source of Russian culture and values. The strong potential of the radio in particular in structuring identities and realities of its listeners is relayed by what linguistic anthropologist Debra Spitulnik describes as "ways of seeing and interpreting the world, ways that ultimately shape their very existence and participation within a given society."[30] And, as Faye Ginsburg reminds us, "understanding radio requires attention not only to the sonic . . . but also to the ways that radio is embedded in and sometimes constitutive of 'inaudible' social practices such as kinship, religion, technology, personhood, and social movements."[31] The actualization of such abstractions is likewise mirrored in other clandestine radio efforts, including that which materialized during the Algerian Revolution (1954–1962), in which "listening in on the Revolution, the Algerian existed with it, made it exist."[32] Similarly, the entire project of Radio Liberty rested on the hope that its programs would present and subsequently inculcate an émigré alternative to Soviet reality and incite an overthrow of the Soviet regime.

The disembodied voice specific to radio broadcasts, moreover, adds transgressive potential to this process, as the radio can "play with the subversive potential of unseen voices, challenging and even mocking conventional social norms."[33] Within the context of the Cold War specifically, the disembodied element of Radio Liberty broadcasts played perhaps an equally important protective role, enabling the transmission of otherwise unutterable and potentially lethal information from the (relatively) safe distance of its recording studios in Europe and the United States.[34]

The symbolic realm of the voice itself presents a further layer of signification to Radio Liberty's broadcasts. Indeed, Radio Liberty operated explicitly on the subversive potential of the *émigré voice*, as it simultaneously signified Russian (insider) and dissenter (literal and symbolic outsiders to the Soviet Union). As an example of the "musical and linguistic expressivity" ethnomusicologists have assigned the voice, the case of Radio Liberty broadcasts further qualifies the voice as "the embodied site of . . . social distinction" as it "links the materiality of sound to the sociality of vocal practice."[35] As Radio Liberty's voice was constitutive of insider/dissenter, it maximized the subversive potential of the surrogate radio station, situating the diaspora within the intersection of "sound, technology, and power" with which radio engages sociality.[36] Disembodied from the self—as the (exiled) body was separated from the homeland—the émigré voice in Radio Liberty simultaneously signified distance and intimacy, thus compounding its efficacy.

Echoing the nativist philosophy behind the staffing of Radio Liberty, the programs themselves were similarly meant to function in an organic manner, influencing listeners to create a revolution from within so that "one fine day the Soviet government, deprived of its support and prospects, [would] itself die off."[37] Underlying this approach was a respect for the Russian people and an admiration for their culture. Shub, for example, hoped for programming that would "unlock the frozen energy and conscience of a nation whose talents had produced a Pushkin and Tolstoy, a Tchaikovsky and Shostakovich, a Mendeleev and Sikorsky," ultimately toppling the Soviet regime "by its own internal dynamic."[38] Consequently, programs broadcast by Radio Liberty were not to be overt in their propaganda, but were to have a more nuanced approach, as organizers believed that "any crass manipulation by outsiders, any Madison Avenue hectoring, any sloganeering 'anti-Commie crap,' could only harm that process."[39] This freewheeling and adaptive approach to Cold War broadcasting was enabled by loose congressional oversight and differed greatly from that of the Voice of America, whose constant scrutiny by Congress resulted in curtailed content and delayed output.[40]

In addition to broadcasting news otherwise not heard in Soviet Russia, Radio Liberty featured programs on art, literature, history, religion, and other aspects of Russian culture. Émigré broadcasters read works of contemporary Soviet writers and those in the emigration; they aired funeral services of renowned émigré artists; and they featured lectures on such varied topics as Sergei Diaghilev, the Russian Civil War, and the persecution of Jewish artists in the Soviet Union. Program executives strove to incorporate multiple viewpoints in their shows, inviting such guests as Alexandra Tolstoy, who was imprisoned by the Bolsheviks in 1920 and who fled Soviet Russia in 1929; Alexander Galich, dissident bard musician; and Angelica Balabanoff, who had worked with Lenin in the early years of the Bolshevik regime. Attempting for a semblance of balance, moreover, Radio Liberty broadcasts scrutinized not only the Soviet Union but also examined the shortcomings of the United States with such lectures as "The Imperfections of Capitalism."[41]

The relative weakness of Radio Liberty's signal prohibited broadcasting music of any considerable duration until better transmitters were set up in the early 1960s.[42] Subsequently, entire programs were devoted to music that ranged from classics of the Russian nineteenth-century canon to songs of Soviet bard musicians to Western jazz and rock.[43] In 1962, program executives swiftly responded to Nikita Khrushchev's crackdown on jazz by launching a program entitled "This Is Jazz." Even with this most American of genres, however, Radio Liberty continued to underscore its Russian-oriented programming, as it featured the voice of Boris Orshansky, a Soviet army captain who defected after World War II, and included forbidden music of Soviet jazz composers.[44]

By contrast, the Voice of America already aired the wildly popular "Jazz Hour," delivered by the smooth baritone of Willis Conover, whose voice became a sonic emblem of the United States.[45] The difference in approaches between Radio Liberty and the Voice of America can be found even in something as seemingly basic as the theme song of each jazz program. While Conover's program symbolized the mission of its respective station of "telling America's story" by opening each show with the American standard "Take the A Train," Orshansky's echoed Russia's clandestine version by featuring a jazz tune written by an unidentified Soviet composer (later disclosed to be Gennadi Golshtein) and forbidden in the Soviet Union.[46]

With numerous connections in the world of American jazz, it was Joe Valerio, Dukelsky's future contact at Radio Liberty, who asked members of the Benny Goodman group to record this underground music for the inaugural program of "This Is Jazz" and who would be central in getting the program off the ground. With the idea of Russian-made jazz having been launched at Radio Liberty, the time was ripe for someone connected both to Russia and to American vernacular music to enter the stage. Soon enough, Valerio would be soliciting Vernon Duke as the ideal candidate for the job.

Popular Music, Soviet Style

Other than a short, cordial note from Radio Liberty's New York program director thanking Dukelsky for his interview with Radio Liberty in 1955, very little transpired between Dukelsky and Radio Liberty for nearly a decade. By 1964, however, the radio station had undergone a sea change that in turn transformed its relationship with the composer. The "Amcomlib" letterhead had been replaced by "Radio Liberty Committee," signaling the growing stature of its new incarnation; jazz had been officially launched at Radio Liberty; and Valerio and other program executives were busy seeking innovative ways to attract Soviet listeners. By this time, Dukelsky had also made a notable amendment in his life: after spending more than fifty years as a bachelor, he married Kay McCracken, a Northwestern University graduate and voice student of Lotte Lehman.

It was also in 1964 that Dukelsky began to work regularly with Radio Liberty. After airing some of his poetry on the station (his failure to be recognized as a composer and as a poet is underscored cleverly in his poem entitled "April Fool"—"among poets I am a composer, and among composers a poet"), Dukelsky began working on a project that was to merge his musical talent with Radio Liberty's goal of putting "communism on the spot" (an objective written prominently on its letterhead of the time). Out of this merger came another Duke pop song, "*Pora domoi* [Time to Go Home]"—his first composition for Radio Liberty.[47]

Whether the song project was instigated by Duke or by Radio Liberty is not clear, although later press releases suggest that Radio Liberty pursued Duke, rather than the other way around. Indeed, Duke's very position as a Russian émigré who succeeded in the world of American show business—traversing Russian and American cultures with unusual ease—apparently drew Radio Liberty to seek out the composer. A press release describing the song project underscores the organization's objective of finding a composer who was fluent in both spheres: "What Radio Liberty wanted was an American tunesmith of Russian descent and thoroughly familiar with the style of music acceptable to Soviet fans."[48]

The goals of the project were made clear from the earliest stages of the collaboration: 1) to present a song that engaged the themes of home and travel in an effort to influence Soviet travel policy; and 2) to provide the

Russian people with a good pop tune. In a letter written to Duke in March 1964, Valerio sums up the official purpose of the project in an effort to prep Duke for interviews: "The 'true story,' as we see it, is that Soviet citizens are denied freedom of travel and nurture a longing to experience those very things that your lyrics convey. In addition, the Soviets are stepping up their complaints about the lack of good 'pop' music being turned out by their own composers."[49]

Broadcasting an appealing song, in turn, would not only satisfy Radio Liberty's effort to promote culture produced by Russian émigrés but would also generate enough enthusiasm and interest to act on the travel-themed lyrics. As Valerio wrote: "by playing up the theme of travel, seeing, knowing everything, at best we may in some small way generate pressures from within on the regime to loosen up on travel restrictions. At least you have symbolized in song the longings of millions of Soviet citizens."[50] The idea of instigating (or, at minimum, reflecting) a longing among Soviet listeners through a catchy pop tune epitomized Radio Liberty's strategy of subtle propaganda.

Duke responded in kind to Valerio's call, writing music and lyrics that reflect the idea of travel. The text of "*Pora domoi*," for example, states:

Khizhina il' khoromy?	Whether in a hut or a haughty palace
Uiut rodnovo ugla	Domestic bliss in one's own cozy corner
Il' gorodok ne znakomyi?	Or an unknown town?
Liubov' moia dom moi	Wherever my love abides, that's where I'll be at home.
Gde b ona ni zhila.	
Khochu proslyt' kovboem iz Montany,	I would like to be known as a cowboy from Montana,
Poekhat' v Rim veseluiu vesnoi,	Or travel to Rome some springtime so fine,
Iskolesit' ves belyi svet,	Circumnavigate the whole wide world,
Berega drugikh planet,	And the shorelines of distant planets, too,
Pridet liubov' togda: pora domoi!	Yet when love arrives: it is time to go home!
Menia maniat Vezuvii, Monblany,	Various Vesuviuses and Monblancs entice me,
Poliarnyi led, Bermudy leghkii znoi.	As do the Polar icecaps, and the warm breezes of Bermuda.
Zateiu vol'nuiu igru ot Parizha do Peru	My untrammeled game takes me from Paris to Peru
Pridet liubov' togda: pora domoi!	But, when love arrives: then it is time to go home!

Mne iasno, zemlia prekrasna:	I understand, the world is grand: but how
no kak ee obniat'?	does one embrace it?
I sgoraiu neterpen'em,	I burn with anticipation,
Vse uvidet', vse uslyshat', vse uznat'.	To see it all, hear it all, know it all.
Ia kazhdyi den' kudanibud' na	I am ready at the drop of a hat to take an
samolete gotov letet'	airplane any place
Besstrashnyi molodoi,	I, who am fearless and young,
Madagaskaru otdal dan' ia,	I've paid tribute to Madagascar, and the
Riv'era, dosvidan'ia!	Riviera, too—goodbye, I am off!
Ty prishla liubov', teper' pora	Yet you came, love, and now it is time to
domoi!	go home!

The instructions Duke received for composing "*Pora domoi,*" at least as he relays publicly, were simple enough: "[Radio Liberty] asked me to write songs with Russian words (of my own creation, incidentally), to an American-type melody with a beat that is characteristic of our popular music."[51] Duke's interpretation of an "American-type" melody and beat presents an insight into his sound view and into Valerio's idea of what style of music would be acceptable for broadcasting. Opening with a series of seventh chords, syncopated rhythms, and rapid key changes, Duke's propensity for jazz is made evident from the very first bars of "*Pora domoi.*" The first section of the song conveys a wistfulness, with a series of minor and major seventh and ninth chords and one harmony gliding into the next (see example 4.1). This harmonic elusiveness suggests a journey of sorts, as there is no sense of "home" with the frequent and rapid key changes. In turn, the lyrics in this section relay an abstract, almost philosophical idea of home—that "home" can be a "hut or palace" or anywhere in which the narrator's love is found.

Although retaining the jazzlike quality of the opening, the second section of "*Pora domoi*" abruptly shifts the mood to one of adventure, signaled by the C-major chord that begins the section, the unusual chordal progression (C-D-a), and the series of open fifths that dot the bass part (see example 4.2). The harmonic ambiguity of the piece continues in this section, as the C-major chord can be heard as either a tonic or a subdominant, and is followed abruptly by a stepwise upward motion to a D-major chord. The open fifths and wide harmonies in this section convey an arid sound that is reinforced by the lyrics that begin the section ("I want to be known as a cowboy in Montana"). It is only at the end of this section that the listener arrives "home" at long last, finally encountering a strong G-major (tonic) chord

Example 4.1. Vernon Duke, "*Pora domoi*," measures 1–12. Box 75, Vernon Duke Collection, Music Division, Library of Congress.

that falls on the word "home" (i.e., "time to return home!"). Just as quickly, however, the listener is thrown back into the dreamy world of travel and adventure with an F-natural that distorts the tonic chord and returns the song to the C-D-a progression.

The appeal of a popular song with "American-type" melody and rhythm was to serve a purpose even more surreptitious and specific to Radio Liberty's goals. Initially unknown even to Duke, "*Pora domoi*" was to help Radio Liberty with one of its greatest challenges: determining the makeup and number of its listeners. As funding provided secretly from the CIA could only continue with evidence of effective programming, Radio Liberty was constantly thinking of creative ways to gauge the size of its audience

Example 4.2. Vernon Duke, "*Pora domoi*," measures 12–16. Box 75, Vernon Duke Collection, Music Division, Library of Congress.

and efficacy of its broadcasts.[52] The "*Pora domoi*" project presented a new means of tallying Radio Liberty listeners: in order to live up to its goals of "maximum exposure and mileage" of the song, Radio Liberty would promise free recordings of the song to all requesters.[53] The strategy was to serve not only a pragmatic function but also a capitalist one, as the "acetate giveaway" was merely the first step in creating a pop sensation that would sweep both the Soviet Union and the United States in a fashion similar to the "Moscow Nights" phenomenon of the late 1950s.[54] The initial Russian sensation would then prompt an English version and leave Duke as a celebrated composer and triumphant cold warrior.

Although seemingly giving Duke agency in the compositional process of "*Pora domoi*," Valerio subtly manipulated the framing of the song in public presentations. Valerio insisted, for example, that the song was inspired by Soviet poet Evgeny Evtushenko (b. 1933), going plainly against Duke's claim of being inspired by the lesser-known émigré poet Vladimir Varshavsky (1906–1977). In response to Duke's protests, Valerio writes: "the word 'suggested' [referring to an earlier statement made by Valerio that Evtushenko himself suggested the song's theme] might have been softened. But, again, we did discuss [Evtushenko's] Prologue and there are certain similarities of allusion in Prologue and Pora."[55] In support of Valerio's assertion, one may find a similarity between "Pora" and "Prologue" in the feverish listing of various cities from around the world found in Evtushenko's poem:

Mne nelovko	It's awkward
Ne znat' Buenos-Airesa, N'iu-	Not to know Buenos Aires and New
Iorka.	York.
Khochu shatat'sia,	I'd like to wander
skol'ko nado, Londonom	As much as I please through London
So vsemi govorit'—puskai na	To converse, however brokenly, with
lomanom.	everyone.
Mal'chishkoi, na avtobuse povisshim,	Like a kid, hanging on to a bus
Khochu proekhat' utrennim Parizhem!	Ride through Paris at daybreak![56]

The weight of restriction, however, is expressed ever more explicitly in Evtushenko's poem, perhaps further explaining Valerio's push for an alignment between the two works. Indeed, associating the piece with Evtushenko may have been a means of presenting cutting-edge (and more widely recognized) Soviet culture to Radio Liberty's listeners.

The discussion over the source of inspiration for "*Pora domoi*" reflects a broader open-endedness relating to the song that caused disagreement throughout the collaborative process between Duke and Valerio. Something as seemingly straightforward as the title, "*Pora domoi*," for example, proved to be problematic. While Duke initially refers to the English title as "Time to Go Home" (reflecting the literal translation), Valerio insists on the more romantically oriented, "The Girl Who Will Keep Me Home," explaining that the new title would help avoid the "risk of misinterpretation."[57] Although Valerio does not elaborate, one need not go far to read his statement as a well-founded concern over its insinuation of a return to Soviet Russia. As Duke writes in a letter to Valerio dated February 23, 1964, the "initial point" of the song's subject matter was to ensure that the idea of home would not be identified with Soviet Russia, which he implemented by writing a verse that would convey the idea that "'home is where your heart is' and that might be *anywhere*" (emphasis in original). For a radio organization staffed by recent Soviet escapees to air a song about "return" without any further qualification could indeed have been interpreted as being odd and even counterproductive.

Although Duke may have assuaged fears of misinterpretation by his fervent declarations, the final version of "*Pora domoi*" remains relatively ambiguous in its meaning. This ambiguity is especially evident when considering the different ways the song has been described by Radio Liberty personnel. Duke's ambiguous assertion that home "might be anywhere," for example, is taken to an extreme in a press release that states, "Although the song is titled 'Pora Domoy' ('Time to Go Home'—or in Ogden Nash's brilliant English version 'A Girl to Keep Me Home'), the main point behind the title is that 'home is where your heart is'; in other words, that when a young Soviet citizen falls in love he doesn't *have* to do so at home, in Russia" (emphasis in the original).[58] This ambiguity likewise permeates retrospective reflections on the piece. In his 2002 memoir, then New York program director Gene Sosin describes the piece as "a sentimental song, which expressed the joy one feels on returning home after wandering abroad for years."[59]

On the one hand, the various interpretations of the piece may simply reflect Duke's successful implementation of Radio Liberty's strategy of sophisticated, nuanced messaging. One cannot blame Duke for adhering to such instructions as "Unsubtle propaganda such as extolling America's riches or the true freedom enjoyed by our fellow-citizens was out."[60] Yet the ambiguity inherent to the piece may have actually contributed to its lukewarm reception as, despite the initial "very encouraging and extremely complimentary messages" about the "Pora" project from Radio Liberty headquarters in Munich, the song appears to have missed the grand impact it was anticipated to create.[61]

In response to Duke's inquiries regarding Soviet reception to a May 1964 concert he organized that featured "*Pora domoi*," Valerio stated, "there were no echoes. This is *most* unusual. I have learned not to judge these things in terms of US Nielsens and Trendexes. Our audience response comes in strange and startling ways" (emphasis in original).[62] Valerio immediately followed this somber thought, however, on a more hopeful note, stating, "After a repeat of one of our interviews with you, followed by 'Pora,' we did receive a letter asking for more on Russian composers living in the US and the popularity of Russian music in general in the US."

Whether Valerio's update on the project was meant to placate Duke or to underscore the difficulty Soviet listeners faced in communicating with Radio Liberty, it is clear that "*Pora domoi*" did not create the stir that was expected. Nevertheless, in April of the following year, Duke received further encouragement from Valerio, who relayed the following words from New York head Howland Sargeant, "Considering the risks and the postal censorship, one letter [referring to the December 1964 correspondence] from the USSR is equivalent to a thousand from a free country."

The apparently meager reception of *"Pora domoi"* may have also been a result of Duke's haste in publicizing his work for Radio Liberty. As early as February 1964, Duke wrote Valerio that he had been assured by his publicist that the "Pora" project would be "headline stuff" for journalists.[63] By March, it appears that Duke was pushing for a public press release regarding *"Pora domoi,"* considered premature by Valerio. In an effort to dissuade Duke from going forward, Valerio wrote, "It is still our feeling that a discernable reaction in the USSR would really provide impact to the story." Perhaps attempting to hedge his bets by giving Duke choice in the matter, Valerio went on to say, "But if you think that placing the story with a syndicated columnist would not dilute the effect of a later story, the choice is yours to make."[64]

And choose he did. By May, small blurbs began appearing in music magazines on the new "Duke ditties" composed for Radio Liberty and beamed to the Soviet Union.[65] In June, Duke met with gossip columnist Cobina Wright to discuss the project, which resulted in further articles detailing Duke's work with the Cold War radio station. With titles like, "New Voice Gets Ear of Soviets," the articles present Duke as a liberator whose insider perspective as a Russian émigré enables him to write songs that tap into the yearnings of the Russian people. Positioned as a noble cold warrior, Duke is portrayed as a composer whose music would help liberate "captive Russia" and as someone who works tirelessly for such a "worthy cause."[66]

Although it is impossible to assess the extent to which this publicity may have diminished, as Valerio feared, the impact made by *"Pora domoi,"* it is evident that Duke utilized the project as a platform for self-promotion. Taken within a broader context of Duke's association with the radio station, a definitive pattern emerges in which Radio Liberty serves as an outlet for Duke's seemingly boundless quest for recognition rather than merely an ideological venue for an émigré's anticommunist efforts.

Waging War through Atonality:
Dukelsky's Lermontov Cycle

Although Duke reported on his interviews about *"Pora domoi"* to Valerio with much enthusiasm, he concludes his writing on the work with an emphatic plea: "I need at least 10 more Radio Liberty folders" (emphasis in original).[67] Indeed, from his earliest interactions with Valerio, Duke consistently sought out means of promoting his music through his Radio Liberty connection. In one of his earliest requests, Duke repeatedly asked Valerio to use his position as program director at Radio Liberty to bolster the 1964 revival of his musical, *Cabin in the Sky*. From asking to plug the musical in Radio Liberty broadcasts and press releases to requesting a mass outing to the show ("at reduced ticket prices") for Radio Liberty personnel, Duke attempted to make the most of his relationship with the radio organization.[68]

Yet Duke went beyond merely seeking support for his music through Radio Liberty. Shortly after establishing a relationship with Valerio, Duke proposed an entire series in which he would serve as organizer and point person. Pitched initially as a single evening of poetry read by Russian émigrés, the event would evolve into a multiyear endeavor involving the Los Angeles chapter of Litfund, the émigré benevolent organization that assisted Russian writers in the diaspora. Outlining the program as one in which émigré poets now residing along the West Coast could broadcast their works to Soviet Russia, Duke's conception of the event aligned with Radio Liberty's objectives. As Duke stated in a letter in February 1964, "I think that an hour's broadcast, say, with an illuminating forward [*sic*] by Gaievsky [Ukrainian essayist and émigré] presenting the poets about to appear in person and on tape, followed by samples representative of the given poets' output, without necessarily any political implications, might be very effective."[69]

Despite the seeming compatibility between the anticommunist objectives of Radio Liberty and the Russian emigration as a whole, Duke's idea of broadcasting the poetry reading was met with resistance by a number of Los Angeles–based émigrés precisely on the grounds of the radio organization's political entanglements. After avoiding Duke, for example, Litfund's chairperson asked Gaievsky whether or not he thought it "a good idea to mix Litfund's charitable activities with political propaganda?"[70] In response to the minor mutiny, Duke requested from Valerio Radio Liberty pamphlets "for purposes of a 'last stand.'"[71] Positioning himself as an outsider, in this case, Duke distanced himself not only from the Litfunders but from Russians as a whole as he wrote, "You and I know that the moment you get mixed up with Russians, trouble, intrigue, and various forms of back-biting will ensue."[72] Beyond the local implications of Duke's response, the Litfund/Radio Liberty episode demonstrates the diversity of views with regard to political engagement that existed within the Russian emigration as a whole.

Although Duke initially adhered to his plan of the poetry reading, he soon guided the Litfund evening in a direction beneficial to himself. Gaievsky's "illuminating forward" would be written by Duke ("poetry not being [Gaievsky's] strong point"), while the list of poets suddenly included Duke himself.[73] Going further afield, Duke soon proposed to change the poetry-only event into an evening of poetry and music. Outlining the new program, Duke writes: "The second half—surprise!—will consist of Kay McCracken, my wife, with self at the piano in a short vocal recital."[74] Although the concert would include several works of other Russian composers, the majority of the program featured a combination of Duke/Dukelsky pieces, including an aria from his *Mistress into Maid [Baryshnia-Krestianka]* opera, "April in Paris," and "*Pora domoi.*" Ending his letter to Valerio with the optimistic, "I think there would be enough entertainment value in such a poetico-music evening," Duke seamlessly metamorphosed the Litfund evening of poetry into a Duke-centered event.

Attesting to Duke's willpower, the inaugural Litfund/Radio Liberty evening not only went on as planned, but would begin a long affiliation between the two organizations.[75] From finding performers to conceiving the program themes to coordinating the recording details, the Litfund/Radio Liberty collaboration presented a fitting venue for Duke's seemingly limitless drive. Perhaps most useful for the composer, the Litfund series for Radio Liberty allowed Duke to feature music otherwise seldom played (if at all) in American concert halls, in this respect paralleling his endeavors as founder and president of the Society for Forgotten Music. For his programs, Duke went to great lengths to first identify little-known Soviet and Russian émigré composers of quality and then to locate scores of their works, an undertaking Valerio cleverly dubbed "Operation-Note-Search" ("*noty*" being the Russian word for "score").[76] It was through these efforts that listeners in the Soviet Union heard excerpts from Nicolas Nabokov's ballet-oratorio *Ode*, Alexei Haieff's "*Ekho kolybel'noi* [Echo from the Lullaby]," and the haunting "Chinese Song" by Alexander Cherepnin.

Duke naturally included the works of Dukelsky in these concerts, showcasing among other pieces selections from his cool *Parisian Suite*, which combined Prokofiev's athleticism with dreamy Ravel-like harmonies and the Anglophone songs from his "American Series." One work for which Duke particularly advocated was his Lermontov song cycle. Completed in late 1964, the cycle consists of six pieces set to the poetry of Mikhail Lermontov. Rather than choose some of Lermontov's better-known poems, Duke instead selected works more obscure and idiosyncratic in their content, claiming to choose pieces that illustrated the lyricism of the poet's prose. The set includes, for example, the erotic "*Stansy*" (1829), which details the narrator's joy as he watches his lover flush and sigh in ecstasy, and the misogynist-toned "*K glupoi krasavitse* [To the Stupid Beauty]" that begins with the words:

Toboi pleniatsia izdali	To admire you from a distance
Moe vse zrenie gotovo,	My eyes are fully ready,
No slyshat' bozhe sokhrani,	But, God forbid, that I am forced to hear
Mne ot tebia odno khot' slovo.	Just one word uttered from your mouth.

Duke's settings of these poems further their idiosyncratic impression, as the atonal sounds present a seemingly jarring contrast to the more classically situated literary figure.[77] Although Duke interweaves traces of tonality throughout the works, the overall feeling is one of atonality, with no clear tonal center and frequently clashing vocal and piano parts. The pieces are also interjected with moments of humor, such as the conspicuously conventional tonic chord ending the otherwise atonal "*K glupoi krasavitse*" and the burlesquelike waltz that opens the third piece of the cycle, "*K drugu.*"

Perhaps prompted by Duke's modern, even cheeky, setting of the classical author's poetry, Valerio stressed the strong potential appeal of the work for broadcasting to the Soviet Union. In a letter from December 23, 1964, Valerio writes: "I'm anxious to *depart from the routine meat-and-potatoes programs to do something really startling* for Radio Liberty. Therefore, I was anxious to talk to you about your Lermontov cycle" (emphasis added). Preceded by a paragraph regarding Duke's "*Pora domoi,*" one can interpret Valerio's statement as one typical of Cold War discourses that privilege classical, and especially atonal, music as a means of promoting democracy.[78] In particular, the "indecorousness" and "flouting of conventions" associated with modern, avant-garde music that could be applied to Duke's Lermontov cycle signaled freedom to listeners, especially in contrast to the Socialist Realist music that predominated in the very geographic regions targeted by Radio Liberty.[79] Danielle Folser-Lussier underscores the correlation between avant-garde music and the notion of "freedom" among listeners in the Eastern bloc: "In Eastern Europe, where avant-garde music was long the subject of diatribes and occasional state-ordered suppression, US officials could use this music to challenge socialist musical standards and to connect with listeners, particularly young people, who wanted alternatives to socialist realism. . . . As a result of previous suppression, [avant-garde music and jazz] had acquired an appealing association with freedom that remained potent even after the music had begun to become officially acceptable again."[80]

Although Valerio's statement about Duke's Lermontov cycle coincides with and may have been informed by prevailing Cold War ideology, approaching it more locally reveals the added complexities of personal motivation at play in the programming of Duke's song cycle. When it came to Radio Liberty programming, Valerio and Duke constantly discussed and negotiated, engaging in a dance of epistolary exchanges in which the two men simultaneously strove for delicacy and efficacy. With regard to Duke's Lermontov cycle specifically, the exchange reveals a particularly carefully crafted mediation. The first mention of the cycle occurs in December 1964, with Valerio writing: "I sense you must be angry because you've written music for possible use over Radio Liberty and didn't let me know."[81] Valerio's words seem to present a gracious backpedaling, as if to remedy a potentially awkward rejection of Duke's work.

Perhaps as a means of saving face, Duke immediately responded: "I am certainly not angry on account of my Lermontov songs not being taped by Radio Liberty. This, frankly, never entered my mind."[82] Yet Duke's ever-shrewd manner comes through even in the face of rejection, for later in the letter he informs Valerio of his completion of the Lermontov cycle and plugs the idea of recording the work for Radio Liberty with soprano Irina Nikolai, a "young and attractive Ukrainian girl," suggesting Valerio pay the singer fifty dollars for recording Duke's cycle. It was to this series of exchanges that Valerio responded with his note about recording something "startling" for Radio Liberty—framing the use of the song cycle as his own innovative idea, perhaps as a means of preserving the relationship.

Did Duke win this exchange? Perhaps temporarily, he did, for Nikolai was paid and the pieces were recorded. Yet, it is not evident whether Duke's Lermontov cycle was ever aired by Radio Liberty. Almost as if admitting his guilt, Valerio began buying time immediately after expressing interest in the Lermontov project, once again seemingly veiling his agenda under a cloak of political rhetoric: "Inasmuch as you are going to be tied up with other commitments for a while, I will have a chance to plan the [Lermontov] project so we take advantage of the breaks in timing, cultural events in the USSR, best propagation time of the year (early autumn) and a number of other factors that increase the chance for success."[83]

By June of the following year, Duke was still waiting for Valerio's reaction to the work, to which Valerio responded with the following evasive statement: "A review from me is meaningless. It's like asking your public relations consultant for a character reference. I am convinced that someday, through Vernon Duke, Radio Liberty will do something big in terms of nudging the course of events in the USSR one bloody millimeter toward greater cultural diversity and artistic freedom."[84]

Whether Valerio attempted to merely appease Duke with his statements or whether his words reflect his belief in Duke's efficacy in reaching Radio Liberty's goals, Duke seemed to faithfully adhere to Radio Liberty's objectives as laid out to him by Valerio: "All Radio Liberty is interested in doing is to inform its listeners of the cultural heritage and activities of former Russians now living in the US. . . . If we can broadcast a program which showcases the quality of the cultural contribution that former Russian citizens have made and continue to make, if we can give some hint of the talent they possess, then we are filling in some of the omissions in the Soviet media."[85] By showcasing the poetry and music of Russians in the emigration, Duke promoted the notion of a lively cultural milieu existing beyond Russia's borders. The June 11, 1966 Litfund program, for example, featured Soviet Estrada singer Vladimir Malinin performing songs by Duke as well as pieces that align more closely with the underground bard music then popular in the Soviet Union. Accompanied by a guitarist from Carmen Miranda's Los Angeles–based Brazilian band, Malinin sung, for example, the cool bossa nova, "*Popugai* [Parrot]," to the sharp-witted lyrics of Radio Liberty satirist and Soviet dissident, Leonid Pylaev.

In introducing Litfund's programs, moreover, Duke engaged in the type of subtle propaganda for which Radio Liberty writers strove. In introducing the "Chinese Song" of Cherepnin on the "Poetry and Music of the Emigration" program, for example, Duke underscores the commonality between Russians at home and in the diaspora, noting that, an "unquestionable Russianness" permeates the piece and that "*Kak ne kak, a russkimi ostalis' my vse* [No matter how you slice it, but Russians all of us remain]."[86] Likewise, Duke utilized his ever-sharp wit in getting his points across. In his introductory remarks for "New Voices of Russian Poetry and Music," for example, Duke criticizes the Soviet musical system for keeping the works of its young composers away from Western stages. Instead of using pedantic language, however, Duke employs a clever pun in blaming the lack of variety in Soviet music on then Secretary of Union of Soviet Composers Tikhon Khrennikov, exclaiming, "*delo pakhnit Khrennikom* [In a word, the entire outfit smells of Khrennikov]" (whose root, "*khren,*" means "horseradish" and is also slang for "old fogey").[87]

Duke's nuanced approach to the Litfund programs was exactly the kind of soft power in which Valerio hoped to engage through Radio Liberty's broadcasting. In response to the evening of new Russian works, for example, Valerio wrote: "Coming at this particular time when US-USSR relations are undergoing new strains, such an evening proves that there are still some areas left for meaningful exploration and that it is not necessary to judge every single activity in terms of Viet Nam. The Litfund shows scored a subtle propaganda point especially after the Soviets cancelled the track meet in L.A.—a propaganda disaster."[88] Referring to the sudden boycott in 1966 by the Soviet Union of the annual US-USSR track and field competition in protest of US involvement in Vietnam, Valerio underscores the quiet potency of broadcasting internal culture.[89] Indeed, Litfund's programs presented a far cry from the sports arena, introducing Radio Liberty listeners to little-known, underground, and even oppositional Russian artists in programs presented by thoughtful and intelligent émigrés who had rejected the Soviet Union and were now living beyond its borders. The "knowledgeable-guest-in-the-living-room"[90] feel that Radio Liberty strove to convey in its broadcasts, moreover, stands as an example of the "human connections" that Danielle Fosler-Lussier posits as being the "essence" of soft power.[91]

Yet, for all of the work Duke undertook for molding Litfund programs to satisfy the needs of Radio Liberty, it was only in his next and final project for Valerio that Duke reached the pinnacle of his work for the Cold War radio station.

"Beaming Broadway": Radio Liberty's Musicomedy Series

"Diksilendskii regtaim marsh [Dixieland Ragtime March]"—with these words, Vernon Duke transformed Irving Berlin's "Alexander's Ragtime Band" into a song he saw fit for Soviet consumption. Thinking the original reference to "Alexander" too confusing for the Russian listener, Duke shifted the well-known ragtime march to the realm of "Dixieland" rather than a figure radio listeners might associate with Russia's former Imperial regime.

The Duke-Berlin amalgam was just one of nearly seventy American show tunes that Duke set to Russian for Radio Liberty over the course of two years. First broadcast on October 3, 1966, the "Fifty Years of American Musical Comedy" series (or "Musicomedy" as it was referred to by Duke and Valerio), was conceived by Duke to present listeners in the Soviet Union with a history of American musical comedy, beginning with the life and works of Sigmund Romberg and featuring such notable songwriters as Jerome Kern, Cole Porter, and Frank Loesser. As part of this gargantuan task, Duke wrote the scripts, played the piano, and translated and set more than sixty tunes to Russian.

Seeking to "preserve the spirit of the original while also making the themes comprehensible for Russian listeners," Duke changed American standards into tunes that would make sense both rhythmically and thematically.[92] Hence, George Gershwin's "Fascinating Rhythm" became "*Neponiatnii ritm* [Incomprehensible Rhythm]," as Duke claimed that Russian lacks the word for "fascinating."[93] Duke's own "April in Paris" morphed into "*Letom v Parizhe* [Summer in Paris]," as the accent in the Russian "*Aprel'*" falls on the second, and hence, rhythmically incorrect, syllable, and anyway, as Duke jested, "April in Paris is much too cold and rainy."[94] Rodgers and Hammerstein's "People Will Say We're in Love" became "*Liudi uznaiut o nas* [People Will Find Out about Us]."

Of the major projects Duke undertook for Radio Liberty, Musicomedy made the most of the composer's abilities. As the project relied on a flawless and reciprocal understanding of English and Russian and an insider's knowledge of the American musical, Musicomedy demanded a most unusual triptych of skills, all mastered by Duke. Hence the Duke-Dukelsky divide that seemed to all but torment the composer for most of his adult life was finally put to ideal use—his lot as a Russian émigré thrown into the domain of American show business finally reconciled and maximized.

As for the purpose of the Musicomedy series, it was to acquaint Russians with American musical comedy and to correct the notion that American tunesmiths lack the ability to write a good melody.[95] As "something new and therefore thrilling" to the Soviet listener, the American show tunes, in turn, would serve as a kind of cultural bridge between the Soviet Union and the United States.[96] Explaining that the Soviet musical remained stuck in the "Viennese light opera" style, Duke contrasted the outmoded Soviet operetta with the upbeat Broadway musical, which entailed a "verve and freshness" that would speak "directly to Russian youth."[97] According to Duke, it was not simply good melodies that would attract the Russians, but the captivating rhythms for which American tunesmiths were known that would ultimately charm the otherwise common-time listeners. In an interview regarding the project for Monitor Records, Duke points out the importance of the rhythmic element, claiming: "An American jazz tune, and especially one that probably would not be considered as such by the real New Orleans fanciers as 'Fascinating Rhythm,' which is a highly individual sort of a number, is almost unknown to the Russians. They'd find it probably difficult not only to sing, but even to play it. And yet the exhilaration of that rhythm excites them."[98]

The idea of cultural reconciliation through Broadway show tunes may have originated, as Duke claims in a write-up of the project, from Sergei Prokofiev, who allegedly suggested that his friend set a number of Gershwin tunes to Russian.[99] Yet Duke's 1955 autobiography tells another story. In this version, Duke is approached in 1929 by Soviet music critic Boris Assafiev to translate Gershwin's *Lady Be Good* and *Funny Face* with the following tantalizing proposition: "who knows, you may be instrumental in revolutionizing our entire light-music production."[100] Regardless of whether it was Prokofiev or Assafiev who first proposed the idea, Duke's reaction as he relays it in his autobiography reveals his stated views on the persuasive potential of American show tunes in conquering the Soviet enterprise: "I felt that no better anti-Soviet propaganda could be imagined than a big, healthy dose of Gershwin music, and all the good American things it stands for."[101] Although Duke otherwise writes very little about musical propaganda in his autobiography, this episode reveals that kernels of Duke's Musicomedy idea had been germinating since at least 1955, if not the late 1920s.

By the time Musicomedy was broadcast by Radio Liberty, Duke was not alone in his conviction of the potential of Broadway show tunes for battling communism. By this time, the US State Department had reluctantly recognized the benefit of using excerpts of musical comedies in their Cultural Presentation programs to provide the necessary entertainment value and thus broad appeal alongside pieces that were deemed more serious and therefore more prestigious than their lighter counterparts.[102] Soviet audiences had also demonstrated their adoration of the American musical, with sold-out performances of *My Fair Lady* in Moscow, Leningrad, and Kiev in the show's 1960 run. A Russian language version of the musical even appeared as early as 1959, perhaps priming Russian listeners for pieces like Duke's "*Tovo i zhdi poidut dozhdi v Ispanii*" (i.e., The Rain in Spain).[103] Although the official production of *My Fair Lady* would not be put on until 1964, the American Embassy in the Soviet Union fully supported the unofficial undertaking, noting that the show greatly helped promote the idea of "a vital, many-sided, free, expressive and multi-talented force, which is part of our way of life."[104] Although more controversial among State Department circles because of its depiction of ethnic tension and urban life, *West Side Story* also produced a sensation, its 1959 unofficial performance practically devoid of music and dancing yet devoured by Soviet audiences.[105]

With the persuasive potential of Broadway show tunes established and the Soviet audience ripe for the taking, it is little wonder that Valerio responded so enthusiastically to Duke's project of "beaming Broadway" through the Iron Curtain. In response to Duke's first set of scripts, Valerio writes: "Vernon, I think we're on to a real hot series. You are really delivering the goods."[106] The emphatic sentiment is conveyed not only by Valerio's words but also by Valerio's addressing Duke by his first name in the body of the letter, something that rarely occurred within their correspondence. Merely two days later, Valerio exclaimed, "The way it is shaping up I believe the series will be a Radio Liberty cultural milestone."[107] Valerio's continued and eager enthusiasm for Musicomedy would surpass that of any other project Duke undertook for Radio Liberty.

Yet for all of its potential for furthering Radio Liberty's objectives and the apparent ease with which Duke tackled the demanding project, Musicomedy was not able to escape the fallout of the ongoing give and take between Duke's personal goals and the institutional aims of Radio Liberty. For one thing, Duke continued to use non-Russian singers in recording the Russian renditions of the Broadway tunes. Although Duke used Vladimir Malinin, the "Soviet Vic Damone," for the primary parts (a choice that Valerio deemed to be "perfect"), he shortly introduced the idea of using his wife, Kay, and American tenor Arthur Ross-Jones, to sing several selections (duets with Malinin, in the case of Kay). In a delicate style of rescinding similar to his approach to the Lermontov matter, Valerio soon responded with the following words: "We at Radio Liberty have long sought to project the knowledgeable-guest-in-the-living-room concept. I believe we will demonstrate this concept with all of its ramifications for the first time. And I'm afraid if the duet device becomes a feature it may get a bit crowded AT THE PIANO [pun on the series name, all caps in original]."[108] The following month, Valerio wrote Duke with an appeal more emphatic and direct: "I'm afraid I've failed to make clear a point of policy. The sustaining . . . series U Royalya ["At the Piano," the formal name for Musicomedy] differs considerably from an occasional Litfund program. But it is precisely this degree of Russian-ness in the former that sets us apart from the Voice of America, the BBC, or Vatican Radio. So whereas Kay and Ross-Jones are great in a semi-annual Litfund show, we do run the risk of aggravating some 'inside' problems concerning the image of our sustaining shows."[109] Valerio and Duke spent the course of the next month arguing over the matter, Duke countering Valerio's reprimand asking, "just *where* this 'degree of Russian-ness' will be harmed or jeopardized" by using Kay, whose Russian "when singing, is certainly adequate."[110] The situation was resolved in a manner similar to that of the Lermontov episode: after Valerio and Duke both asserted their positions, they agreed to a compromise, with Duke omitting one of the two duets and the series proceeding as planned.

Beyond trying to convince Soviet listeners of the appeal of American values and way of life through strands of *"Khalo Dolli* [Hello, Dolly]" and other Broadway songs, Musicomedy also served a function that targeted the very genre that it engaged: the beaming of show tunes was to pressure the Soviet Union to recognize international copyright laws. As one project in a long line of attempts to compel the Soviet Union to recognize foreign copyrights, the Musicomedy series was intended to pressure the Soviet Union to ratify the 1886 Berne Convention by raising public awareness of the lack of compensation for foreign songwriters for Soviet performances of their works, while Soviet counterparts enjoyed the benefit of royalties when their works were performed abroad.[111] Duke used the publicity for Musicomedy to underscore the duplicitous nature of the situation, noting that, "What's good for the composer of 'Moscow Nights' should also be good for the composer of 'Night and Day.'"[112] By December 1967, Valerio pushed the connection between Musicomedy and Soviet copyright policy, giving Duke specific instructions to present this angle in subsequent interviews about the project.[113]

This kind of public awareness campaign was precisely the type of work believed to hold the most potential in convincing the Soviet Union to recognize international copyright laws. An article published in the *Duke Law Journal* in 1965, for example, notes, "The focusing of greater publicity on the immorality of the Soviet position on international copyright apparently offers the best hope for change. Those in the best position to create such publicity are foreign government officials, persons engaged in cultural missions to the USSR and, most important of all, authors whose works have been pirated by the Soviets."[114] Duke's position as a recognized songwriter and public figure hence maximized his potential in furthering the copyright cause.

The entire Musicomedy project, however, rested on a fundamental contradiction, for the translation and broadcasting of the Musicomedy songs were conducted without the knowledge and, presumably consent, of the original composers and lyricists. Repeatedly asking Valerio to publicize his efforts, Duke expressed his discomfort in the endeavor: "I find it extraordinarily trying to perform a gargantuan and *valuable time-consuming* job without it being known to and approved by ASCAP and my fellow members. . . . I don't like being [a candidate for the ASCAP Board of Directors] while anonymously carrying on with my R. L. activities *directly involved* with the output of my fellow ASCAP members" (emphasis in original).[115]

Duke can hardly be implicated for his illegal entanglements, for Valerio's broad application of fair play was but one of a longer series of occasions in which those implementing American ideals in the Soviet Union turned a blind eye toward copyright infringement. With regard to Broadway shows in particular, such egregious disregard is evident as early as 1960, when the American consul championed the unofficial production of *My Fair Lady* in the name of US-Soviet goodwill.[116] Although the Soviet Union never paid royalties for the production, the enthusiastic tone of the American embassy's dispatch report suggests that the United States government was more than willing to overlook the copyright infringement, a point that is made further evident by the continued illegal American productions of *My Fair Lady* and *West Side Story* until their official Soviet tours in 1964.[117]

Conclusion

Vernon Duke's four-year engagement with Radio Liberty reveals much about the underlying dynamics of the United States Cold War propaganda efforts. We see the tension between praxis and ideology play out within local contexts (as represented by the constant negotiating between Duke and Valerio) and on the broader plane of Cold War tactics (America's overlooking of Soviet copyright infringement, for example). Peeping out from behind the grand narrative of anticommunism that informed Cold War rhetoric and the Russian émigré diaspora, the self-serving aspect of Cold War efforts specifically suggests that the umbrella of "Western values" championed by cold warriors was upheld by a multitude of more prosaic spokes. Within this constellation of power plays, music emerges not only as an instrument of ideology, vacillating, as Danielle Fosler-Lussier asserts, between operating as "information propaganda" and "nonpolitical human contact," but also as a tool for actualizing highly practical, individualist acts.[118]

The case of Vernon Duke demonstrates the messy, often tangled motivations at play in Cold War efforts. While Duke clearly sought recognition and a performance venue for his compositions through his Radio Liberty connection, he also shared the ideological goal of fighting the Soviet Union. Indeed, his secretary of the time, Asta Aristova, notes the extent to which Duke valued and took pride in his work with Radio Liberty, which she describes as being spurred by his ardent anticommunism and his fervent love of Russian culture, a point only reinforced by his monetary donations to the organization.[119] Duke responded to the specific task of writing an appealing pop tune that would rouse Soviet citizens to pressure their government to ease travel restrictions. The Litfund concerts organized by Duke and on which he showcased many of his compositions present the image of a lively, creative milieu of Russian émigrés, thereby suggesting a viable, diasporic alternative to Soviet Russia. Finally, the dozens of show tunes Duke translated, set, and performed for the Musicomedy series convey the appeal of the American way of life as well as serve to point out the unfair nature of the Soviet approach to international copyright laws.

On January 20, 1969, not a month since the last correspondence between Duke and Valerio had transpired, Radio Liberty's Munich Headquarters sent an urgent telegraph to its New York branch. In the place of the regular broadcast, "On Musical Themes," the New York office was to air the obituary of the late Vernon Duke, whose sudden death during an operation for lung cancer shocked his "many friends and admirers" at Radio Liberty. A handwritten note on the telegraph from Joe Valerio to Duke's widow furthered the sentiment and formally ended the correspondence between him and the spirited composer: "Dear Kay, I think this speaks for itself. Joe V."[120]

Duke's death coincided with the beginning of the unraveling of the myth of a privately funded Cold War radio station. Almost exactly two years to the day of Duke's death, the CIA's hand in funding Radio Liberty was fully and publicly disclosed, leading its executives to scramble to keep the organization in existence. Not only did they succeed in keeping Radio Liberty functioning, but ultimately, after more than thirty years, the organization played a primary role in bringing about the collapse of the Soviet regime. An exploration of the intimate history behind this effort discloses Duke's contribution and place in this endeavor, demonstrating the confluence of personal and institutional agendas at work behind the disembodied émigré voice echoing through the vast ether of the abandoned but never forgotten homeland: "*Govorit Radio Svoboda* [Radio Liberty is speaking]."

Notes

1. Michelangelo Capua, *Yul Brynner: A Biography* (Jefferson, NC: McFarland and Company, Inc., 2006), 16.

2. Concert Program for The Cappella Russian Male Chorus, May 26, 1956, Box 6, Christ the Savior Papers, The Archives of the Orthodox Church in America, Syosset, New York.

3. Vincent Giroud, *Nicolas Nabokov: A Life in Freedom and Music* (Oxford: Oxford University Press, 2015), 120–121, 168.

4. Nicolas Nabokov, quoted in Giroud, *Nicolas Nabokov*, 106.

5. Danielle Fosler-Lussier, "Instruments of Diplomacy: Writing Music into the History of Cold War International Relations," in *Music and International History in the Twentieth Century*, edited by Jessica C. E. Gienow-Hecht (New York: Berghahn Books, 2015), 122.

6. Ibid., 119.

7. Peter J. Schmelz, "Intimate Histories of the Musical Cold War: Fred Prieberg and Igor Blazhkov's Unofficial Diplomacy," in *Music and International History in the Twentieth Century*, edited by Jessica C. E. Gienow-Hecht (New York: Berghahn Books, 2015), 192.

8. Two notable exceptions are Simo Mikonnen's study of early American efforts to recruit Soviet émigrés for anti-Bolshevik work [Simo Mikkonen, "Exploiting the Exiles: Soviet Émigrés in U.S. Cold War Strategy," *Journal of Cold War Studies*, 14, no. 2 (Spring 2012): 98–127] and Vincent Giroud's recent work on Nicolas Nabokov [Giroud, *Nicolas Nabokov*]. See also Benjamin Tromly, "The Making of a Myth: The National Labor Alliance, Russian Émigrés, and Cold War Intelligence Activities," *Journal of Cold War Studies*, 18, no. 1 (Winter 2016): 80–111.

9. Vernon Duke, *Passport to Paris* (Boston: Little, Brown, and Company, 1955), 77.

10. Ibid., 78.

11. Ibid., 77.

12. For a detailed look at the relationship between Dukelsky's popular and classical styles, see Aaron Ziegel, "One person, one music: Reconsidering the Duke-Dukelsky Musical Style," *American Music* 28, no. 3 (Fall 2010): 320–345.

13. Duke, *Passport to Paris*, 85.

14. Ibid., 87.

15. Ibid., 90.

16. Ibid., 103.

17. Ibid., 121, 123.

18. Ibid., 130.

19. Vernon Duke, "The History of an Effort—The Society for Forgotten Music," *Downbeat Magazine* (August 1959), 29.

20. Scott Holden, "The 'Adventures and Battles' of Vladimir Dukelsky (a.k.a. Vernon Duke)," *American Music* 28, no. 3 (Fall 2010): 316.

21. Duke, *Passport to Paris*, 92.

22. Curiously, Duke's comment about returning to Russia in response to a Radio Liberty staffer's facetious quip of "*Zima v moskve* [Winter in Moscow]" was edited out of the final version. Reel #17 ("Interview with Vernon Duke") and Reel #44 ("Victoria Monditch interview with Vernon Duke"), Vernon Duke Collection, Music Division, Library of Congress, Washington, DC [hereafter, "Vernon Duke Collection"].

23. Joe Valerio to Vernon Duke, September 7, 1966, "Radio Liberty Correspondence (English)," Box 128, Vernon Duke Collection.

24. Gene Sosin, *Sparks of Liberty: An Insider's Memoir of Radio Liberty* (University Park: The Pennsylvania State University Press, 1999), 1; Radio Liberty [http://www.rferl.org/info/history/133.html], accessed May 23, 2016.

25. For an excellent discussion of the creation and early development of Amcomlib, see Mikkonen, "Exploiting the Exiles."

26. Sosin, *Sparks of Liberty*, 8.

27. Ibid., 50.

28. Radio Liberty [http://www.rferl.org/info/history/133.html], accessed May 23, 2016; Simo Mikkonen, "Radio Liberty—The Enemy Within?: Disseminating Western Values through U.S. Cold War Broadcasts," in *Europe – Evropa: Crosscultural Dialogues between the West, Russia and Southeastern Europe*, edited by Juhani Nuorluoto and Maija Könönen (Uppsala, Sweden: Uppsala University, 2010), 245.

29. Sosin, *Sparks of Liberty*, 2; Mikkonen, "Exploiting the Exiles," 107, 122.

30. Debra Spitulnik, "Anthropology and Mass Media," *Annual Review of Anthropology* 22 (October 1993): 294.

31. Faye Ginsburg, "Radio Fields: An Afterword," in *Radio Fields: Anthropology and Wireless Sound in the Twenty-First Century*, edited by Lucas Bessire and Daniel Fisher (New York: New York University Press, 2012), 269.

32. Frantz Fanon, "This Is the Voice of Algeria," in *The Sound Studies Reader*, edited by Jonathan Sterne (New York: Routledge, 2012), 333.

33. Michele Hilmes and Jason Loviglio, "Introduction," in *Radio Reader: Essays in the Cultural History of the Radio*, edited by Michele Hilmes and Jason Loviglio (New York: Routledge, 2002), xiii.

34. The physical distance of Radio Liberty's broadcasters from the Soviet Union provided relative, though not absolute, safety, as Soviet agents infiltrated Radio Liberty, in some cases threatening and even murdering its employees [see, for example, James Critchlow, "Moscow Strikes Back," in *Radio Hole-in-the-Head: RL: An Insider's Story of Cold War Broadcasting* (Washington, DC: The American University Press, 1995), 55–67].

35. Steven Feld, Aaron A. Fox, Thomas Porcello, and David Samuels, "Vocal Anthropology: From the Music of Language to the Language of Song," in *A Companion to Linguistic Anthropology*, edited by Alessandro Duranti (Malden, MA: Blackwell, 2004), 340.

36. Lucas Bessire and Daniel Fisher, "Introduction," in *Radio Fields: Anthropology and Wireless Sound in the Twenty-First Century*, edited by Lucas Bessire and Daniel Fisher (New York: New York University Press, 2012), 10.

37. Sosin, *Sparks of Liberty*, 39.

38. Critchlow, *Radio Hole-in-the-Head*, 14.

39. Ibid.

40. David F. Krugler, *The Voice of America and the Domestic Propaganda Battles, 1945–1953* (Columbia: University of Missouri Press, 2000), 49, 159.

41. "Radio Liberty (Radio Svoboda) Russian Broadcast Recordings," Vera and Donald Blinken Open Society Archives, Central European University [http://www.osaarchivum.org/digital-repository/osa:89898864–78b7–4cf9–b4f7–aaf218f85599], accessed June 6, 2016.

42. Sosin, *Sparks of Liberty*, 101.

43. For more on Soviet bard musicians, see, for example, J. Martin Daughtry, "'Sonic Samizdat': Situating Unofficial Recording in the Post-Stalinist Soviet Union," *Poetics Today* 30, no. 1 (2009): 27–65; Vladimir Frumkin, *Pevtsy i vozhdi* [Singers and Leaders] (Nizhnii Novgorod: Dekom, 1995).

44. The music was smuggled out of the Soviet Union by members of the Benny Goodman ensemble during their 1962 tour. The use of forbidden Russian music on an unofficial radio station acquired through an official US-sponsored music tour presents a compelling intersection of official and unofficial uses of music in Cold War programming.

45. On the significance of Conover's voice with regard to influencing listeners, see Rüdiger Ritter, "Broadcasting Jazz into the Eastern Bloc—Cold War Weapon or Cultural Exchange? The Example of Willis Conover," *Jazz Perspectives* 7, no. 2 (2013): 117.

46. Sosin, *Sparks of Liberty*, 103.

47. From here forward, I address Dukelsky as Duke to remain consistent with the name by which he was referred at Radio Liberty from 1964 onward.

48. Unmarked, undated press release, "Radio Liberty Correspondence (English)," Box 128, Vernon Duke Collection.

49. Valerio to Duke, March 20, 1964, "Radio Liberty Correspondence (English)," Box 128, Vernon Duke Collection.

50. Ibid.

51. Reel #47, "Interview," Vernon Duke Collection.

52. Strategies used by Radio Liberty to determine its listenership included enticing listeners to request free programming booklets, asking for fan and hate mail, and discreetly discussing Radio Liberty with tourists from the Soviet Union. In addition to strategies reflected in individual Radio Liberty broadcasts, see also Sosin, *Sparks of Liberty*, 38–39; Critchlow, *Radio Hole-in-the-Head*, 99–112.

53. Valerio to Duke, February 19, 1964, "Radio Liberty Correspondence (English)," Box 128, Vernon Duke Collection.

54. To create an American-friendly version of "*Pora domoi*," Valerio insisted on the involvement of American poet Ogden Nash (1902–1971) in devising an English translation of Duke's lyrics.

55. Valerio to Duke, March 9, 1964, "Radio Liberty Correspondence (English)," Box 128, Vernon Duke Collection.

56. Original Russian text from "Evgenii Evtushenko: Stikhi," http://www.evtushenko .poet-premium.ru/stihi.html [accessed February 20, 2017].

57. Valerio to Duke, March 9, 1964, "Radio Liberty Correspondence (English)," Box 128, Vernon Duke Collection.

58. "Radio Liberty Clippings (English)," Box 128, Vernon Duke Collection.

59. Sosin, *Sparks of Liberty*, 103.

60. Unmarked press release, "Radio Liberty Correspondence (English)," Box 128, Vernon Duke Collection.

61. Valerio to Duke, February 19, 1964, "Radio Liberty Correspondence (English)," Box 128, Vernon Duke Collection.

62. Valerio to Duke, December 23, 1964, "Radio Liberty Correspondence (English)," Box 128, Vernon Duke Collection.

63. Duke to Valerio, February 23, 1964, "Radio Liberty Correspondence (English)," Box 128, Vernon Duke Collection.

64. Valerio to Duke, March 20, 1964, "Radio Liberty Correspondence (English)," Box 128, Vernon Duke Collection.

65. These blurbs appear in such magazines as *Music Business* (May 9, 1964) and *Hollywood Reporter* (May 29, 1964). Although Duke's publicity campaign was deemed untimely, Duke nevertheless abided by the parameters set out by Valerio in what he was and was not to discuss, including emphasizing the private ownership of the station, its goals of beaming material otherwise censored in the Soviet Union, and keeping silent about the listenership aspect of the project [Valerio to Duke, March 20, 1964, "Radio Liberty Correspondence (English)," Box 128, Vernon Duke Collection].

66. Cobina Wright, "Radio Liberty: Two Songs for the Russians" and Dale Munroe, "New Voice Gets Ear of Soviets," *Citizen News*, July 8, 1964 ["Radio Liberty Clippings (English)," Box 128, Vernon Duke Collection].

67. Duke to Valerio, June 19, 1964, "Radio Liberty Correspondence (English)," Box 128, Vernon Duke Collection.

68. Duke to Valerio, February 23, 1964, "Radio Liberty Correspondence (English)," Box 128, Vernon Duke Collection. Although Duke expresses surprise in the lack of success of the *Cabin* revival, the musical's appearance in 1964 in the midst of the civil rights era most likely would have been viewed as outdated, a point that is articulated by Howard Taubman in his review for the *New York Times* [Theater: "Cabin in the Sky," *New York Times*, January 22, 1964, 32].

69. Duke to Valerio, February 23, 1964, "Radio Liberty Correspondence (English)," Box 128, Vernon Duke Collection.

70. Duke to Valerio, April 11, 1964, "Radio Liberty Correspondence (English)," Box 128, Vernon Duke Collection.

71. Ibid.

72. Ibid.

73. Duke to Valerio, March 23, 1964, "Radio Liberty Correspondence (English)," Box 128, Vernon Duke Collection.

74. Ibid.

75. In the process of organizing the first Litfund/Radio Liberty event, Duke was also solicited to become president of the Los Angeles Litfund chapter—a point that he relays to Valerio with much surprise.

76. Valerio to Duke, June 4, 1964, "Radio Liberty Correspondence (English)," Box 128, Vernon Duke Collection.

77. For an overview of different musical settings by Russian composers of Lermontov's poetry, see Arnold McMillin, "Setting Lermontov: Some Musical Versions of the Poet's Works," *New Zealand Slavonic Journal* Vol. 43 (2009): 3–22.

78. For an excellent history of the rise between the concepts of modernism and freedom within the sphere of music in the United States, see Ian Wellens, *Music on the Frontline: Nicolas Nabokov's Struggle Against Communism and Middlebrow Culture* (Ashgate: Hants, England, 2002), especially pages 93–134. For a historiography of the association between musical style and Cold War politics, see Emily Abrams Ansari, "Musical Americanism, Cold War Consensus Culture, and the US-USSR Composers' Exchange, 1958–1960," *Musical Quarterly* 97, no. 3 (Fall 2014): 360–362.

79. Danielle Fosler-Lussier, *Music in America's Cold War Diplomacy* (Oakland: University of California Press, 2015), 32.

80. Ibid.

81. Valerio to Duke, December 4, 1964, "Radio Liberty Correspondence (English)," Box 128, Vernon Duke Collection.

82. Duke to Valerio, December 8, 1964, "Radio Liberty Correspondence (English)," Box 128, Vernon Duke Collection.

83. Valerio to Duke, December 23, 1964, "Radio Liberty Correspondence (English)," Box 128, Vernon Duke Collection.

84. Valerio to Duke, July 14, 1965, "Radio Liberty Correspondence (English)," Box 128, Vernon Duke Collection.

85. Valerio to Duke, May 5, 1964, "Radio Liberty Correspondence (English)," Box 128, Vernon Duke Collection.

86. Reel #10, "Radio Liberty Programs based on Litfund Evening of 6/11/1966," Vernon Duke Collection.

87. Reel #4, "Radio Liberty Program based on Litfund Evening of 6/11/66"; program from Box 129, Vernon Duke Collection.

88. Valerio to Duke, July 15, 1966, "Radio Liberty Correspondence (English)," Box 128, Vernon Duke Collection.

89. For more on the US-USSR track meets, see Joseph M. Turrini, "'It Was Communism Versus the Free World': The USA-USSR Dual Track Meet Series and the Development of Track and Field in the United States, 1958–1985," *Journal of Sport History* (Fall 2001): 427–471.

90. Valerio to Duke, September 7, 1966, "Radio Liberty Correspondence (English)," Box 128, Vernon Duke Collection.

91. Fosler-Lussier, *Music in America's Cold War Diplomacy*, 21.

92. Vernon Duke quoted in Stanley Green, "Beaming Broadway to the Volga," unmarked typescript, "Radio Liberty Lyrics (Russian)," Box 129, Vernon Duke Collection.

93. Reel #47, "Interview," Vernon Duke Collection.

94. Vernon Duke quoted in Stanley Green, "Beaming Broadway to the Volga," unmarked typescript, "Radio Liberty Lyrics (Russian)," Box 129, Vernon Duke Collection.

95. Vernon Duke, "Talks at the Keyboard (50 Years of American Musical Comedy)," "Radio Liberty Miscellaneous (English)," Box 129, Vernon Duke Collection.

96. Recording of Duke's interview with Charlie Holmes (Monitor Records), Reel #47, "Interview," Vernon Duke Collection.

97. Duke quoted in Green, "Beaming Broadway to the Volga."

98. Reel #47, "Interview," Vernon Duke Collection.

99. Duke, "Talks at the Keyboard."

100. Duke, *Passport to Paris*, 218.

101. Ibid.

102. Fosler-Lussier, *Music in America's Cold War Diplomacy*, 37.

103. "Russians Ask for *My Fair Lady*," *The Age*, May 7, 1959, 10.

104. Edward L. Freers, "Despatch from the Embassy in the Soviet Union to the Department of State," July 18, 1960, Office of the Historian, US Department of State website [https://history.state.gov/historicaldocuments/frus1958–60v10p2/d29#fn:1.3.3.1.4.45.4.5], accessed July 1, 2016.

105. Elizabeth A. Wells, *West Side Story: Cultural Perspectives on an American Musical* (Lanham, MD: The Scarecrow Press, Inc., 2011), 226.

106. Valerio to Duke, June 3, 1966, "Radio Liberty Correspondence (English)," Box 128, Vernon Duke Collection.

107. Valerio to Duke, June 8, 1966, "Radio Liberty Correspondence (English)," Box 128, Vernon Duke Collection.

108. Valerio to Duke, September 7, 1966, "Radio Liberty Correspondence (English)," Box 128, Vernon Duke Collection.

109. Valerio to Duke, October 7, 1966, "Radio Liberty Correspondence (English)," Box 128, Vernon Duke Collection.

110. Duke to Valerio, October 12, 1966, "Radio Liberty Correspondence (English)," Box 128, Vernon Duke Collection.

111. Allan P. Cramer, "International Copyright and the Soviet Union," *Duke Law Journal* 1965, no. 3 (Summer 1965): 536–539.

112. Duke quoted in Stanley Green, "The New Russian Hit Parade," August 26, 1967, "Radio Liberty Lyrics (Russian)," Box 129, Vernon Duke Collection.

113. Valerio to Duke, December 7, 1967, "Radio Liberty Correspondence (English)," Box 129, Vernon Duke Collection.

114. Cramer, "International Copyright," 544.

115. Duke to Valerio, January 27, 1967, "Radio Liberty Correspondence (English)," Box 129, Vernon Duke Collection.

116. Freers, "Despatch from the Embassy in the Soviet Union." For further contemporary views on the impact of cultural exchange (including productions of *My Fair Lady*) on US-Soviet goodwill, see Stephen S. Rosenfeld, "Soviet-American Exchanges—Tit-for-Tat Goodwill," *Science* 143, no. 3613 (March 27, 1964): 1413–1417.

117. Wells, *West Side Story*, 226–227.

118. Folser-Lussier, *Music in America's Cold War Diplomacy*, 12.

119. Asta Aristova, telephone interview with author, July 25, 2016.

120. Telegraph to Kay McCracken, "Radio Liberty Lyrics (Russian)," Box 129, Vernon Duke Collection.

5

OLD RUSSIA AT THE PIERRE

Music, Enchantment, and the Dancing Body in Twenty-First Century New York

MAY 2016. NEARLY A CENTURY HAS PASSED SINCE the Bolshevik Revolution of 1917 and subsequent civil war shattered the society of Imperial Russia, bringing White Russian émigrés to Harlem. More than twenty years have elapsed since military trucks rolled into Red Square, signaling the beginning of the end of the Soviet Union, and with it the disappearance of the raison d'être of the First Wave Russian emigration. Radio Liberty, while still in existence, has broadened its scope to include the Middle East and South Asia. Russian Harlem has disappeared, the descendants of its original members scattered along the suburbs of Long Island, New Jersey, and Westchester County. Vernon Duke, Sergei Prokofiev, and Sergei Rachmaninoff—musicians who experienced life in Russia as it existed before the Bolshevik Revolution and who played an active role in Russia Abroad—are now, outside of their music, only the stuff of books.

And yet, the guests continue to trickle in to the opulent Pierre Hotel, its beautiful stone façade facing Central Park on an upscale stretch of Fifth Avenue. The event: the thirty-seventh annual ball of the Russian Nobility Association (RNA), an organization originally founded in New York in 1933 to raise money for the Russian émigrés who had come to the United States after fleeing Bolshevik Russia. I am nervous, as I stand at the entrance to the ballroom, watching men in tuxedos and women in full-length gowns walk by. One man in particular catches my attention—he is impeccably dressed, with a large medal dangling on a black sash around his neck and white mustache pomaded to a perfect point at each tip. As I enter the hall, I hear the canned sounds of a cover of "The Way You Do the Things

You Do," followed by the orchestra playing a restrained version of the Russian gypsy classic, "*Ochi chernye* [Dark Eyes]."

Although I do not know them by face, an earlier interview with one of the RNA board members alerted me to the presence of descendants of the Romanoff family and other Russian noble families—a group whose predecessors helped make up the post-Bolshevik "First Wave" emigration. After I speak with a number of guests, it is clear that this RNA Ball, similar to other Russian balls I have attended in my fieldwork, likewise includes Russians from more recent emigration waves, as well as American socialites, eager to catch a glimpse of Russian nobility, fulfill a philanthropic obligation for their companies, or simply interested in having an elegant evening on the town.

The $450 dinner tickets, available by invitation only, assure at least the semblance of exclusivity. Crystal chandeliers twinkle high above the guests, while candles shed a soft glow among the arrangements of roses and lilies standing like graceful flamingos within the tall crystal vases on each table. A large flag bearing the imposing double-headed eagle, the insignia of Tsarist Russia, hangs prominently over the dance floor. The orchestra soon begins to play the tango, "*Utemlenye solntsem* [Exhausted by the Sun]," at which point the guests descend onto the dance floor in full force.

American businessmen, children of today's globetrotting Russians, and descendants of yesterday's aristocrats dancing side by side to a Stalin-era classic (originally a 1930s Polish dance tune) all under the aegis of the Imperial eagle—Russia Abroad today is in no way a less complex cultural phenomenon than it was in the 1920s. Nearly a century after Russian Harlem was established by destitute exiles, New York's First Wave Russian scene continues to exist, despite an ever-increasing fracturing of its meaning and connection to the prerevolutionary Russian homeland. This chapter examines the ways a mythologized, prerevolutionary "Old Russia" that had once been central to defining the First Wave Russian diaspora is enacted, performed, and represented in New York today. Focusing specifically on the Russian-themed ball, this chapter explores the role of music and dance in engendering conceptions of continuities of identity and community through this seemingly anachronistic activity.

Although 1920s New York abounded with sites of cultural production organized around the idea of prerevolutionary Russia (see chap. 1 and 2), today, First Wave–related activities centering around "Old Russia" belong to one of three primary categories: balls, summer camps, and Russian

Orthodox parish events, such as weddings and pre-Lenten *maslenitsa* (Mardi Gras) celebrations. Although the means by which Old Russia is signified differs in each case, all three are centered on the body, pointing to the importance of corporeal engagement for enabling latter-generation diasporans to connect with a mythical homeland. In each setting, the somatic dimensions of enacting and engaging with cultural roots becomes evident, as the body, with its kinetic gestures, culinary tastes, and aural and vocal proclivities, engages in activities that are emotionally and socially compelling, despite the loss of most political and even linguistic markers of the historical homeland.[1]

Based on fieldwork and interviews conducted between 2007 and 2016 with guests and organizers of Russian balls in New York and Washington, DC, this chapter examines enactments of Old Russia as they occur within the context of social dance. Focusing specifically on the intersections between music, dance, and "the cultural body," this chapter explores ways in which participants at Russian-themed balls bring the trope of Old Russia to life, thus situating the dancing, listening body as a crucial signifier in performing particular iterations of Russianness.[2] Approaching the body as a site for expressing the discursive and for engaging the kinetic within the context of dance provides a framework for thinking about ways that the past as collective symbol can be enacted and experienced and of the central role of music in mediating this process.

The ball in particular presents myriad ways in which ideas of Old Russia are conveyed. Featuring people in Russian folk costumes, men with medals pinned to their chests, and ball gowns ranging from the elegant to the gaudy, New York's Russian balls fall into what Colleen McQuillen has described as zones of "sanctioned play among adults."[3] From this perspective, the ball presents a forum in which discourses surrounding Old Russia take shape through the ways participants present themselves and confer meaning through the body. As Mauro Van Acken writes in his study of the *Dabkeh* dance among Palestinians in Jordan, "[the body] expresses identity and difference; it is a public marker of status; it displays terms of identity otherwise censured or implicitly silenced."[4] Studies ranging from reconstructions of traditional Lemkos dancing to those on the Los Angeles salsa scene have looked to the dancing body for signifying extrasomatic concepts like class, gender, race, and ethnicity.[5] A study of balls in the Russian diaspora contributes to this scholarly conversation, as it explores the ways economies of class, power, and migration history are enacted and managed on the dance floor.

Simultaneously, Russian balls in New York are sites in which the body serves as a mechanism for physically experiencing the abstract notion of prerevolutionary Russia. Since Allegra Fuller Snyder first suggested dance to be a "way of knowing," a growing number of scholars have looked to the body as a means of understanding how culture is "passed down, or embodied" through dance.[6] Following this line of thought, this chapter examines dance as a kinetic enactment of and engagement with Old Russia. The ball is not only constitutive of the performing body but is a space in which one can experience a mythologized past through the act of dance, thus presenting a potent intersection of the physical and representational realms. The kinetic realm enables the dancer to come in contact with Old Russia in the smooth turn of a heel, the clasp of a waist, and the athletic demands of the traditional *kazachek* dance, gestures both mediated through and propelled by music. These balls emerge as sites in which to see, watch, hear, touch—in short, to encounter—Old Russia as it is imagined and performed in twenty-first century New York.

Ultimately, I argue that the dancing, listening body is a vehicle through which to experience the temporary enchantment on which much of the idea of the Old Russian ball rests. This is a moment whereby the representational and physical intertwine, bringing a respite from the modern disenchantment of the world so prominently asserted by Max Weber at the start of the twentieth century.[7] Indeed, such moments of "re-enchantment" like the ball serve as "exceptional events which go against (and perhaps even alter) the accepted order of things."[8] The paradoxical nature of Russian balls in New York helps enable and usher in this state of enchantment, as these sites are simultaneously entrenched in the past and acutely of the present; richly semiotic while imbued with a physicality that seemingly transcends the representational; conducive to producing feelings of ethnicity while underscoring the performativity of this endeavor. These balls fulfill multiple functions for their participants, simultaneously offering a forum for people to actively shape collectivities around ideas of Old Russia (an act of affirmation) as well as a space for a deliberate performance of Russianness (an act of demonstration or even subversion). In these instances, the line between performance and experience, nostalgia and spectacle, insider and outsider, re-creation and presentation is blurred, allowing the Russian ball to remain resonant in twenty-first century New York for the dancing, listening bodies through which its staging is performed.

Russian Balls in New York City

It was not until the White Russian emigration made its presence in New York in the early 1920s that Russian-themed balls began taking place with any regularity.[9] One of the earliest balls organized by the recent exiles was the "Russian Fair." Held in February 1922 at the Regiment Armory (Thirty-Fourth Street and Park Avenue), the Russian Fair was meant to simulate the jovial atmosphere of the Russian countryside. Guests wandered through groves of artificial trees. A traditional puppet show was performed. Waiters wearing masks of Russian literati Alexander Pushkin and Nikolai Gogol served traditional delectables. In addition to featuring a faux forest, the armory was decorated with a Russian inn (copied from a painting by Nikolai Remisoff, set designer for the *Chauve-Souris* show then taking Broadway by storm—see chap. 2) and was lined with kiosks selling traditional Russian arts and crafts.

The Russian Fair of 1922 would inaugurate what would become typical of the numerous Russian-themed balls to follow. Enticing guests with simulated encounters with a mythologized Russia (intimated through such things as Russian folk music orchestras, folktale themes, or the presence of nobility suggested by the titles of patrons and organizers featured prominently on invitations), these events have centered on creating a multisensory experience of Old Russia. This encounter with Old Russia is predicated on a self-deception that Ian MacMillen (following Oliver Harris) has described as a kind of "meaningful blindness" inherent to such moments of "fascination."[10] The enchanted setting of the ball intensifies this process, as balls are already framed by a high level of fantasy through fairytales and depictions in films, not to mention the particular place balls hold in the plots of Russian literary classics like *War and Peace*, *Anna Karenina*, and *Eugene Onegin*.

The balls, as they take place in the present day, typically begin with guests sipping cocktails to the sounds of a balalaika ensemble playing Russian folk music. Following cocktails, a silent auction takes place, during which guests place bids on such goods as amber necklaces, Russian-themed paintings, and yearlong memberships to the Faberge-filled Hillwood Museum in Washington, DC. Once guests have had a chance to consume

Russia through their eyes, hands, and pocketbooks, they are summoned to dinner (sometimes Russian-themed) that is accompanied by colorful singing and dancing, the specifics of which I describe below. The evening then culminates with dancing, which is dominated by ballroom steps (tangos, waltzes, foxtrots) and a traditional Russian dance segment.

The guests attending today's Russian balls come from a range of professional and ethnic backgrounds and attend for a variety of reasons. At the 2007 Petroushka Ball, I met a young American banker as he stood in line for a cocktail. In response to what brought him to the event, he answered that it was a "fun" way to engage in philanthropy. (The ball is affiliated with the Russian Children's Welfare Society, which today primarily donates money to orphans in Russia and presents one of the most public examples of remittance in the First Wave Russian diaspora.) At the 2016 Russian Nobility Association Ball, I encountered an exuberant visual artist from Russia who had immigrated to the United States almost twenty years earlier. When it was time for the traditional Russian dance segment, he was one of the first to dance, energetically showing off athletic moves, with a stylized touch of humor. Earlier that evening, a man in his seventies invited me to tango and told me that he "ball hops" and prefers the Petroushka to the RNA ball, as it is more "lively." The previous year, I met a descendant of Russian princes who works as an attorney in the Boston area, does not speak Russian, but who grew out his beard for the event to look "more Russian."

Although not in New York, the most unexpected encounter I experienced during my fieldwork was at the 2015 Old Russian New Year Ball, which was held that year at the Cosmos Club in Washington, DC. This serendipitous meeting involved the great-great grandson of composer Sergei Rachmaninoff (1873–1943). Although Jordan Wanamaker Javier (whose great-grandmother, Irina, was the composer's oldest daughter) did not take part in more conventional displays of Russianness, such as speaking Russian or Russian dancing, he clearly held a position of distinction at the event, as he was announced at the conclusion of a short vocal recital of Rachmaninoff's works and made his way to the center of the ballroom to the sound of enthusiastic applause. Conversing with him afterward, I learned that Jordan, although not raised speaking Russian, was forced to take piano lessons as a child and now worked as a managing partner at a successful DC-based construction firm.

The balls today also include a considerable number of descendants of First and Second Wave Russia émigrés who maintain active involvement in the institutions once founded by their grandparents and great-grandparents, including the balls themselves and parish-based Russian schools, where many learn the traditional dance steps they later showcase at the balls. As a twenty-one-year-old woman told me, she and her friends look forward to the balls as a forum to show off their dance moves, see their friends, dress up, and follow the traditions of their grandparents. As she explains, "If our grandparents hadn't started the tradition [of the ball], then it's probably not something we would do."[11]

Although Russian balls in New York today in many ways resemble their predecessors, several key changes have taken place since their inception in the 1920s. Most notably, the balls have become more inclusive and subsequently more diverse in their patronage, allowing entry to anyone able to pay the price of a ticket.[12] A descendant of First Wave Russian émigrés who came to the United States from Yugoslavia through Europe's displaced persons (DP) camps following World War II recalls the impediments in place for such recently arrived Russians as herself in attending the earlier balls. Contrasting the ease with which people attend balls today, she states: "It wasn't like, '*Davai poedim na belyi ball* [Let's just go to the White Ball]' unless you had relatives or friends who were already in that kind of [circle] . . . And to what? To hobnob with Governor Rockefeller?"[13] Underscoring the difference between Russian DPs and the Russians who had come to the United States in the 1920s, she explains:

> [You had] this group, made up of the nobility, and all these highfalutin names . . . you had these grand balls, they were the White Russian balls. . . . And I would say that the average, run-of-the-mill Russian DP, or whatever, didn't really attend those balls, they'd stay in their little—and I don't mean to belittle it, in no way, I'm just trying to show the difference—they stayed in their church hall *podval* [basement], *kakoi-to konsert v kakom-to* YMCA, *ili shto-to takoe* [some kind of concert in some kind of YMCA, or something along those lines]. A ball that really wasn't a ball, but people just got dressed up and went. . . . And those were the two different kind of worlds.

Emblematic of a deeper division between the two communities of post-Bolshevik Russian émigrés in New York (see chap. 3), the contrasting ball scenes point to a significant difference in monetary and social status, levels of insularity, and intermingling with New York elite.

Similar to the expansion of attendees, the organizers too now come from a wider range of backgrounds. While early ball organizers like Prince Serge Obolensky (m. Alice Astor) and Princess Dolly Obolensky (m. Hans Spitzer) brought much attention to the balls within New York City's social circuit, thanks to their titles and intermarriage with wealthy social-ites, today's balls are organized by less sensational individuals, including Americans and Russians of various descent and from different emigration waves—in this way no longer belonging to the sole provenance of First Wave Russians. Indeed, only a tiny fraction of the organizers are descendants of New York's 1920 White Russian community.

Moreover, where once New York abounded with Russian balls ranging from lavish affairs at the Plaza Hotel to intimate evenings at Harlem's Rus-sian Club, these dances have dwindled in number down to four primary events: the Petroushka Ball, the Ball of the Russian Nobility Association, and the annual ball of the two major Russian scouting organizations in the United States (ORUR and NORR). As the two largest balls that draw from the broader public, I focus on the Petroushka and RNA balls, whose annual number of attendees near seven hundred and four hundred guests respectively.

Despite the smaller number of balls, these events continue to stand as important social occasions among the Russian émigré community in New York. As one Russian-American living on Long Island put it, "If you love anything to do with Russia, you'll go to the balls."[14] And so, we come to the question of what exactly is this notion of "Russia"—how is it displayed, and how does the ball serve as a means for bringing its participants in touch with this abstract concept?

Vignette I: Gypsies, Georgians, and the Imperial Russian Imagination

"At our *baly* [balls], they have Russian culture—whether it is opera, whether it is dance, ballet, folk, *chirkassy* [Circassian dances]—whatever—it's show-casing our culture. And our culture is very rich—from classical to folk to gypsy."[15]

Classical ballet, dagger dances, gypsy music—the bewildering array of genres reveals a range of symbols at play in creating "Russian culture." Spo-ken by a middle-aged woman of Russian descent who has spent countless hours organizing balls in New York, these words reveal a multivalent under-standing of Russianness that informs the way Russia is frequently defined and presented at balls today. As the most public, deliberate, and managed display of Russia, the formal entertainment described by this consultant and observed during my fieldwork suggests a strong exotic-imperialism at work in conveying Old Russia.

Figure 5.1. Prince David Chavchavadze, Eugenie Chavchavadze, Lado Babishvili, and Prince Alexis Obolensky at the Old Russian New Year Ball, c. 1980. Private Collection, Courtesy of Marusya Chavchavadze.

Whether presenting Circassian, Georgian, or Gypsy themes, the integration of non-Russian Others into a broader Russianness has long been part of the Russian ball scene in New York. In November 1938, for example, a group of young émigrés (The Russian Students Organization) held a gypsy-themed ball at the Plaza Hotel. Forgoing the typical setting of an Imperial Russian court, which had served as the ball's theme in the past, the "Night with Russian Gypsies" featured a "gypsy campfire fete"; the young Russian and American organizers in shoulder-baring blouses, long skirts, colorful necklaces and headscarves; and a "Gypsy" ensemble of singers and dancers.[16] The annual "White Ball" organized by Serge Obolensky beginning in the 1930s was likewise marked with an exotic twist. Each year, the ball opened with the Caucasian *lezginka* danced by former members of the Russian nobility dressed in the dashing *cherkasska* (Circassian uniform, complete with dagger tucked into belt)—a trend that simultaneously took place at émigré balls in Paris, Brussels, London, and later, Washington, DC. Like many men of his parents' generation, for example, Prince David Chavchavadze regularly wore a Circassian uniform to the Old Russian New Year Ball in Washington, DC. Each year, the ball would commence with Chavchavadze dancing the *lezginka* with his wife, Eugenie de Smitt, also the child of First Wave émigrés and whose grandfather was the primary founder of the Russian church in Harlem (see fig. 5.1). A descendent of both Russian and Georgian royal lines whose grandfather had led the Circassian Regiment in the World War I, Chavchavadze's costuming suggests the complex nature of these enactments, a point on which I elaborate later in this section.

Although guests at Russian balls today no longer wear stylized Gypsy dress or *cherkassy*, Georgian and especially Russian Gypsy music ensembles are a standard feature of the formal entertainment, pointing to the long interest in and subsumption of a stylized "gypsy" culture by Russians (see chap. 1 and 2). The 2009 Petroushka Ball, for example, featured the Brooklyn-based Romashka ensemble. A play on words referencing both the Rom people and the Russian word for daisy, "*romashka*," the very name of the ensemble signals a linguistic appropriation of Romani into the Russian lexicon. The manner in which the ensemble is described in the ball's program makes an obvious attempt to present this group as exotically alluring, yet comfortably hip: "The musicians are a wild bunch of virtuoso rhythm-throttling chop-splitting, Brooklyn-dwelling world music aficionados . . . the band channels their raw musical energy to create an infectious Eastern European gypsy dance party!" Eastern Europe is equated with a "raw" energy and made synonymous with the Romani culture. Situating Romashka within the ever-trendy Brooklyn and as a group of worldly music lovers, however, the program balances this otherness with cosmopolitan chic and accessibility. Guests at these balls are likewise often treated to a show of "gypsy" dancing, with members of the ensembles creating mesmerizing displays of multicolored skirts and bright scarves swept up into dizzying patterns.

In part, this drive to deliver an exotic product comes from the organizers' desire to impress guests and ensure a proper level of flair. As the chairwoman of one of the balls described to me, "I want [the dinnertime entertainment] to be active. I want it to be happy. I don't want anything mundane that people will start talking. . . . It's a twenty minute show. I need people to jump out of their seats."[17] Another organizer stressed, "We have colorful, loud dancing. . . . All kinds of national folk dances and so on and so forth. Because people perk up to that."[18] As these examples illustrate, there is a deliberate positioning of Russia as an exotic sum of its parts—a choice that is, in part, driven by marketing sensibilities of attracting and satisfying the high-paying guests.

Beyond the immediate explanation offered by ball organizers, the display of non-Russian Others at New York's balls can be situated within a longer history of Imperial subsumption and entanglement with the ethnic Other. An impulse in part propelled by the numerous military conquests that Russia has undertaken and to which it had been subject, the Russian position as both conqueror and conquered has long obfuscated the geopolitical and cultural lay of the land. From Scythians to Mongol vanquishers, non-Slavic Others have been deeply implicated in Russia's history and have been highlighted at times within discourses of national identity.

By the nineteenth century, the Caucasus in particular presented a focal point of military and, soon after, cultural subsumption. Russia's aggressive military campaign, culminating with the "final" imperial conquest of the Caucasus in 1859, only furthered the incorporation of Eastern Other into the Russian cultural and geographic landscape, with the increased presence of Russian subjects in the region resulting in the Caucasus being considered as Russia's "'own' orient."[19] While the presence of Romani peoples within Imperial Russia was not a consequence of Russian military conquest, but rather a result of Rom migration to the region, the existence of this group in Russia since the mid-fifteenth century and its strong connection with the sphere of elite entertainment from late eighteenth century onward has likewise had a profound influence on the way Russian culture has been imagined and produced (see chap. 1).[20]

The "Orient" as an aspect of the prerevolutionary Russian imagination was as much a consequence of conquest as it was a product of artistic musings. Susan Layton, Orlando Figes, and others have argued that Russia's nineteenth-century military campaign against the Caucasus prompted an outpouring of literature and art that left a profound imprint on Russian conceptions of the region. The works of Pushkin, Lermontov, and Tolstoy depicting impassioned Gypsy subjects were similarly treated as authentic renderings of Romani life.[21] Through romanticized imagery, simulated ethnographic accounts, and, in the case of Alexander Pushkin, "mellifluous verse" that enlivened the reading experience, this body of literature tended to be read as authoritative accounts rather than imagined constructions of Orientalized subjects.[22]

If classical literature presented a romantic image of the non-Russian Other, music gave it its voice. Russia's classical composers relished the sound of steppes, Gypsies, and Circassians just as these tropes engulfed the sphere of popular song, oftentimes utterly obscuring the provenance of this music. As Alaina Lemon writes in her study of Romani people in Russia and in the Russian imaginary, "It was culture as art that defined Gypsies; it was manifest in Gypsy song and dance because *Russian* literature found it there (italics in original)."[23] Richard Taruskin's definitive treatment of this subject elaborates on the specific musical elements that became codes of Orientalism in Russian music, whose heavy hints of languor would color Russian perceptions of the East for generations to come.[24] Romashka and the other dance ensembles that enact Russia's Imperial subjects at today's balls continue this obfuscation between simulacra and reality, the corporeality of the performers further bringing imagined peoples into the living present.

The intersection between Russian and Eastern Other is likewise rooted in a duality that has long informed Russian national identity. The extensive political, cultural, and in some cases genealogical entanglements with subjects associated with the "Orient" at times led to identification with the very Others that Russians encountered and raised a fundamental question of national identity (Is Russia East or West?).[25] Of this long-held intersection with the East and its bearing on Russian national identity, Susan Layton writes, "In the light of such considerations, a Russian could not believe in the alterity of the orient as readily and invariably as a European might."[26] Depending on current trends, this ambiguity with regard to national identity at times led Russians to flaunt and even feign Eastern roots. Between the fifteenth and seventeenth centuries, Russians adopted Turkic names in response to the influential Tatar domination; after the prolonged Caucasian military campaign of the nineteenth century, Russian men began to wear Circassian uniforms; and the Orientalist designs of the *Ballets Russes* left an indelible imprint on the Western imagination of what constituted Russia. These outward displays of otherness were but symptoms of an underlying Orientalist perspective coupled with an internal uncertainty with regard to national identity and deliberate separation from the West—a sentiment that reached its literary apotheosis with Alexander Blok's revolutionary battle cry: "Yes, Scythians—are we!"[27]

From this perspective, the enactment of exoticism at balls in the emigration at once reflects long-held Orientalist and Imperialist tendencies while pointing to the sometimes-murky overlap between Russia and the Others enveloped culturally, politically, and genealogically by the Empire and the way these entanglements have been strategically positioned to present a particular image of Russianness.

Vignette II: Princess Obolensky's *Kokoshnik*

Walking into the second, more intimate hall of the Waldorf Astoria Hotel (the first being reserved for ballroom dancing at the Petroushka Ball), I cannot help but notice the large Russian folk ensemble seated on stage, the players' red satin costumes radiating a shiny gloss under the stage lights. The men wear red satin shirts, black pants, and knee-high boots, and the women wear traditional red jumpers, or *sarafany*, their rich raspberry hue accentuated with deep forest greens and bright-yellow stripes sewn artfully onto their blouse sleeves and skirts. Accentuating the already-conspicuous presence of the contrabass balalaika, the large triangle-shaped instrument taking up an inordinate amount of space on the crowded stage, the player wears a tall conical hat with fur trim and a richly embroidered open frock—a look echoing the early Muscovite nobility and adopted most notably by Tsar Nicholas II at the renowned 1903 *Bal costumé au Palais d'Hiver*. Hanging noticeably over the stage, and bringing the spectator back to the twenty-first century, a sign in English enthusiastically reads, "It's Barynya Time!"—referring to the name of the ensemble regularly hired to perform at Russian balls in New York. The incongruence and anachronisms of the Russian émigré ball once again jump to the foreground.

Although the folk ensembles performing at New York's balls occasionally play lesser-known traditional songs in a style that signals a historic authenticity (using such signifiers as belting chest voice, folksy lyrics, and minimal choreography), the ensembles lean toward established folk standards, including the Ukrainian *Hopak*, "*Riabinushka*," and "*Kalinka*," as well as folklike songs from the Soviet period, such as "Moscow Nights" and "Blue Kerchief." The dance routines often accompanying these selections mirror the amalgamation of traditional and studied, featuring stylized movements that merge seemingly traditional steps with ballet technique. Pointed toes, fast spins, and tight choreography balance out the geometric foot moves, athletic squats, and the spontaneous clapping and whistling coming from the exuberant audience, to create an overall folksy yet polished effect.

Despite the crafted nature of these folk renderings, the folk element plays a central role in framing New York's Russian balls as portals to Old Russia. As an outward and longstanding symbol of an idyllic, timeless Russia, folk motifs (whether sartorial or musical) signal a link to this mythical idea, a point that I examine with regard to music in detail in chapter 1. With regard to costuming, folk dress has long positioned its wearers as part of an older, elemental Russia. Indeed, costumes worn at national-themed balls beginning in the late eighteenth century provided an "illusion of historical continuity" between their wearers and a long-gone past.[28]

Within the context of today's Russian émigré diaspora, this idea of historical continuity through costuming signals a display not of a current Russia but rather an imagined Russia of the past. Operating on a "shared cultural literacy for the communication of meaning," the notion of Old Russia imparted through folk music, costumes, and dancing is codified further through clues embedded elsewhere—including in the conspicuous inclusion of aristocratic titles of ball organizers and patrons in invitations and in announcements made throughout the evening, prominent displays of the Russian Imperial flag, and in the common commencement of each ball with the Tsarist anthem, "*Bozhe tsaria khrani* [God save the tsar]."[29]

Although Russian-themed costume balls abounded among guests in prerevolutionary Russia and in the early years of the First Wave diaspora in New York City, currently aside from the performing ensembles, few guests wear traditional Russian costumes. Two regular instances of such dressing hence deserve attention, as these individuals stand out against the otherwise tuxedo- and gown-clad guests. First, at certain balls, Russian costumes are worn by girls and boys—typically children of the organizers—selling raffle tickets. The young age of these mummers lends an innocence to their otherwise-anachronistic garb (see fig. 5.2). With last names like Ossourgine and Pouschine, many of these youngsters are descendants of Russian noble

Figure 5.2. Young attendee (Olya) at the 2007 Petroushka Ball. Photograph by author.

Figure 5.3. Selene Obolensky with ball attendee, Katherine Potapov, at the 2008 Old Russian New Year Ball. Photograph by author.

families. Yet the combination of braces and thick New York accents fore-grounds the symbolic stylization of the billowy blouses and bright-blue shiny shirts.

Second, and even more distinct, has been the regular appearance of Princess Selene Obolensky (1929–2014) in traditional Russian costume at the Old Russian New Year Ball in Washington, DC. An Alabama native with a lilting southern drawl who married into the renowned Russian family, Obo-lensky's position as head organizer suggests that with the proper connec-tion and costume, entry into Old Russia is not restricted to those of Russian descent (see fig. 5.3). Like the German-born Catherine the Great, Obolensky's background—an American from Birmingham—could possibly have com-promised her position within the Russian émigré scene. Yet, much beloved and respected, Selene became one of the primary movers within DC's Russian ball culture, a process I argue that was furthered by her regular wearing of an elaborate kokoshnik and Russian gown. As with Catherine the Great, whose wearing of traditional Russian dress was "a type of sartorial propaganda that symbolically enshrined her allegiance by showing her as a native daughter," the wearing of Russian costumes by figures like Selene Obolensky and the American children of Russian descent makes "native daughters" of them all.[30]

Vignette III: Of Class and Carnival

And yet, Old Russia as it is displayed at these balls is not simply an overtly exotic showcase. A more implicit aspect of this performance is the desire to present an upperclassness associated with a bygone era. From the names of counts and princesses included in ball programs and invitations to the lavish, old-style goods covering the tables of the silent auctions to the Pushkin-era dances performed on occasion by men in cravats and women in empire-waist dresses as part of the dinner entertainment, the accouter-ments of old-world refinement underlies the Russianness exhibited at these balls. One of the members of the RNA board stressed the importance of this aesthetic as a defining aspect of the ball experience: "We try to keep the ball elegant because we want to, as much as possible, given the circumstances, to emulate what a ball would have been like in those quote good old days. And so, we want that elegance."[31] Class is equated with and serves as a gateway to recreating an idyllic, golden past.

One of the most prominent ways that class is signaled at Russian balls is by the wearing of medals. From large brass crosses to an array of medals carefully pinned along white sashes, many types and sizes of medals adorn guests at Russian balls. As specified in the invitations, the white-tie dress allows guests to wear medals as part of their ensembles, which can confer gravitas on their possessors. When asked about the significance of these medals, a descendant of Second Wave émigrés in her early thirties who has attended balls since she was a teenager noted that medals are a way for their wearers to "revel in the fact that they come from nobility."[32] Another young Russian-American, a descendant of First Wave émigrés from a renowned prerevolutionary family, similarly linked medal-wearing to an exhibition of one's alleged upper-class background, a move that she simultaneously saw as being anachronistic: "So you'll see these old men wearing these medals. . . . It's so funny. You lose your title when you come to America."[33]

Yet, the reality of the acquisition of and meaning behind these medals often gets swept away into the carnival undercurrent dominating these balls. A man wearing a large medal around his neck at the 2016 RNA Ball turned out to be not Russian at all but from Bulgaria and a member of the philanthropic Order of St. John of Jerusalem, through whose membership he received the medal. In response to my inquiry into the order, the man invited me to join at the following year's initiation ceremony—a move I attribute to an interest in enlisting female members rather than to any assessment of my background. When asked about the large crosslike medal adorning his tuxedo, a male guest at the 2015 Old Russian New Year Ball told me that he was wearing the medal of the Order of St. George (a medal at one point in time granted to certain members of the White Army, among other instances), adding in jest that he has been "well preserved." I quickly followed up as to how he acquired the medal, which, he revealed, he had purchased at a local expo show. I was particularly struck by an attendee at the 2008 Old Russian New Year Ball whose sheer number of medals pinned carefully across his chest automatically made him stand out from the crowd. Approaching him to learn about his family history, I soon discovered that he had no Russian roots at all but was a collector of Russian paraphernalia as well as a regular attendee of the ball.

To learn that the medals dangling on lapels originate from sources as disparate as benevolent orders and local auctions points to the success of such enactments and the extent to which guests are invested in performing Old Russia. Whether displaying medals, folk costumes, or Circassian daggers, in these instances, the body emerges as a "legible exhibition space" onto which meaning can be projected and read.[34] Indeed, participants at balls are both active agents and passive recipients in generating sartorial significance. Drawing on Cindy Garcia's concept of the "sequined" salsa dancer, who relies more on "affect, speculation, and desire" than on monetary wealth to gain social status within the salsa sphere, so too is it possible for guests at Russian balls to assert their place in the social hierarchy with the proper outward signs of class, past, and ethnicity.[35]

False counts, kokoshnik-wearing Southern belles, and Russian-Americans who dance but do not speak Russian—the many ways people perform Old Russia at balls today suggests a strong element of masquerade at work.[36] As one young member of the RNA board put it, "for an evening you are playing somebody else."[37] In her work on costume balls in Imperial Russia, Colleen McQuillen notes the power of masquerade in character animation: "When the wearer dons and animates his costume, he plays a corresponding role, enacting his newly adopted identity."[38] Although masking at Russian balls today happens more often on a subtle rather than overt plane, the balls nevertheless offer enhanced spaces for a "strategic performance of social identity in the public sphere."[39] Yet outward significations of Russianness are only part of the total effect of New York's balls, as the embodied experience plays a central role in bringing Old Russia to life.

The Kinetic Realm: Russian Dancing

"The thing that gets everyone going is the Hopak. And it's the thing that makes the event more Russian than anything."[40]
"I could Hopak before I could walk."[41]

Sol—do—mi. As the last waltz of the 2016 RNA ball fades out, I hear the telltale opening motive. Sol—do—mi—re mi fa re mi do. The reedy sound of the accordion only confirms the signal. It is none other than the beginning of the "Hopak," the dance of Ukrainian origin that is a standard part of today's Russian ball. The opening teaser gradually accelerates to a pace conducive to dancing. As if instinctively, the guests assemble in a circle, awaiting the first souls to brave the athletic dance. I inch my way through the onlookers to the very front—the liminal zone between spectator and participant, where one can quickly interchange with the other. A couple in their early thirties takes to the floor. The husband, a member of the RNA board and librarian at a nearby Russian monastery, squats to the floor and begins to execute the so-called *mel'nitsa*—swinging one leg deftly around his body like a windmill for which the move is named. In a deep-blue gown,

Figure 5.4. A couple dancing as the circle of onlookers cheers at the 2016 Russian Nobility Association Ball. Photograph by author.

pearls, and high heels, his wife circles around him, sprightly shifting weight between left and right legs while opening and closing her arms. Meanwhile, the onlookers clap to the rhythm of the dance, with sharp staccato beats of two complementing the woman's footwork of steps in three.

After approximately ten seconds or so, the next act begins. A man who appears to be in his twenties gingerly enters the circle, moving his feet to the rhythm and opening his arms. Gaining momentum, he leaps up, raising his torso and spreading his legs in a momentary levitation. Upon returning to the ground, he smoothly opens his arms, as if at once acknowledging his success and presenting himself to the circle of onlookers. With each descent, the onlookers erupt in cheers (see fig. 5.4). Next to enter the circle is a group of four young women, their arms intricately crossed and their feet likewise following a crisscross pattern. Two young men swiftly descend below them. Holding each other by one arm with the other arm raised, the men execute the notoriously difficult *sobachki* ("little dogs")— moves requiring rapid alterations between left and right legs, all while in a squatting position. The swapping of dancers, gestures, and couples continues for approximately ten minutes, as onlookers clap to the rhythm and shout with glee between sipping drinks, glancing at their cell phones, and scheming their next moves.

The seeming ease with which the traditional portion of the Russian ball is imbued—dances that are, in this case, historically Ukrainian but that have been coopted under the guise of "Russian dancing" in yet another example of cultural subsumption—points to an inherent duality. Echoed in the quotes cited at the beginning of this section, the traditional dancing at Russian balls illustrates the "slippage" described by Ann Cooper-Albright between "somatic identity (the experience of one's physicality) and cultural identity (how one's body—skin, gender, ability, age, etc.—renders meaning in society)," for these dances are at once emblematic of a traditional, seemingly archetypal Russianness, while also being corporeal, immediate experiences.[42] Indeed, Russian dancing is understood as being highly symbolic ("more Russian than anything") while also something inborn ("I could Hopak before I could walk").

Applying Susan Leigh Foster's idea of "bodily reality" to the Russian ball, this section looks at the "body's role in the production of narrative, in the construction of collectivity, [and] in the articulation of the unconscious."[43] The ideas revolving around New Epic Dance as analyzed by Cooper-Albright in particular may be fruitfully applied to the above phenomenon to elucidate how embodied practices can inform collective understandings of the past. As staged dances that can "enact and rework" the myths, histories, and sense of collectivity associated with a particular group, New Epic Dance creates a space for "expressions of cultural identity which call upon mythic and archetypal, as well as historical, images."[44]

Engaging with the "mythic and archetypal" offers a useful framework for understanding how dance can evoke an idealized homeland among groups of migrants and their descendants. Relying on Toni Morrison's distinction between "truth" and "fact," Cooper-Albright demonstrates how dance can engage a collective sense of identity informed and enacted through a certain level of mythology. As Cooper-Albright writes: "It is not the primacy of the historical text that is so important for Morrison, but the potency of the embodied image. History is written about past events. Stories are told in order to connect the knowledge of the past and hopes for the future with one's experiences of present realities. . . .This redeployment of history is predicated on a collective consciousness of cultural identity—a sense of self that is connected to a sense of one's peoples."[45]

The "embodied image" as expressed through dance allows both an immediacy rooted in individual experience and a collectivity engendered through communal effort, creating a salient and seemingly shared engagement with the past in a way that resonates in the present. According to Cooper-Albright, the connection between an individual and the group initiated through dance speaks both to the "present moment and a historical continuity—defining who your community is at present and who your community was several hundred years ago."[46] Cooper-Albright bolsters this idea through Audre Lorde's *biomythography*, the "re-creation of history as myth, as tales that embody common ideals."[47] Looking at two renditions of African-American New Epic performance, Cooper-Albright shows how these enactments depict dance as eliciting "memory and history," taking its executors to a place that would be otherwise wholly "a dream place—distant and unreal."[48]

Although not staged in a traditional sense, the Russian dancing segment at New York's balls presents a performance based on steps often rehearsed throughout the year at regular dance practices.[49] Framed by the Old Russia theme that is signaled by the music, costumes, aristocratic titles, Imperial Russian flags, and dinner entertainment, the Russian dance likewise engages a mythologized Russia of the past. This "re-creation of history as myth" through Russian dancing rests on three primary processes: an evocation of an idyllic, bygone Russia (and, by extension, a deep-rooted Russianness); a powerful, if momentary, ecstasy brought about through the physical act of dance; and a camaraderie between the dancers as well as between dancers and onlookers.

The connection between traditional dance and an idyllic Russia has been long held in the Russian imaginary. After the Napoleonic Wars, Russian dancing was introduced at court balls as a means of the elite becoming "more 'Russian.'"[50] Yet, these dances were not seen as superficial enactments but rather were positioned as extensions of an essential Russian self. Princess Elena Golitsyn, for example, relayed her dancing of a traditional *pliaska* at a ball in mid-nineteenth-century Novgorod as follows: "Nobody had taught me how to dance the *pliaska*. It was simply that I was a 'Russian girl.'"[51]

The discourses framing stylized traditional dancing as a physical expression of an innate, deep-rooted Russianness continue to the present day. A young man then in his late teens—one of the most agile and showy dancers I had seen among the New York crowd—told me that the music of the Hopak in particular made him "feel Russian."[52] Another woman in her early twenties noted the ubiquity of the Hopak at Russian events as well as the seemingly intrinsic response to the music: "the classic folk song [Hopak] comes on and everyone knows you've got to go to the dance floor because a circle is going to form and people are going to gather in the middle and dance. And everyone's clapping. . . . *For some reason, everyone knows what to do*. Even if you never actually took folk dancing classes, which is hard to believe, but even if you have no idea what's going on and you gather in the middle, you start twirling around in the middle, and people love it (italics mine)."[53]

As something not requiring sustained commitment, as does language, for example, Russian dancing is a vibrant and key component for evoking Old Russia. The growing popularity of Russian dance lessons among people of Russian descent in the New York area, moreover, points to the increased salience of dance for informing a diasporic identity for today's Russian Americans. Vladimir Galitzine, descendant of a renowned Russian aristocratic family and former organizer of the RNA whose grandchildren now take part in Russian dancing at balls, has noted the efficacy of dancing for instilling a connection to a Russia of the past among émigré descendants in New York. Unlike speaking Russian, which far from all are able to do, most young people in New York's Russian émigré community are raised learning traditional dance steps, a point that brings solace to Galitzine: "You know that that's going to be passed on. *Malen'ki kusochik* [a little piece] that is being passed on."[54] A "little piece" of Russia, encapsulated, expressed, and experienced through dance. Galitzine's momentary code switching into Russian and use of diminutive for "little piece," moreover, lend his words an earnestness and echoes the idea of an inherent connection between traditional dance and a mythologized Russia.

Similar to other embodied practices that engender associations with an "aristocratic or courtly golden age," Russian dance thus functions in this regard as a "means through which this cultural memory is preserved and reproduced."[55] Indeed, the Russian dancing that occurs at balls in twenty-first century New York at once signifies a connection to a bygone Russia and rests on a physicality that contributes to a sense of community among participants. This is *biomythography* in the making—a process that continues to resonate with its creators, whether Russian elites in the nineteenth century or participants at Russian balls in twenty-first century New York. This juxtaposition between imagined past and immediate present generated through dance is not unique to Russian balls and can be found, for example, within *Dabkeh* wedding dances among Palestinians in Jordan. Pointing out the interplay between past and present at work in these dances, Mauro Van Acken writes, "*Dabkeh* represents a continuous reinvention of tradition. It is displayed and perceived as a symbol of ancient tradition connected to the lost villages and lost land of Palestine. At the same time, it is a sign of an intimate present identity since it is linked to marriage parties, relations of solidarity, feasts and ritual."[56]

The particular moves specific to Russian dancing at balls only reinforces this sense of myth and collectivity, as the high level of coordination necessary in executing Russian dance steps lends itself to a representation of physical and social unity. The line of women with arms intercrossed and feet executing similarly crossed patterns must be in sync, lest one member impedes on the flow or trips over her neighbor's feet. The intertwined arms of the men quickly alternating between standing and squatting or sweeping their feet while on their haunches creates an aesthetic unity as well as physical support, with the dancers literally and figuratively leaning on one another. Less demanding physically but far more precarious are the spinning numbers. The simpler ones consist of two dancers facing each other and holding arms in a crisscross fashion, whirling rapidly about and, on occasion, spinning out of control into the circle of onlookers. The more involved spinning move entails four dancers in a circle, with two men propping two women on their arms. As the group gains momentum, the women lean back—a sort of spinning lotus. One false move and the assembly falls, the formation fails, and one or all of the dancers can be injured. No mere passive spectators, the onlookers contribute to the esprit de corps, clapping to the music, encouraging the dancers, and whooping in response to particularly daring demonstrations. The reciprocal feedback between spectators and dancers as well as the circle itself elicits camaraderie, framing this "little corner" of Old Russia with social, symbolic, and geometric unity.

The sheer energy elicited through the demanding spins, gravity-defying jumps, and rapidly alternating steps of Russian dance, moreover, engenders momentum, which may, on reflection, signal a vibrant, living ethnicity rather than a static symbol of the past. In their work on the intersections between dance and ethnicity, Anthony Shay and Barbara Sellers-Young ask, "How do we know race and ethnic identity through dance in a way we do not know it [through] any other form of performance?"[57] As but one example, Russian dancing offers a physicality—complete with endorphins, racing heart, and sense of accomplishment—that is often absent in other forms of ethnic signification, such as speaking and reading, likely explaining why many Russian-Americans today dance enthusiastically but do not speak Russian and identify traditional dance as a primary means of engaging Russianness.

The case of Russian dancing also illustrates how a highly symbolic, studied act like dance can generate an elation free of extrasomatic signifiers that helps position that very act as a conduit for collectivity. I argue that a central aspect of Russian dancing in New York is the interplay between the representational ("we are Russian dancing") and what Graham St. John and others have described as a moment of "ecstasy," in which one engages with a "non-reflective awareness autonomous in its 'freedom' from ideology, language, and culture."[58] In such instances, participants approach the "experience of *being* other [rather] than *performing* otherness (italics in original)" as the "ludic reversal or reconfiguration of structure and language common to festival and carnival performance is replaced with the dissolution of language and meaning, with a raw experience of self-dissolution or 'surrender.'"[59] Such state of surrender, in which one engages completely in the immediacy of the moment, helps, in retrospect, to index Russian dancing as something inborn, naturalizing both the act of dancing itself and the Russianness with which it is associated.

The "surrender" made possible through the act of dance can be elicited not only by traditional Russian dancing but also through the more inclusive ballroom dancing making up the major portion of each ball. From this perspective, even those who either do not wish to brave the circle or have not had formal dance training or, by extension, those who may not otherwise take part in Russian émigré cultural life (such as in the weekly Russian dance lessons) can engage in the elation made possible through dance and the music that accompanies it. Returning, for example, to the 2016 RNA ball and the sounds of the 1930s classic tango "Exhausted by the Sun," executed by sharp, staccato chords that punctuate the rhythm, I watch as couples step, slide, and twirl each in their own way, seemingly lost to the world around them. Some dancers are rather clunky, accentuating the underlying rhythm with heavy footsteps; others incorporate moves more appropriate for salsa dancing, while still others appear as studied and as put together as competition ballroom dancers (a perfection almost eerie in its juxtaposition against the more relaxed dancing that dominates the floor). I watch as the dance floor becomes especially heated for *"Schast'e vdrug* [Suddenly

Happiness]," from the 1973 classic Soviet film *Ivan Vasil'evich meniaet professiiu* [Ivan Vasilevich Changes Professions]. Although some people simply dance energetically to the upbeat tempo, others enthusiastically sing along, relaying their knowledge of this particular example of Soviet popular culture. Young women and men raise their arms high in the air at particular moments of the text, while others dance together in small groups or happily mouth the words to their partners.

I argue that these moments of surrender allow anyone, regardless of cultural, ethnic, or migratory background, to engage in the Old Russia that frames these balls. Indeed, the kinetic experience is a central point of entry to various collectivities across cultural processes. In his work on the participation of Americans in the Bulgarian Koprivshtitsa festival, Ian MacMillan has noted the central place of the dancing body for encountering Bulgarianness, even for those who do not share this background. He states, "In overcoming the difficulties of Balkan meters and harmonies, as well as those of the rhythms and other musical parameters that are associated with them, many Balkanites engage in a musical embodiment that moves beyond imitation to a becoming-Other that they experience with great affect."[60] Similarly, Natasha Pravaz presents a compelling case for the potential of the (often non-Brazilian) body in engaging Brazilian "modes-of-being" through samba participation in Toronto, demonstrating how long-held enactments can be transmitted cross-culturally as well as cross-corporeally.[61]

In these examples, the body emerges as a vessel for harboring gestures that have come to register as expressions of and connections to extrasomatic collective identities, whether of ethnicity, of the past, or of a broader otherness. This embodied memory is in line with Paul Connerton's *bodily social memory* and echoes Pierre Bourdieu's *bodily hexis*—acts repeated, naturalized, and having acquired particular values, indicative (whether reflexively or unreflexively) of a particular collectivity.[62] The writing of Paul Connerton in particular offers a useful framework for approaching the junction between individual bodies, collective memory, and the interplay between the symbolic and the physical. According to Connerton, an important bridge between the body and social memory is the "commemorative ceremony," as it presents a site for collective "re-enactments of the past" in which "master narratives" can be articulated and performed.[63] Although Connerton recognizes the role of the representational in conferring an idea of the past in such events, he calls for the acknowledgment of the corporeal in creating social memory, a synthesis he labels *bodily social memory*. For Connerton, the body as creator of such reenactments is not merely something inscribed with meaning but is also a repository of habits, which "cannot be thought without a notion of bodily automatisms."[64] As he writes, "Our bodies, which in commemorations stylistically re-enact an image of the past, keep the past also in an entirely effective form in their continuing ability to perform certain skilled actions . . . Many forms of habitual skilled remembering illustrate a keeping of the past in mind that, without ever adverting to its historical origin, nevertheless re-enacts the past in our present conduct."[65]

The buoyant dance steps executed by Princess Elena in the nineteenth century and ball attendees in the twenty-first are a prime example of such sedimented habits—as they confer a collectively recognized connection to a mythologized Russia while being perceived as something innate, something as inherent and as inborn as, in reference to the consultant cited earlier, "walking." More broadly, the body (which, through dance can reach a state of "surrender," thus, in retrospect, indexing that moment as something real) can bring a collectively understood past into the present through public performances or "commemorative ceremonies" like the ball. The range of musical selections at New York's Russian balls, including American and Soviet pop tunes alongside prerevolutionary Russian gypsy romances and folk songs, makes room for multiple subjectivities within the overarching framework of Old Russia that dominates these events.

Conclusion

The idea of "Russia" today is far from the fashionable image it once was in New York's aristocrat-fueled Russian vogue of the 1920s. This lack of favor is encountered today among ball organizers, for whom the mention of a "Russian" ball among potential donors is often more of a liability than an asset.[66] The idea of Russian nobility is, at minimum, anachronistic and something that has caused even certain members of the Russian Nobility Association board to question the place of the word in the title of the organization.

Why, one might ask, do people from a multitude of backgrounds continue to organize and attend balls evocative of an Old Russia? Although today's ball attendees are far from the hapless refugees of nearly a century ago and likely not a single person is old enough to have had personal contact with prerevolutionary Russia, there continues to be an attraction to the enchantment associated with this mythical place that is largely propelled by the synthesis of music and dance. Indeed, I argue that the multisensory world of the ball rests on the kinetic and musical realms working in tandem to create an enchantment that brings an idea of an idyllic, prerevolutionary Old Russia "sensuously to the present."[67]

Russian balls in New York present a prime exploration of the intersection of music, dance, and the body as it engenders representations and experiences of an imagined place lodged in the recesses of an imagined past. Indeed, these balls function as sites in which the past is constantly being produced and reproduced, framed by an overarching idea of an idyllic, bygone Russia. As such, Russian balls in New York present a prime example of what Sydney Hutchinson has described as "the intensity with which place and community are produced through bodily practices," and specifically, "the intimate ties between body and place as constructed through dance."[68] Beyond the specific geographic sites discussed by Hutchinson, the "place" of Old Russia is one imagined rather than actual, offering entry to a utopian realm through the dancing, listening body and a place that is continually reconceived and rearticulated in the self-fashioning that permeates the balls. Indeed, evoking Hutchinson's *kinetopia*, or, "zones of movement that, at best, may have utopian dimensions, as when they imagine a world in which multiple cultures can coexist peacefully and beautifully, even within the same body," the Russian ball presents a realm of paradox, in which multiple presents and pasts, whether historic, migrational, or one of identities, can coexist within and between the bodies at play.[69]

Notes

1. See, for example, Natalie K. Zelensky, "Sounding Diaspora through Music and Play in a Russian-American Summer Camp," *Ethnomusicology Forum* 23, no. 3 (December 2014): 306–330.

2. Anthony Shay and Barbara Sellers-Young, "Dance and Ethnicity: Introduction," in *The Oxford Handbook of Dance and Ethnicity*, edited by Anthony Shay and Barbara Sellers-Young (New York: Oxford University Press, 2016), 3.

3. Colleen McQuillen, *The Modernist Masquerade: Stylizing Life, Literature, and Costumes in Russia* (Madison: The University of Wisconsin Press, 2013), 4.

4. Mauro Van Acken, "Dancing Belonging: Contesting *Dabkeh* in the Jordan Valley, Jordan," *Journal of Ethnic and Migration Studies* 32, no. 2 (March 2006): 220.

5. See, for example, Cindy Garcia, *Salsa Crossings: Dancing Latinidad in Los Angeles* (Durham, NC: Duke University Press, 2013); Cathy Black, "The Dance of Exile: Jerzy Starzyński, Kyczera, and the Polish Lemkos," *Dance Research Journal* 40, no. 2 (Winter 2008): 41–55.

6. Allegra Fuller Snyder cited in Tomie Hahn, *Sensational Knowledge: Embodying Culture through Japanese Dance* (Middletown, CT: Wesleyan University Press, 2007), 6; Hahn, *Sensational Knowledge*, 1.

7. Max Weber, "Science as a Vocation," in *From Max Weber: Essays in Sociology*, edited and translated by H. H. Gerth and C. Wright Mills (Oxford: Oxford University Press, 1946), 129–156.

8. Joshua Landy and Michael Saler, "Introduction: The Varieties of Modern Enchantment," in *The Re-Enchantment of the World: Secular Magic in a Rational Age*, edited by Joshua Landy and Michael Saler (Stanford: Stanford University Press, 2009), 2.

9. Despite the rich history of costume balls in New York, and even several Russian-themed dances that took place around the *Ballets Russes* craze of the early 1910s, Russian balls did not become a regular occurrence until after the arrival of Russian exiles in the 1920s. The several Russian-sponsored balls that did take place before the arrival of the émigrés, such as a ball organized by Russian socialists in 1911 or the Waldorf Ball held by Ambassador Boris Bakhmeteff for the aid of Russia in 1916, included few or no overt ethnic markers.

10. Ian MacMillen, "Fascination, Musical Tourism, and the Loss of the Balkan Village (Notes on Bulgaria's Koprivshtitsa Festival)," *Ethnomusicology* 59, no.2 (Spring/Summer 2015): 241.

11. Sophia Geringer, telephone interview with the author, August 5, 2016.

12. To this day, nevertheless, the dinner portion of the RNA Ball, for example, is by invitation only.

13. Xenia Woyevodsky, interview with the author, Bethesda, MD, February 19, 2007.

14. Valentina Mickle, interview with author, Sea Cliff, NY, August 6, 2006.

15. Name withheld, interview with author, Oakland, NJ, August 15, 2006.

16. "Novel Setting Will Enhance Annual Russian Ball Nov. 30: 'A Night with Russian Gypsies' Will Be the Theme of a Colorful Benefit Planned by Former Nobility and Large Society Group," *New York Times*, November 13, 1938, 49.

17. Name withheld, interview with the author, Syosset, NY, July 9, 2016.

18. Name withheld, telephone interview with the author, August 23, 2016.

19. G. Semin, *Sevastopol': istoricheskii ocherk* (Moscow: Voennoe izdatel'stvo, 1955), 24, cited in Susan Layton, *Russian Literature and Empire: Conquest of the Caucasus from Pushkin to Tolstoy* (Cambridge: Cambridge University Press, 1994), 1.

20. Alaina Lemon, *Between Two Fires: Gypsy Performance and Romani Memory from Pushkin to Postsocialism* (Durham, NC: Duke University Press, 2000), 7.

21. See, for example, Lemon, *Between Two Fires*, 31.

22. Layton, *Russian Literature and Empire*, 19, 16.

23. Lemon, *Between Two Fires*, 34.

24. See, most notably, Richard Taruskin, "'Entoiling the Falconet,'" in *Defining Russia Musically: Historical and Hermenuetical Essays* (Princeton, NJ: Princeton University Press, 1997), 152–185.

25. See, for example, Layton, *Russian Literature and Empire*, 73–74.

26. Ibid., 75.

27. Aleksandr Blok, *Skify* [Scythians] (1918).

28. McQuillen, *Modernist Masquerade*, 67.

29. Ibid., 146.

30. Ibid., 67.

31. Name withheld, interview with the author, Syosset, NY, July 9, 2016.

32. Name withheld, interview with author, Arlington, VA, December 17, 2006.

33. Name withheld, interview with author, New York, NY, August 12, 2006.

34. McQuillen, *Modernist Masquerade*, 33.

35. Garcia, *Salsa Crossings*, 14.

36. Although phony nobility began surfacing at Russian balls practically as soon as these events were organized, such posturing attests to the continued salience of the trope of "the noble." The most recent of such known enactments was that of Alan Z. Feuer, who regularly attended both the Petroushka and RNA balls among other New York society events posing as an Austrian aristocrat. Remembered fondly as "the last true society gentleman," it was not until after his death in 2012 that his performance was exposed (Alan Feuer, "The Secret Life of a Society Maven," *New York Times*, April 21, 2012, http://www.nytimes.com/2012/04/22 /nyregion/the-secret-life-of-alan-z-feuer.html, [accessed December 28, 2016]).

37. Michael Perekrestev, interview with the author, Jordanville, NY, July 16, 2016.

38. McQuillen, *Modernist Masquerade*, 32.

39. Ibid., 31.

40. Name withheld, interview with the author, Brighton Beach, NY, August 13, 2006.

41. Name withheld, interview with the author, Oakland, NJ, August 15, 2006.

42. Ann Cooper-Albright, "Introduction: Situated Dancing," in *Engaging Bodies: The Politics and Poetics of Corporeality* (Middletown, CT: Wesleyan University Press, 2013), 10.

43. Susan Leigh Foster, "Introduction," in *Corporealities: Dancing Knowledge, Culture and Power*, edited by Susan Leigh Foster (London: Routledge, 1996), xi, xv.

44. Cooper-Albright, "Embodying History: Epic Narrative and Cultural Identity in African-American Dance," in *Engaging Bodies*, 148.

45. Ibid., 150.

46. Ibid., 169.

47. Ibid., 149.

48. Ibid., 169; Jewelle Bomez, *The Gilda Stories* (Ithaca, NY: Firebrand Books, 1991), 39, cited in Cooper-Albright, "Embodying History," 165.

49. Vladimir Galitzine, telephone interview with the author, August 24, 2016; Sophia Geringer, telephone interview with the author, August 5, 2016.

50. Figes, *Natasha's Dance*, 104–105.

51. Ibid., 105.

52. Name withheld, interview with the author, Oakland, NJ, August 15, 2006.

53. Name withheld, telephone interview with the author, August 5, 2016.

54. Vladimir Galitzine, telephone interview with the author, August 24, 2016.

55. Chloë Alaghband-Zadeh, "Listening to North Indian Classical Music: How Embodied Ways of Listening Perform Imagined Histories and Social Class," *Ethnomusicology* 61, no. 2 (Summer 2017): 224.

56. Van Acken, "Dancing Belonging," 206.

57. Shay and Sellers-Young, "Dance and Ethnicity," 4.

58. Graham St. John, "Trance Tribes and Dance Vibes: Victor Turner and Electronic Dance Music Culture," in *Victor Turner and Contemporary Cultural Performance*, edited by Graham St. John (New York: Berghahn Books, 2008), 153; J. Landau, "The Flesh of Raving: Merleau-Ponty and the 'Experience' of Ecstasy," in *Rave Culture and Religion*, edited by Graham St. John (London: Routledge, 2004), 113 (cited in St. John "Trance Tribes," 153).

59. St. John, "Trance Tribes," 153.

60. MacMillen, "Fascination," 246.

61. Natasha Pravaz, "Transnational Samba and the Construction of Diasporic Musicscapes," in *The Globalization of Musics in Transit: Music, Migration, and Tourism*, edited by Simone Krüger and Ruxandra Trandafoiu (New York: Routledge, 2014), 282.

62. See, in particular, Bourdieu, "Structures and the Habitus," 93–94.

63. Paul Connerton, *How Societies Remember* (Cambridge: Cambridge University Press, 1989), 72, 70.

64. Ibid., 5.

65. Ibid., 72.

66. Ball organizer, name withheld, interview with the author, Syosset, NY, July 9, 2016.

67. Lila Ellen Gray, *Fado Resounding: Affective Politics and Urban Life* (Durham, NC: Duke University Press, 2013), 10.

68. Sydney Hutchinson, "Dancing in Place: An Introduction," in *Salsa World: A Global Dance in Local Contexts*, edited by Sydney Hutchinson (Philadelphia: Temple University Press, 2015), 4, 2.

69. Sydney Hutchinson, "Breaking Borders/*Quebrando Fronteras*: Dancing in the Borderscape," in *Transnational Encounters: Music and Performance at the US-Mexican Border*, edited by Alejandro Madrid (Oxford: Oxford University Press, 2012), 59.

EPILOGUE

I CONCLUDE THIS BOOK WHERE I STARTED, WITH the question posed by William Safran (and undoubtedly by diaspora communities across time and space): how long can a diasporic consciousness last, and what is necessary for its survival? A study of the First Wave Russian émigré community in New York City from its formation in Harlem through the present day demonstrates the central role played by music in this process. Ultimately, the sustainability afforded through music within this diaspora is framed by a paradox, as its continuity has been largely enabled through change while still being rooted around an idea of prerevolutionary Russia.

The period surrounding the founding of the Russian émigré community in Harlem demonstrates the importance of musical performance (specifically, Russian gypsy and folk songs) as a forum through which a diasporic metacommentary can be constructed. This music was positioned in public discourses as something that could transport its listeners back to the precataclysmic homeland and served to promote nostalgia and an idealized vision of the homeland. Yet, far from remaining bound to a static idea of "Russian music" (i.e., that which originated in prerevolutionary Russia), the émigrés took to creating new music, including composing their own Russian gypsy romances and new numbers for Nikita Balieff's production of *Chauve-Souris*. The creative impulse helped make the Russian émigré music culture viable and of interest within the new context of exile (New York City) and brought both financial and social capital to the recent refugees.

The possibility afforded by new music in sustaining the First Wave diaspora comes sharply into focus in the World War II era. While Russian Harlem began to dissolve, the introduction of First Wave émigrés from Europe as well as the Second Wave of emigration from the Soviet Union gave new life to the waning community. Central to this process was the introduction of Soviet songs during this time, as this inauguration expanded the definition of Russian music within the diaspora—and, by extension, the boundary surrounding Russia Abroad—and supplied second-generation émigrés with living culture from the now-abstract homeland.

We also see the potential of music to serve as a means for diasporans to engage in homeland-hostland politics. This kind of involvement was particularly apparent among Russians living in the United States during the Cold War era. Engaging both the practical and ideological realms, émigré musicians were able to utilize their craft as a means of influencing their Russian compatriots living on the other side of the Iron Curtain. In this regard, music production provided diasporans with a purpose (one complementary to their ur-myth) as well as a paycheck.

The real test to Safran's inquiry as it applies to the First Wave Russian diaspora, however, is whether community activities structured around some semblance of prerevolutionary Russia continue to take place and resonate for their participants. The Russian balls that have occurred in New York down to the present offer one such example of an activity that still pivots around discourses of a prerevolutionary Russia. Demonstrating the importance of the dancing body in informing an understanding of Old Russia, we see how the corporeal realm presents participants with a means of engaging with an imagined past that is simultaneously salient and immediate, while not requiring sustained commitment. Moreover, the events pivoting around an idea of prerevolutionary Russia today involve Russian music from a range of periods and diasporans from multiple waves, in this way further sustaining the First Wave diaspora through enriching and broadening the very ideas of a musical Russianness and Russia Abroad.

By chance, this book neared its completion around the centennial of the 1917 Bolshevik Revolution. As the catalyst event from which the First Wave emigration came into existence, the revolution remains a historic and symbolic landmark within the emigration's history. It is yet to be seen how the revolution will be marked within the Russian diaspora (or by the current Russian government). How will the First Wave émigrés fit into narratives of the centennial? Whose voices will inform official discourses about this event? And, following Su Zheng, in what capacity will Russians in the United States "claim diaspora" in this particular period of American and Russian geopolitical and cultural history?[1]

By examining the Russian émigré community in New York over the better part of a century, this book has demonstrated the importance of music in maintaining diasporic consciousness of events that took place one hundred years ago but whose collective memory continues to structure certain social and cultural discourses down to the present. While the gatherings organized by the White Russian exiles in a church basement in Harlem are by now historical accounts, music continues to diversify and broaden the number of ways to identify with the historic, mythical homeland and to be Russian abroad.

Note

1. Su Zheng, *Claiming Diaspora: Music, Transnationalism, and Cultural Politics in Asian/ Chinese America* (New York: Oxford University Press, 2010), 10.

BIBLIOGRAPHY

Alaghband-Zadeh, Chloë. "Listening to North Indian Classical Music: How Embodied Ways of Listening Perform Imagined Histories and Social Class." *Ethnomusicology* 61, no. 2 (Summer 2017): 207–233.

Alajaji, Sylvia Angelique. *Music and the Armenian Diaspora: Searching for Home in Exile.* Bloomington: Indiana University Press, 2015.

Aleksandrov, E. A., ed. *Russkie v Servernoi Amerike: biograficheskii slovar'* [Russians in North America: A Biographical Dictionary]. Hamden, CT: n.p., 2005.

Anderson, Benedict. *Imagined Communities: Reflections on the Origin and Spread of Nationalism.* London: Verso, 1991.

Andreyev, Catherine, and Ivan Savicky. *Russia Abroad: Prague and the Russian Diaspora,1918–1938.* New Haven, CT: Yale University Press, 2004.

Ansari, Emily Abrams. "Musical Americanism, Cold War Consensus Culture, and the US-USSR Composers' Exchange, 1958–1960." *Musical Quarterly* 97, no. 3 (Fall 2014): 360–362.

Aristova, Asta. *Chto sokhranila pamiat': vospominania o zhizni v Germanii, 1945–1949* [What Memory Has Preserved: Memoirs of Life in Germany, 1945–1949]. n.p., 2003.

Baily, John, and Michael Collyer. "Introduction: Music and Migration." *Journal of Ethnic and Migrational Studies* 32, no. 2 (March 2006): 167–182.

Bakhtin, Mikhail. "Forms of Time and of the Chronotope in the Novel." In *The Dialogic Imagination: Four Essays*, edited by Michael Holquist, translated by Caryl Emerson and Michael Holquist, 84–258. Austin: University of Texas Press, 2006.

Barth, Fredrik. "Introduction." In *Ethnic Groups and Boundaries: The Social Organization of Culture Difference*, edited by Fredrik Barth, 9–38. Boston: Little, Brown and Company, 1969.

Bernadskii, G. G. *Russkaia kolonia v Soedinnenykh Shtatakh* [The Russian Colony in the United States]. New York: n.p., 1992.

Bertensson, Sergei, and Jay Leyda. *Sergei Rachmaninoff: A Lifetime in Music.* Bloomington: Indiana University Press, 2001.

Bessire, Lucas, and Daniel Fisher. "Introduction." In *Radio Fields: Anthropology and Wireless Sound in the Twenty-First Century*, edited by Lucas Bessire and Daniel Fisher, 1–47. New York: New York University Press, 2012.

Black, Cathy. "The Dance of Exile: Jerzy Starzyński, Kyczera, and the Polish Lemkos." *Dance Research Journal* 40, no. 2 (Winter 2008): 41–55.

Blejwas, Stanislaus A. "Old and New Polonias: Tensions Within an Ethnic Community." *Polish American Studies* XXXVIII, no. 2 (Autumn 1981): 55–83.

Blizniuk, Mikhail. *Prekrasnaia Marusia Sava: russkaia emigratsiia na kontsertnykh ploshchadkakh i v restoranakh Ameriki* [The Wonderful Marusia Sava: The Russian Emigration on the Concert Stages and Restaurants of America]. Moscow: Russkii Put', 2007.

Bomez, Jewelle. *The Gilda Stories.* Ithaca, NY: Firebrand Books, 1991.

Bowlt, John. "Introduction." In *The Salon Album of Vera Sudeikin-Stravinsky*, edited and translated by John Bowlt, ix–xxx. Princeton, NJ: Princeton University Press, 1995.

Boym, Svetlana. *The Future of Nostalgia.* New York: Basic Books, 2001.

Braziel, Jana Evans, and Anita Mannur. "Nation, Migration, Globalization: Points of Contention in Diaspora Studies." In *Theorizing Diaspora: A Reader*, edited by Jana Evans Braziel and Anita Mannur, 1–22. Malden, MA: Blackwell Publishing, 2003.

Brown, Malcolm. "Native Song and National Consciousness in Nineteenth-Century Russian Music." In *Art and Culture in Nineteenth-Century Russia*, edited by Theofanis George Stavrou, 57–84. Bloomington: Indiana University Press, 1983.

Brynner, Rock. *Empire and Odyssey: The Brynners in Far East Russia and Beyond.* Hanover, NH: Steerforth Press, 2006.

Bufalino, Brenda. "Russia: A Warm Tap Welcome After the Cold War." *On Tap* 13, no. 2 (Fall 2002): 9–11.

Bulgakowa, Oksana. "The 'Russian Vogue' in Europe and Hollywood: The Transformation of Russian Stereotypes through the 1920s." *Russian Review* 64, no. 2 (April 2005): 211–235.

Bumgardner, Eugenia S. *Undaunted Exiles.* Staunton, VA: McClure Co., 1925.

Butler, Judith. "Performative Acts and Gender Constitution: An Essay in Phenomenology and Feminist Theory." *Theatre Journal* 40, no. 4 (December 1988): 519–531.

Capua, Michelangelo. *Yul Brynner: A Biography.* Jefferson, NC: McFarland and Company, Inc., 2006.

Chamberlain, Lesley. *The Philosophy Steamer: Lenin and the Exile of the Intelligentsia.* London: Atlantic Books, 2006.

Chavchavadze, David. *Crowns and Trenchcoats: A Russian Prince in the CIA.* New York: Atlantic International Publications, 1990.

Chavchavadze, Paul. *Father Vikenty: The Story of an Impulsive Russian Priest Leading His Flock in a New World.* Cambridge, MA: Houghton Mifflin Company, 1955.

Chavchavadze, Sasha. *Museum of Matches.* Brooklyn, NY: Proteotypes, 2011.

Clifford, James. *Routes: Travel and Translation in the Late Twentieth Century.* Cambridge, MA: Harvard University Press, 1997.

Cohen, Robin. *Global Diasporas: An Introduction.* 2nd ed. New York: Routledge, 2008.

Connerton, Paul. *How Societies Remember.* Cambridge: Cambridge University Press, 1989.

Cooper-Albright, Ann. "Introduction: Situated Dancing." In *Engaging Bodies: The Politics and Poetics of Corporeality*, 1–17. Middletown, CT: Wesleyan University Press, 2013.

Cramer, Allan P. "International Copyright and the Soviet Union." *Duke Law Journal* 1965, no. 3 (Summer 1965): 536–539.

Crist, Stephan A. "Jazz as Democracy?: Dave Brubeck and Cold War Politics." *Journal of Musicology* 26, no. 2 (Spring 2009): 133–174.

Critchlow, James. *Radio Hole-in-the-Head: RL: An Insider's Story of Cold War Broadcasting.* Washington, DC: The American University Press, 1995.

Crowe, David M. *A History of the Gypsies of Eastern Europe and Russia.* 2nd ed. New York: Palgrave Macmillan, 2007.

Daughtry, J. Martin. "'Sonic Samizdat': Situating Unofficial Recording in the Post-Stalinist Soviet Union." *Poetics Today* 30, no. 1 (2009): 27–65.

Davenport, Lisa A. *Jazz Diplomacy: Promoting America in the Cold War Era.* Jackson: University Press of Mississippi, 2009.

Denikin, Ksenia. "*Stranitsy iz dnevnika* [Pages from a Diary]." *Novyi Zhurnal* 20 (1948): 256–269.

Doherty, Thomas. *Hollywood and Hitler, 1933–1939.* New York: Columbia University Press, 2013.

Douglas, Ann. *Terrible Honesty: Mongrel Manhattan in the 1920s.* New York: Farrar, Straus and Giroux, 1995.

Dubinets, Elena. *"Motsart otechestva ne vybiraet": O muzyke sovremennogo russkogo zarubezh'ia* [Mozart Does Not Choose a Homeland: On the Music of the Contemporary Russian Emigration]. Moscow: Muzizdat, 2016.

Duke, Vernon. *Passport to Paris.* Boston: Little, Brown, and Company, 1955.

Evtuhov, Catherine, and Richard Stites. *A History of Russia: Peoples, Legends, Events, Forces.* Boston: Houghton Mifflin Company, 2003.

Fanon, Frantz. "This Is the Voice of Algeria." In *The Sound Studies Reader,* edited by Jonathan Sterne, 329–335. New York: Routledge, 2012.

Feingold, Henry L. *Silent No More: Saving the Jews of Russia, the American Jewish Effort, 1967–1989.* Syracuse, NY: Syracuse University Press, 2007.

Feld, Steven, Aaron A. Fox, Thomas Porcello, and David Samuels. "Vocal Anthropology: From the Music of Language to the Language of Song." In *A Companion to Linguistic Anthropology,* edited by Alessandro Duranti, 321–345. Malden, MA: Blackwell, 2004.

Figes, Orlando. *Natasha's Dance: A Cultural History of Russia.* New York: Metropolitan Books, 2002.

Fischer, George. "The New Soviet Emigration." *Russian Review* 8, no. 1 (January 1949): 289–295.

Fokine, Michel. *Fokine: Memoirs of a Ballet Master.* Boston: Little, Brown, and Company, 1961.

Foner, Nancy. *From Ellis Island to JFK: New York's Two Great Waves of Immigration.* New Haven, CT: Yale University Press, 2000.

Fosler-Lussier, Danielle. "Instruments of Diplomacy: Writing Music into the History of Cold War International Relations." In *Music and International History in the Twentieth Century,* edited by Jessica C. E. Gienow-Hecht, 118–139. New York: Berghahn Books, 2015.

———. *Music in America's Cold War Diplomacy.* Oakland: University of California Press, 2015.

Foster, Susan Leigh. "Introduction." In *Corporealities: Dancing Knowledge, Culture, and Power,* edited by Susan Leigh Foster, xi–xvii. London: Routledge, 1996.

Frank, Stephen P. "Confronting the Domestic Other: Rural Popular Culture and Its Enemies in Fin-De-Siècle Russia." In *Cultures in Flux: Lower-Class Values, Practices, and Resistance in Late Imperial Russia,* edited by Stephen P. Frank and Mark D. Steinberg, 74–107. Princeton, NJ: Princeton University Press, 1994.

Frolova-Walker, Marina. "Music of the Soul?" In *National Identity in Russian Culture,* edited by Simon Franklin and Emma Widdis, 116–131. Cambridge: Cambridge University Press, 2004.

Frumkin, Vladimir. *Pevtsy i vozhdi* [Singers and Leaders]. Nizhnii Novgorod: Dekom, 1995.

Gans, Herbert J. "Symbolic Ethnicity: The Future of Ethnic Groups and Cultures in America." In *Theories of Ethnicity: A Classical Reader,* edited by Werner Sollors, 425–459. New York: New York University Press, 1996.

Garcia, Cindy. *Salsa Crossings: Dancing Latinidad in Los Angeles.* Durham, NC: Duke University Press, 2013.

Geldern, James von, and Louise McReynolds, eds. *Entertaining Tsarist Russia: Tales, Songs, Plays, Movies, Jokes, Ads and Images from Russian Urban Life, 1779–1917*. Bloomington: Indiana University Press, 1998.

Geldern, James von, and Richard Stites, eds. *Mass Culture in Soviet Russia: Tales, Poems, Songs, Movies, Plays, and Folklore, 1917–1953*. Bloomington: Indiana University Press, 1995.

Genizi, Haim. *America's Fair Share: The Admission and Resettlement of Displaced Persons, 1945–1952*. Detroit: Wayne State University Press, 1993.

Gidal, Marc. "Musical Boundary-Work: Ethnomusicology, Symbolic Boundary Studies, and Music in the Afro-Gaucho Community of Southern Brazil." *Ethnomusicology* 58, no. 1 (Winter 2014): 83–109.

———. *Spirit Song: Afro-Brazilian Religious Music and Boundaries*. New York: Oxford University Press, 2015.

Gill, Jonathan. *Harlem: The Four Hundred Year History from Dutch Village to Capital of Black America*. New York: Grove Press, 2011.

Ginsburg, Faye. "Radio Fields: *An Afterword*." In *Radio Fields: Anthropology and Wireless Sound in the 21st Century*, edited by Lucas Bessire and Daniel Fisher, 268–278. New York: New York University Press.

Giroud, Vincent. *Nicolas Nabokov: A Life in Freedom and Music*. Oxford: Oxford University Press, 2015.

Gitelman, Zvi. *A Century of Ambivalence: The Jews of Russia and the Soviet Union, 1881 to the Present*. Bloomington: Indiana University Press, 2001.

Gitelman, Zvi, ed. *The New Jewish Diaspora: Russian-Speaking Immigrants in the United States, Israel, and Germany*. New Brunswick, NJ: Rutgers University Press, 2016.

Glad, John. *Russia Abroad: Writers, History, Politics*. Washington, DC: Birchbark Press, 1999.

Glenny, Michael, and Norman Stone. *The Other Russia: The Experience of Exile*. New York: Viking Penguin, 1990.

Goldmark, Daniel. *Tunes for 'toons: Music and the Hollywood Cartoon*. Berkeley: University of California Press, 2005.

Gray, Francine du Plessix. *Them: A Memoir of Parents*. New York: Penguin Books, 2005.

Gray, Lila Ellen. "Memories of Empire, Mythologies of the Soul: Fado Performance and the Shaping of Saudade." *Ethnomusicology* 51, no. 1 (Winter 2007): 106–130.

———. *Fado Resounding: Affective Politics and Urban Life*. Durham, NC: Duke University Press, 2013.

Greeley, Andrew M. *Ethnicity in the United States: A Preliminary Reconnaissance*. New York: John Wiley and Sons, 1974.

Guevara, Gema R. "'La Cuba de Ayer/La Cuba de Hoy': The Politics of Music and Diaspora." In *Musical Migrations: Transnationalism and Cultural Hybridity in Latino/a America*, edited by Frances R. Aparicio and Cándida F. Jáquez, 33–46. New York: Palgrave, 2003.

Gurock, Jeffrey S. *When Harlem Was Jewish, 1870–1930*. New York: Columbia University Press, 1979.

Guterl, Matthew Pratt. *The Color of Race in America, 1900–1940*. Cambridge, MA: Harvard University Press, 2001.

Hahn, Tomie. *Sensational Knowledge: Embodying Culture through Japanese Dance*. Middletown, CT: Wesleyan University Press, 2007.

Halbwachs, Maurice. *On Collective Memory*. Edited and translated by Lewis A. Coser. Chicago: The University of Chicago Press, 1992.

Hall, Stuart. "Cultural Identity and Diaspora." In *Theorizing Diaspora: A Reader*, edited by Jana Evans Braziel and Anita Mannur, 233–246. Malden, MA: Blackwell Publishing, 2003.

Harper, Marjory. "Introduction." In *Emigrant Homecomings: The Return Movement of Emigrants, 1600–2000*, edited by Marjory Harper, 1–14. Manchester: Manchester University Press, 2005.

Hassell, James. *Russian Refugees in France and the United States Between the World Wars*. Philadelphia: American Philosophical Society, 1991.

Hill, Constance Vallis. *Tap Dancing America: A Cultural History*. New York: Oxford University Press, 2010.

Hilmes, Michele, and Jason Loviglio. "Introduction." In *Radio Reader: Essays in the Cultural History of the Radio*, edited by Michele Hilmes and Jason Loviglio, 1–20. New York: Routledge, 2002.

Hohman, Valleri J. *Russian Culture and Theatrical Performance in America, 1891–1933*. New York: Palgrave Macmillan, 2011.

Holden, Scott. "The 'Adventures and Battles' of Vladimir Dukelsky (a.k.a. Vernon Duke)." *American Music* 28, no. 3 (Fall 2010): 297–319.

Horowitz, Joseph. *Artists in Exile: How Refugees from Twentieth-Century War and Revolution Transformed the American Performing Arts*. New York: HarperCollins Publishers, 2008.

Hutchinson, Sydney. "Breaking Borders/*Quebrando Fronteras*: Dancing in the Borderscape." In *Transnational Encounters: Music and Performance at the US-Mexican Border*, edited by Alejandro Madrid, 41–66. Oxford: Oxford University Press, 2012.

———. "Dancing in Place: An Introduction." In *Salsa World: A Global Dance in Local Contexts*, edited by Sydney Hutchinson, 1–25. Philadelphia: Temple University Press, 2015.

Iubileinyi sbornik Khrama Khrista Spasitelia v N'iu Iorke [The Tenth-Anniversary Booklet of Christ the Savior Cathedral in New York]. New York: Rossiya Pub. Co., 1934.

Iubileinyi sbornik sobornavo Khrama Khrista Spasitelia v N'iu-Iorke, 1924–1949 [The Twenty-Fifth-Year-Anniversary Booklet of Christ the Savior Cathedral in New York, 1924–1949]. n.p., n.d.

Ivanovič's, Kosik. "*Russkii teatr v restorane: Belgrad 20-h gg. XX v* [Russian Theater in the Restaurants: Belgrade in the 1920s]." *Godišnjak za društvenu istoriju* 12, no. 1–3 (2005): 111–127.

Jacobson, Matthew Frye. *Whiteness of a Different Color: European Immigrants and the Alchemy of Race*. Cambridge, MA: Harvard University Press, 1998.

Jahn, Hubertus F. *Patriotic Culture in Russia During World War I*. Ithaca, NY: Cornell University Press, 1995.

———. "'Us': Russians on Russianness." In *National Identity in Russian Culture: An Introduction*, edited by Simon Franklin and Emma Widdis, 51–73. Cambridge: Cambridge University Press, 2004.

Jaroszynska-Kirchmann, Anna D. *The Exile Mission: The Polish Political Diaspora and Polish-Americans, 1939–1956*. Athens: Ohio University Press, 2004.

Johnston, Robert. *New Mecca, New Babylon: Paris and the Russian Exiles, 1920–1945*. Kingston, ON: McGill-Queen's University Press, 1988.

Jones, David R., and Boris Raymond. *The Russian Diaspora, 1917–1941*. Lanham, MD: Scarecrow Press, 2000.

Jordan, Pamela A. *Stalin's Singing Spy: The Life and Exile of Nadezhda Plevitskaya*. Lanham, MD: Rowman and Littlefield, 2016.

Karlowich, Robert. *We Fall and Rise: Russian-Language Newspapers in New York City, 1889–1914*. Metuchen, NJ: Scarecrow Press, 1991.

Kayyali, Randa A. *The Arab Americans*. Westport, CT: Greenwood Press, 2006.

Kazansky, Konstantin. "Russian Chanson in Paris." In *Russkii Parizh, 1910–1960*, edited by Joseph Kiblitsky, E. N. Petrova, and Juan Allende-Blin, 61–63. Saint Petersburg: Palace Editions, 2003.

Kelly, Catriona. "Russian Culture and Emigration, 1921–1953." In *Russian Cultural Studies: An Introduction*, edited by Catriona Kelly and David Shepherd, 297–307. New York: Oxford University Press, 1998.

Kibria, Nazli. *Becoming Asian American: Second-Generation Chinese and Korean American Identities*. Baltimore: Johns Hopkins University Press, 2002.

Kokot, Waltraud, Khachig Tölölyan, and Carolin Alfonso. "Introduction." In *Diaspora, Identity and Religion: New Directions in Theory and Research*, edited by Waltraud Kokot, Khachig Tölölyan, and Carolin Alfonso, 1–8. London: Routledge, 2004.

Kosteliants, B. O., ed. *Apollon Grigor'ev: izbrannye proizvedeniia* [Apollon Grigoriev: Selected Works]. Leningrad: Sovetskii Pesatel', 1959.

Krugler, David F. *The Voice of America and the Domestic Propaganda Battles, 1945–1953*. Columbia: University of Missouri Press, 2000.

Kupfer, Peter. "'Volga-Volga: 'The Story of a Song,' Vernacular Modernism, and the Realization of Soviet Music." *The Journal of Musicology* 30, no. 4 (Fall 2013): 530–576.

Kuznets, Simon. "Immigration of Russian Jews to the United States: Background and Structure." *Perspectives in American History* 9 (1975): 35–124.

Landau, J. "The Flesh of Raving: Merleau-Ponty and the 'Experience' of Ecstasy." In *Rave Culture and Religion*, edited by Graham St. John, 107–124. London: Routledge, 2004.

Landy, Joshua, and Michael Saler, "Introduction: The Varieties of Modern Enchantment." In *The Re-Enchantment of the World: Secular Magic in a Rational Age*, edited by Joshua Landy and Michael Saler, 1–14. Stanford, CA: Stanford University Press, 2009.

Law, Alma. "Nikita Balieff and the Chauve-Souris." In *Wandering Stars: Russian Émigré Theatre, 1905–1940*, edited by Lawrence Senelick, 16–31. Iowa City: University of Iowa Press, 1992.

Layton, Susan. *Russian Literature and Empire: Conquest of the Caucasus from Pushkin to Tolstoy*. Cambridge: Cambridge University Press, 1994.

Lederhendler, Eli. *Jewish Immigrants and American Capitalism, 1880–1920: From Caste to Class*. Cambridge: Cambridge University Press, 2009.

Lemmon, Alfred. "New Orleans Popular Sheet Music Imprints: The Latin Tinge Prior to 1900." *The Southern Quarterly* 27, no. 2 (Winter 1989): 41–57.

Lemon, Alaina. *Between Two Fires: Gypsy Performance and Romani Memory from Pushkin to Postsocialism*. Durham, NC: Duke University Press, 2000.

Lescott-Leszczynski, John. *History of the United States Ethnic Policy and Its Impact on European Ethnics*. Boulder, CO: Westview Press, 1984.

Lotman, Yuri M. *Universe of the Mind: A Semiotic Theory of Culture*. Translated by Ann Shukman. Bloomington: Indiana University Press, 1990.

Lowenthal, David. *The Past Is a Foreign Country*. Cambridge: Cambridge University Press, 2005.

MacFayden, David. *Songs for Fat People: Affect, Emotion, and Celebrity in the Russian Popular Song, 1900–1955*. Montreal: McGill-Queen's University Press, 2002.

MacMillen, Ian. "Fascination, Musical Tourism, and the Loss of the Balkan Village (Notes on Bulgaria's Koprivshtitsa Festival)." *Ethnomusicology* 59, no.2 (Spring/Summer 2015): 227–261.

Major, Clarence, ed. *Juba to Jive: A Dictionary of African-American Slang*. New York: Penguin Books, 1994.

Marie, Grand Duchess of Russia. *A Princess in Exile*. New York: Viking Press, 1932.

Markowitz, Fran. "The Home(s) of Homecomings." In *Homecomings: Unsettling Paths of Return*, edited by Fran Markowitz and Anders H. Stefansson, 21–33. Lanham, MD: Lexington Books, 2004.

Marks, Steven G. *How Russia Shaped the Modern World: From Art to Anti-Semitism, Ballet to Bolshevism*. Princeton, NJ: Princeton University Press, 2003.

Marullo, Thomas Gaiton, ed. *Ivan Bunin: From the Other Shore, 1920–1933: A Portrait from Letters, Diaries, and Fiction*. Chicago: Ivan R. Dee, Inc.

Matich, Olga. "The White Emigration Goes Hollywood." *Russian Review* 64, no. 2 (April 2005): 187–210.

Mazo, Margarita. "Introduction." In *A Collection of Russian Folk Songs by Nikolai Lvov and Ivan Prach*, edited by Malcolm Brown, 3–76. Ann Arbor, MI: UMI Research Press, 1987.

McMillin, Arnold. "Setting Lermontov: Some Musical Versions of the Poet's Works." *New Zealand Slavonic Journal* Vol. 43 (2009): 3–22.

McQuillen, Colleen. *The Modernist Masquerade: Stylizing Life, Literature, and Costumes in Russia*. Madison: The University of Wisconsin Press, 2013.

McReynolds, Louise. *Russia at Play: Leisure Activities at the End of the Tsarist Era*. Ithaca, NY: Cornell University Press, 2003.

Mikkonen, Simo. "Radio Liberty—The Enemy Within?: Disseminating Western Values through US Cold War Broadcasts." In *Europe-Evropa: Crosscultural Dialogues between the West, Russia and Southeastern Europe*, edited by Juhani Nuorluoto and Maija Könönen, 243–257. Uppsala: Uppsala University, 2010.

———. "Exploiting the Exiles: Soviet Émigrés in US Cold War Strategy." *Journal of Cold War Studies* 14, no. 2 (Spring 2012): 98–127.

Milton, Sybil. "Is There an Exile Art or Only Exile Artists?" In *Exil: Literatur und die Künste nach 1933*, edited by Alexander Stephan, 83–89. Bonn: Bouvier, 1990.

Morrison, Simon. "Semiotics of Symmetry, or Rimsky-Korsakov's Operatic History Lesson." *Cambridge Opera Journal* 13, no. 3 (November 2001): 261–293.

———. *Lina and Serge: The Love and Wars of Lina Prokofiev*. Boston: Houghton Mifflin Harcourt, 2013.

Nabokov, Vladimir. *Speak, Memory: An Autobiography Revisited*. New York: Everyman's Library, 1999.

Nathans, Benjamin. *Beyond the Pale: The Jewish Encounter with Late Imperial Russia*. Berkeley: University of California Press, 2002.

Ochs, Michael. "A Yiddish Operetta Tailored to Its Audience: Joseph Rumshinsky's *Di Goldene Kale*." In *Di Goldene Kale*, edited by Michael Ochs, xiii–lii. Recent Researches in American Music, Vol. 80. Middleton, WI: A-R Editions, Inc., 2017.

Okuntsoff, Ivan K. *Russkaia emigratsiia v Severnoi i Iuzhnoi Amerike* [The Russian Emigration in North and South America]. Buenos Aires: Seiatl', 1967.

Olson, Laura J. *Performing Russia: Folk Revival and Russian Identity*. New York: Routledge Curzon, 2004.

Ong, Aihwa. "Chinese Modernities: Narratives of Nation and of Capitalism." In *Undergrounded Empires: The Cultural Politics of Modern Chinese Transnationalism,* edited by Aihwa Ong and Donald Nonini, 171–202. London: Routledge, 1997.

Pattie, Susan. "At Home in Diaspora: Armenians in America." *Diaspora* 3, no. 2 (Fall 1994): 185–198.

Pedraza-Bailey, Sylvia. "Cuba's Exiles: Portrait of a Refugee Migration." *International Migration Review* 19, no. 1 (Spring 1985): 4–34.

Petrov, Victor. *Russkie v Amerike, XX vek* [Russians in America, the Twentieth Century]. Washington, DC: Russko-Amerikanskoe Istoricheskoe Obshchestvo, 1992.

Petrovskii, Miron. "*Skromnoe obaianie kicha, ili chto est' russkii romans* [The Subtle Charm of Kitsch, or What Is the Russian Romance]." In *Russkii romans na rubezhe vekov* [The Russian Romance at the Boundary of the Century], edited by Valentina Morderer and Miron Petrovskii. Kiev: Oranta-Press, 1997.

Piotrowska, Anna G. *Gypsy Music in European Culture: From the Late Eighteenth to the Early Twentieth Centuries.* Boston: Northeastern University Press, 2013.

Polland, Annie, and Daniel Soyer. *Emerging Metropolis: New York Jews in the Age of Immigration, 1840–1920.* New York City: New York University Press, 2012.

Portes, Alejandro, and Rubén G. Rumbaut. *Immigrant America: A Portrait*, 3rd ed. Berkeley: University of California Press, 2006.

Pospelovskii, Dimitrii. "*O missii russkoi emigratsii* [On the Mission of the Russian Emigration]." In *Sud'by pokoleniia 1920–1930-x godov v emigratsii* [The Fate of the 1920–1930s Generation in the Emigration], edited by Liudmila Flam, 457–466. Moscow: Russkii Put', 2006.

Pravaz, Natasha. "Transnational Samba and the Construction of Diasporic Musicscapes." In *The Globalization of Musics in Transit: Music, Migration, and Tourism*, edited by Simone Krüger and Ruxandra Trandafoiu, 272–297. New York: Routledge, 2014.

Prokhorov, Vadim. *Russian Folk Songs: Musical Genres and History.* Lanham, MD: The Scarecrow Press Inc., 2002.

Rabinovich, Vadim, ed. *Russkii romans.* Moscow: Pravda, 1987.

Radhakrishnan, R. "Ethnicity in an Age of Diaspora." In *Theorizing Diaspora: A Reader,* edited by Jana Evans Braziel and Anita Mannur, 119–131. Malden, MA: Blackwell Publishing, 2003.

Raeff, Marc. *Russia Abroad: A Cultural History of the Russian Emigration, 1919–1939.* New York: Oxford University Press, 1990.

———. "Recent Perspectives on the History of the Russian Emigration (1920–40)." *Kritika: Explorations in Russian and Eurasian History* 6, no. 2 (Spring 2005): 319–334.

Rey, Mario. "Sexuality, Imaging, and Gender Construction in the Music of Exile." In *Queering the Popular Pitch*, edited by Sheila Whiteley and Jennifer Rycenga, 115–130. New York: Routledge, 2006.

Reyes, Adeleida. *Songs of the Caged, Songs of the Free: Music and the Vietnamese Refugee Experience.* Philadelphia: Temple University Press, 1999.

Rischin, Moses. *The Promised City: New York's Jews, 1870–1914.* Cambridge, MA: Harvard University Press, 1977.

Ritivoi, Andreea Deciu. *Yesterday's Self: Nostalgia and the Immigrant Identity.* Lanham, MD: Rowman and Littlefield Publishers, Inc., 2002.

Ritter, Rüdiger. "Broadcasting Jazz into the Eastern Bloc—Cold War Weapon or Cultural Exchange? The Example of Willis Conover." *Jazz Perspectives* 7, no. 2 (2013): 111–131.

Robertson, Stephen, Shane White, and Stephen Garton. "Harlem in Black and White: Mapping Race and Place in the 1920s." *Journal of Urban History* 39, no. 5 (2013): 864–880.

Robinson, Harlow. *The Last Impresario: The Life, Times, and Legacy of Sol Hurok.* New York: Penguin Books, 1994.

———. *Russians in Hollywood, Hollywood's Russians: A Biography of an Image.* Lebanon, NH: Northeastern University Press, 2007.

Roosevelt, Priscilla. *Life on the Russian Country Estate: A Social and Cultural History.* New Haven, CT: Yale University Press, 1995.

Rosenfeld, Stephen S. "Soviet-American Exchanges—Tit-for-Tat Goodwill." *Science* 143, no. 3613 (1964): 1413–1417.

Rothstein, Robert A. "Homeland, Home Town, and Battlefield: The Popular Song." In *Culture and Entertainment in Wartime Russia*, edited by Richard Stites, 77–94. Bloomington: Indiana University Press, 1995.

———. "Death of the Folksong?" In *Cultures in Flux: Lower-Class Values, Practices, and Resistance in Late Imperial Russia*, edited by Stephen P. Frank and Mark D. Steinberg, 108–120. Princeton, NJ: Princeton University Press, 1994.

Rozanov, Ivan, ed. *Russkie pesni XIX veka* [Russian songs of the Nineteenth Century]. Moscow: Gosudarstvennoe Izdatel'stvo Khudozhestvennoi Literatury, 1944.

Russian Orthodox Church of Christ the Saviour in New York: The Tenth Anniversary Book, 1924–1934. New York: Rossiya Publishing Company, 1934.

Rybczynski, Witold. *Home: A Short History of An Idea.* New York: Penguin Books, 1986.

Safran, William. "Diasporas in Modern Societies: Myths of Homeland and Return." *Diaspora* 1, no. 1 (Spring 1991): 83–99.

———. "Deconstructing and Comparing Diaspora." In *Diaspora, Identity and Religion: New Directions in Theory and Research*, edited by Waltraud Kokot, Khachig Tölölyan, and Carolin Alfonso, 9–29. London: Routledge, 2004.

Saul, Norman E. *Friends or Foes?: The United States and Soviet Russia, 1921–1941.* Lawrence: The University Press of Kansas, 2006.

Savaglio, Paula. *Negotiating Ethnic Boundaries: Polish American Music in Detroit.* Warren, MI: Harmonie Park Press, 2004.

Schmelz, Peter J. "Intimate Histories of the Musical Cold War: Fred Prieberg and Igor Blazhkov's Unofficial Diplomacy." In *Music and International History in the Twentieth Century*, edited by Jessica C. E. Gienow-Hecht, 189–225. New York: Berghahn Books, 2015.

Scott, Erik R. "The Nineteenth-Century Russian Gypsy Choir and the Performance of Otherness." Berkeley Program in Eurasian and East European Studies Working Paper (Summer 2008). [http://escholarship.org/uc/item/87w1v9rd].

Segal, Harold B. *Turn-of-the-Century Cabaret: Paris, Barcelona, Berlin, Munich, Vienna, Cracow, Moscow, St. Petersburg, Zurich.* New York: Columbia University Press, 1987.

Shasha, Dennis Elliott, and Marina Shron. *Red Blues: Voices from the Last Wave of Russian Immigrants.* New York: Holmes and Meier Publishers, Inc., 2002.

Shavelson, Melville. *How to Make a Jewish Movie.* Englewood Cliffs, NJ: Prentice-Hall, 1971.

Shay, Anthony, and Barbara Sellers-Young. "Dance and Ethnicity: Introduction." In *The Oxford Handbook of Dance and Ethnicity*, edited by Anthony Shay and Barbara Sellers-Young, 1–14. New York: Oxford University Press, 2016.

Sheffer, Gabriel. *Diaspora Politics: At Home Abroad.* Cambridge: Cambridge University Press, 2003.

Sibley, Katherine A. S. *Red Spies in America: Stolen Secrets and the Dawn of the Cold War.* Lawrence: University of Kansas, 2004.

Silverman, Carol. "Rom (Gypsy) Music." *Garland Encyclopedia of World Music*, Vol. 8, edited by Timothy Rice, 301–324. New York: Garland Publishing Inc., 2000.

———. "Music, Emotion, and the 'Other': Balkan Roma and the Negotiation of Exoticism." In *Interpreting Emotions and in Russia and Eastern Europe*, edited by Mark D. Steinberg and Valeria Sobol, 224–247. DeKalb: Northern Illinois University Press, 2011.

———. *Romani Routes: Cultural Politics and Balkan Music in Diaspora.* New York: Oxford University Press, 2012.

Simpson, Sir John Hope. *The Refugee Problem: Report of a Survey.* London: Oxford University Press, 1939.

Slobin, Greta N. *Russians Abroad: Literary and Cultural Politics of Diaspora (1919–1939).* Brighton, MA: Academic Studies Plus, 2013.

Slobin, Mark. "Icons of Ethnicity: Pictorial Themes in Commercial Euro-American Music." *Imago Musicae* 5 (1988): 129–143.

———. *Tenement Songs: The Popular Music of the Jewish Immigrants.* Urbana: University of Illinois Press, 1996.

———. "The Destiny of 'Diaspora' in Ethnomusicology." In *The Cultural Study of Music: A Critical Introduction*, edited by Martin Clayton, Trevor Herbert, and Richard Middleton, 284–296. New York: Routledge, 2003.

Small, Christopher. *Musicking: The Meanings of Performing and Listening.* Middletown, CT: Wesleyan University Press, 1998.

Smaller, Stephanie. "Pleasure, Danger, and the Dance." In *Russia, Women, Culture*, edited by Helena Goscilo and Beth Holmgren, 246–272. Bloomington: Indiana University Press, 1996.

Smith, Gerald Stanton. *Songs to Seven Strings: Russian Guitar Poetry and Soviet "Mass Song".* Bloomington: Indiana University Press, 1984.

Snyder, John W. *The DP Story: The Final Report of the United States Displaced Persons Commission.* Washington, DC: US Government and Printing Office, 1952.

Solomon, Thomas. "Performing Indigeneity: Poetics and Politics of Music Festivals in Highland Bolivia." In *Soundscapes from the Americas: Ethnomusicological Essays on the Power, Poetics, and Ontology of Performance*, edited by Donna A. Buchanan, 143–163. Burlington, VT: Ashgate, 2014.

Sosin, Gene. *Sparks of Liberty: An Insider's Memoir of Radio Liberty.* University Park: The Pennsylvania State University Press, 1999.

Spitulnik, Debra. "Anthropology and Mass Media." *Annual Review of Anthropology* 22 (October 1993): 293–315.

Spottswood, Richard K. *Ethnic Music on Records: A Discography of Ethnic Recordings Produced in the United States, 1893–1942.* Urbana: University of Illinois Press, 1990.

St. John, Graham. "Trance Tribes and Dance Vibes: Victor Turner and Electronic Dance Music Culture." In *Victor Turner and Contemporary Cultural Performance*, edited by Graham St. John, 149–173. New York: Berghahn Books, 2008.

Starr, S. Frederick. *Red and Hot: The Fate of Jazz in the Soviet Union, 1917–1980.* New York: Limelight Editions, 1985.

Stearns, Marshall, and Dean Stearns. *Jazz Dance: The Story of American Vernacular Dance.* New York: Macmillan, 1968.

Stefansson, Anders H. "Homecomings to the Future: From Diasporic Mythographies to Social Projects of Return." In *Homecomings: Unsettling Paths of Return*, edited by Fran Markowitz and Anders H. Stefansson, 2–20. Lanham, MD: Lexington Books, 2004.

Stites, Richard. "Iconoclastic Currents in the Russian Revolution: Destroying and Preserving the Past." In *Bolshevik Culture: Experiment and Order in the Russian Revolution*, edited by Abbott Gleason, Peter Kenez, and Richard Stites, 1–24. Bloomington: Indiana University Press, 1985.

——. *Russian Popular Culture: Entertainment and Society Since 1900.* Cambridge: Cambridge University Press, 1992.

——. "The Ways of Russian Popular Music to 1953." In *Soviet Music and Society Under Lenin and Stalin: The Baton and Sickle*, edited by Neil Edmunds, 19–32. New York: Routledge, 2004.

Stokes, Martin. "Introduction: Ethnicity, Identity, and Music." In *Ethnicity, Identity and Music: The Musical Construction of Place*, edited by Martin Stokes, 1–27. Oxford: Berg Publishers, 1994.

Strongin, V. L. *Nadezhda Plevitskaia: velikaia pevitsa i agent razvedki* [Nadezhda Plevitskaya: The Great Singer and Secret Service Agent]. Moscow: Ast-Press, 2005.

Summit, Jeffrey A. *The Lord's Song in a Strange Land: Music and Identity in Contemporary Jewish Worship.* New York: Oxford University Press, 2000.

Swift, Anthony. "The Soviet World of Tomorrow at the New York World's Fair, 1939." *Russian Review* 57, no. 3 (July 1998): 364–379.

Tarasar, Constance J., ed. *Orthodox America, 1794–1976: Development of the Orthodox Church in America.* Syosset, NY: The Orthodox Church in America, 1975.

Taruskin, Richard. *Stravinsky and the Russian Traditions: A Biography of the Works Through Mavra.* Vol. 2. Berkeley: University of California Press, 1996.

——. *Defining Russia Musically: Historical and Hermeneutic Essays.* Princeton: Princeton University Press, 1997.

——. *Russian Music at Home and Abroad: New Essays.* Oakland, CA: University of California Press, 2016.

Timofeyev, Oleg Vitalyevich. "The Golden Age of the Russian Guitar: Repertoire, Performance Practice, and Social Function of the Russian Seven-String Guitar Music, 1800–1850." PhD diss., Duke University, 1999.

Tölölyan, Khachig. "Rethinking *Diaspora(s)*: Stateless Power in the Transnational Moment." *Diaspora* 5, no. 1 (Spring 1996): 3–35.

——. "Beyond the Homeland: From Exilic Nationalism to Diasporic Transnationalism." In *The Call of the Homeland: Diaspora Nationalisms, Past and Present*, edited by A.S. Leoussi, A. Gal, and A. D. Smith, 27–45. Leiden, Netherlands: Brill Publishing, 2010.

Tolstoy, Alexandra. "The Russian DPs." *Russian Review* 9, no. 1 (January 1950): 53–58.

Torres, María de los Angeles. *In the Land of Mirrors: Cuban Exile Politics in the United States.* Ann Arbor: University of Michigan Press, 1999.

Tromly, Benjamin. "The Making of a Myth: The National Labor Alliance, Russian Émigrés, and Cold War Intelligence Activities." *Journal of Cold War Studies*, 18, no. 1 (Winter 2016): 80–111.

Tsou, Judy. "Gendering Race: Stereotypes of Chinese Americans in Popular Sheet Music." *Repercussions* 6, no. 2 (Fall 1997): 25–62.

Turino, Thomas. "Introduction: Identity and the Arts in Diaspora Communities." In *Identity and the Arts in Diaspora Communities*, edited by Thomas Turino and James Lea, 3–19. Warren, MI: Harmonie Park Press, 2004.

Turner, Victor. *From Ritual to Theatre: The Human Seriousness of Play*. New York: PAJ Publications, 1982.

Turrini, Joseph M. "'It Was Communism Versus the Free Word': The USA-USSR Dual Track Meet Series and the Development of Track and Field in the United States, 1958–1985." *Journal of Sport History* (Fall 2001): 427–471.

Um, Hae-Kyung. "Introduction: Understanding Diaspora, Identity and Performance." In *Diaspora and Interculturalism in Asian American Performing Arts: Translating Traditions*, edited by Hae-Kyung Um, 1–13. London: Routledge, 2005.

Van Acken, Mauro. "Dancing Belonging: Contesting *Dabkeh* in the Jordan Valley, Jordan." *Journal of Ethnic and Migration Studies* 32, no. 2 (March 2006): 203–222.

Voloshin, A. A. *Na putiakh i pereput'iakh: "dosugi vechernye," Evropa-Amerika, 1921–1952* [On the Pathways and Crossroads: "Evening Leisure," Europe-America, 1921–1952]. San Francisco: Delos, 1953.

Von Eschen, Penny M. *Satchmo Blows Up the World: Jazz Ambassadors Play the Cold War*. Cambridge, MA: Harvard University Press, 2004.

Wallach, Janet. *Chanel: Her Style and Her Life*. New York: Doubleday, 1998.

Weber, Max. "Science as a Vocation." In *From Max Weber: Essays in Sociology*, edited and translated by H. H. Gerth and C. Wright Mills, 129–156. Oxford: Oxford University Press, 1946.

Webster, Jason. *Duende: A Journey into the Heart of Flamenco*. New York: Broadway Books, 2003.

Wellens, Ian. *Music on the Frontline: Nicolas Nabokov's Struggle Against Communism and Middlebrow Culture*. Ashgate: Hants, England, 2002.

Wells, Elizabeth A. *West Side Story: Cultural Perspectives on an American Musical*. Lanham, MD: The Scarecrow Press, Inc., 2011.

Williams, Robert C. *Russia Imagined: Art, Culture, and National Identity, 1840–1995*. New York: Peter Lang Publishing, 1999.

Williams, William H. A. *'Twas Only an Irishman's Dream: The Image of Ireland and the Irish in American Popular Song Lyrics, 1800–1920*. Urbana: University of Illinois Press, 1996.

Witzleben, J. Lawrence. "Review Essay: Music and Diaspora." *Ethnomusicology* 57, no. 3 (Fall 2013): 525–532.

Wulff, Helena. *Dancing at the Crossroads: Memory and Mobility in Ireland*. New York: Berghahn Books, 2007.

Wyman, Mark. *DPs: Europe's Displaced Persons, 1945–1951*. Ithaca, NY: Cornell University Press, 1989.

Zelensky, Natalie K. "Sounding Diaspora through Music and Play in a Russian-American Summer Camp." *Ethnomusicology Forum* 23, no. 3 (December 2014): 306–330.

———. "Russian Church Music, Conundrums of Style, and the Politics of Preservation in the Émigré Diaspora of New York." In *The Oxford Handbook of Music and World Christianities*, edited by Suzel Ana Reily and Jonathan M. Dueck, 361–383. New York: Oxford University Press, 2016.

Zemtsovsky, Izaly. "Russia." In *The Garland Encyclopedia of World Music*, Vol. 8, edited by Timothy Rice, 754–789. New York: Garland Publishing Inc., 2000.

Zheng, Su. *Claiming Diaspora: Music, Transnationalism, and Cultural Politics in Asian/ Chinese America*. New York: Oxford University Press, 2010.

Ziegel, Aaron. "One Person, One Music: Reconsidering the Duke-Dukelsky Musical Style." *American Music* 28, no. 3 (Fall 2010): 320–345.

Zvereva, Svetlana. "*Blogotvoritel'naia deiatel'nost' Sergeia Rakhmaninova v otnoshenii Russkoi Pravoslavnoi Tserkvi* [The Philanthropic Work of Sergei Rachmaninoff in Relation to the Russian Orthodox Church]." In *S. V. Rakhmaninov—natsional'naia pamiat' Rossii* [S. V. Rachmaninov—The National Memory of Russia], edited by S. V. Kostiukova, 23–33. Tambov: Rachmaninovskii Tsentr, 2008.

INDEX

NATALIE K. ZELENSKY is Assistant Professor of Music at Colby College. Her work on music of the Russian diaspora has been published in *The Oxford Handbook of Music and World Christianities*, *Ethnomusicology Forum*, and *Russia Abroad: Music and Orthodoxy*. In 2013, she was a NEH fellow for "America's Russian-Speaking Immigrants and Refugees: 20th-Century Migration and Memory" at Columbia University's Harriman Institute, the research and academic exchange that played an important part in preparing *Performing Tsarist Russia in New York*.

www.ingramcontent.com/pod-product-compliance
Lightning Source LLC
Chambersburg PA
CBHW052000270326
41929CB00015B/2732